Palgrave Macmillan's Digital Education and Learning

Much has been written during the first decade of the new millennium about the potential of digital technologies to produce a transformation of education. Digital technologies are portrayed as tools that will enhance learner collaboration and motivation and develop new multimodal literacy skills. Accompanying this has been the move from understanding literacy on the cognitive level to an appreciation of the sociocultural forces shaping learner development. Responding to these claims, the **Digital Education and Learning Series** explores the pedagogical potential and realities of digital technologies in a wide range of disciplinary contexts across the educational spectrum both in and outside of class. Focusing on local and global perspectives, the series responds to the shifting landscape of education, the way digital technologies are being used in different educational and cultural contexts, and examines the differences that lie behind the generalizations of the digital age. Incorporating cutting-edge volumes with theoretical perspectives and case studies (single-authored and edited collections), the series provides an accessible and valuable resource for academic researchers, teacher trainers, administrators and students interested in interdisciplinary studies of education and new and emerging technologies.

Series Editors:

Michael Thomas is Senior Lecturer at the University of Central Lancashire, UK, and Editor-in-Chief of the *International Journal of Virtual and Personal Learning Environments*.

James Paul Gee is Mary Lou Fulton Presidential Professor at Arizona State University, USA. His most recent book is *Policy Brief: Getting over the Slump: Innovation Strategies to Promote Children's Learning* (2008).

John Palfrey is Head of School at Phillips Academy, Andover, USA, and Senior Research Fellow at the Berkman Center for Internet & Society at Harvard. He is co-author of *Born Digital: Understanding the First Generation of Digital Natives* (2008).

Digital Education: Opportunities for Social Collaboration
Edited by Michael Thomas

Digital Media and Learner Identity: The New Curatorship
By John Potter

Rhetoric/Composition/Play through Video Games: Reshaping Theory and Practice of Writing
Edited by Richard Colby, Matthew S. S. Johnson, and Rebekah Shultz Colby

Computer Games and Language Learning
By Mark Peterson

The Politics of Education and Technology: Conflicts, Controversies, and Connections
Edited by Neil Selwyn and Keri Facer

Digital Technologies for School Collaboration

Anastasia Gouseti

First published in 2014 by
PALGRAVE MACMILLAN®
in the United States—a division of St. Martin's Press LLC,
175 Fifth Avenue, New York, NY 10010.

Where this book is distributed in the UK, Europe and the rest of the world,
this is by Palgrave Macmillan, a division of Macmillan Publishers Limited,
registered in England, company number 785998, of Houndmills,
Basingstoke, Hampshire RG21 6XS.

Palgrave Macmillan is the global academic imprint of the above companies
and has companies and representatives throughout the world.

Palgrave® and Macmillan® are registered trademarks in the United States,
the United Kingdom, Europe and other countries.

ISBN: 978–1–137–37573–5

Library of Congress Cataloging-in-Publication Data

Gouseti, Anastasia.
    Digital technologies for school collaboration / Anastasia Gouseti.
        pages cm
    Includes bibliographical references and index.
        ISBN 978–1–137–37573–5 (hardback)
        1. Web-based instruction—Cross-cultural studies. 2. Internet in
education—Cross-cultural studies. 3. Educational technology—
Cross-cultural studies. 4. Teaching—Computer network resources.
5. Social media. 6. Teacher-student relationships. I. Title.

LB1044.87.G68 2014
371.33′44678—dc23   2013047569

A catalogue record of the book is available from the British Library.

Design by Newgen Knowledge Works (P) Ltd., Chennai, India.

First edition: May 2014

10 9 8 7 6 5 4 3 2 1

For Nicholas

Contents

Preface

As a high-school student on a small Greek island in the early-nineties I spent my childhood and adolescence living entirely offline. I have faint memories of being taught how to use a Word processor at my school's sole computer lab but nothing more than that. Concepts such as instant messaging and Skyping, social networking, and smartphones were unheard if not sci-fi scenarios of a nonexistent reality. Still, some of our teachers—mainly the foreign-language ones—made honest attempts to bring a sense of multiculturalism into the classroom by adopting the use of a range of Teaching English as a Foreign Language resources and tools such as tape and video recordings, the Penguin Young Readers, foreign magazines and newspapers, and so on. We were able to catch a glimpse of the everyday lives of children in the United Kingdom and we were surprised when we watched videos of children going to school wearing uniforms and ties. We learned to recognize the Big Ben and the London Bridge landmarks and sang along to the lyrics of "The Wheels on the Bus" despite the poor sound quality of the recording coming out of what is now considered to be a vintage cassette player. And when our teacher of English suggested getting a pen pal from a foreign country some of us jumped at the opportunity and paid the fee for registering with the agency. Opportunities to link with schools abroad were the exception rather than the rule and the prospect of online collaboration and real-time communication with pupils abroad was unthinkable.

Twenty years later, digital technology has become a familiar element of most aspects of modern life and digital media are now an indispensable feature of most children and young people's leisure-time activities. The use of digital technology has also become a significant component of many forms of teaching and learning. The broader changes in the nature, characteristics, and conditions of digital technologies have led to enthusiastic claims about the potential of the new tools to transform educational practices and processes. In particular, the collaborative and convivial nature of the second wave of "social media" that emerged throughout the 2000s has brought about an enthusiasm that the Internet has created greater opportunities for online school linking and collaboration.

The use of digital technologies is seen to not only provide learners access to a wealth of online information but it can also offer both teachers and students a ready means of communicating with peers at the global level. For instance, claims are often made that students can now benefit more from collaborative practices and form online learning communities with their peers abroad. Moreover, a large number of schools can now boast of having up-to-date computer labs, superfast wireless Internet connection, and laptop carts. All in all, participation in collaborative projects appears to provide a means of promoting global awareness and understanding, improving digital competence, supporting mobility and intercultural learning, enhancing foreign-language skills, sharing expertise and good practices, and many more.

Throughout the course of my academic research I have been both excited and dismayed by the educational potential of digital technologies and web-based school collaboration. On the one hand, I feel excited because I think that there is potential for digital technologies to enhance students' online collaborative practices and offer them opportunities to link with peers abroad and form friendships in a safe online environment. I believe that taking part in a collaborative project can foster cultural links, surpass geographical barriers, open up the classroom, and help teachers and students engage in a wider community of schools. Yet, I am dismayed, because most of the educational discussions regarding school collaboration still focus on deterministic claims that it is the technologies that possess inherent qualities to transform schooling rather than the *ways* teachers and students engage with them. Also, despite the large amounts of funding the area of web-based school collaboration has attracted and the plethora of available programs that has emerged, little research has so far been conducted to explore the issue in depth.

In writing this book I wanted to look at the complex issue of school collaboration and develop rich understandings of the everyday realities of web-based collaborative projects. I also wanted to gain an insight into teachers' and students' experiences from their participation in online collaborative programs and develop a realistic perspective of the range of challenges they face. As such, this book is not a technical guide concerned with "how to" make the best use of digital technology for school collaboration. Instead, this book attempts to capture the "wider picture" of web-based school collaboration and focuses on the people, conditions, and practices that underlie its successful implementation in formal educational settings. In particular, this book aims to identify the host of technological and nontechnological issues that underpin the success of web-based school collaboration and look at the people, policies and other processes, and factors that can shape collaborative environments. This book has been written for anyone interested in the complex albeit exciting world of online school collaboration. All in all, it is hoped that it will inspire readers to look beyond the hype of digital technology use and think more critically about the forms web-based school collaboration might take in the near future.

Acknowledgments

I would like to express my gratitude to the many people who saw me through this book and provided support and encouragement, talked things over, read, offered comments, and assisted in its production.

First and foremost, I would like to thank the pupils and teachers who took part in this study. Without their participation I would not have any material for the book.

I am grateful to Neil Selwyn for his support and guidance in this and other projects over the last few years and for helping me to develop my thinking about education and technology. I am also thankful to colleagues at the Institute of Education with whom I had conversations about the work in and around this book and who often gave advice and encouragement during my doctoral and early academic career—most notably Carey Jewitt, Richard Noss, and John Potter.

I would also like to thank my friends at the Institute of Education for their intellectual and emotional support during our years of doctoral study—especially Rania Al-Nakib, Tereza Markidou, Taciana Pontual, Sunyoung Choi, Sofia Diamantopoulou, and Shuang Zeng.

In terms of writing and production of this book I would like to thank the editors of the *Digital Education and Learning* series. I owe particular thanks to Michael Thomas for encouraging me to persevere with this project. I would also like to thank all of the production and editorial team at Palgrave—notably Sarah Nathan, Scarlet Neath, and Mara Berkoff—as well as the anonymous reviewers for commenting on earlier drafts of the manuscript.

The last and greatest thanks are owed to Theodore, Maria and Dionysios Gousetis as well as Foteini and Kyprianos Konstantinidis for their love and support, and for giving me the time required to write this book while they were looking after little Nicholas.

ANASTASIA GOUSETI
London, October 2013

CHAPTER 1

Web-Based School Collaboration: The Promises and Problems

Introduction

The introduction of digital technologies and the internet in the 1990s raised new challenges and created new opportunities for school collaboration. Moreover, the growth of social media in the 2000s has been a catalyst in the transformation of the ways in which web-based collaboration is perceived. In the context of education, in recent years, a number of educators as well as policy makers and governmental bodies appear to have embraced the potential of new technologies to facilitate school collaboration. This chapter will provide a critical overview of the issues underpinning web-based school collaboration. In particular, it will look at the manifestations of web-based school collaboration at intranational and international levels and will explore the cultural, political, and economic factors that underpin its resurgence.

Based on a review of the existing body of literature, this chapter presents the various existing models of school partnerships and collaborations in primary and secondary education and identifies the various types of school twinning programs that are available online. The purpose is twofold. First, the chapter offers a critical overview of existing models of collaborative programs in order to map out the complex nature of school collaboration and single out the actors and factors that can shape successful implementation into educational practices. Second, the chapter focuses on how the questions and issues underpinning web-based school collaboration can be addressed through the empirical exploration of four collaborative projects across a range of European schools.

Taking a Historical Perspective on School Collaboration

It is imperative to recognize from the outset that current efforts toward the (e)twinning of schools follow on from a long history of school collaboration projects across the past 50 years. Taking a historical approach will allow us to frame the development of collaborative initiatives within a long-term perspective and gain sense of significant long-standing social as well as technical issues that can shape web-based school collaboration. As shall be acknowledged in this chapter, the concept of "twinning" between communities has a long history. In particular, the end of the Second World War saw the rise of the concept of "town twinning" whereby civic and cultural bodies in towns and cities throughout Europe were paired in acts of peace and reconciliation with the aim to enhance communication, foster cultural links, and promote universal mutual understanding (Vion 2002).

Within these civic and cultural efforts, collaboration between schools and other educational institutions was quickly established as an especially appropriate means of breaking down preexisting stereotypes and prejudices and bridging the cultural gap between nations. For example, United Nations Educational, Scientific, and Cultural Organization (UNESCO)'s Associated Schools Project Network (ASPnet), founded in 1953 in the aftermath of the Second World War, is a global network of more than 9,000 educational institutions in 180 countries. It has been one of the first and longest-running collaborative initiatives with the vision of promoting international cooperation and peace through educational exchange (Schweisfurth 2005).

Alongside these political efforts, there has been a long, albeit wide-ranging tradition in the United Kingdom as well as in America and other English-speaking countries of establishing networked communities of educational institutions and promoting school partnerships in order to share knowledge, skills, and good practice (Atkinson et al. 2007; Kerr et al. 2003). On the one hand, collaborative practices have gained recognition as a key component of successful schools (Leonard and Leonard 2001). On the other hand, some authors have gone so far as to argue that collaboration is so "complex and varied in nature" that it "largely resists study" (Hanford et al. 1997, pp. 40–41). As such, categorizing the full range of school collaborative programs that has emerged in the past 60 years and identifying collectively accepted types are not easy tasks. Furthermore, the body of academic literature and research on collaboration appears to be rather poor compared to the abundance of the ongoing twinning and linking projects actually taking place. For these reasons, before we look in more detail at the range of collaborative initiatives that have emerged during the past years, we need to tackle the question of what is actually meant by school collaboration.

What Do We Mean by Web-Based School Collaboration?

In a broad sense, collaboration can be described as a rigorous interaction that encourages educators to open up their beliefs and practices to investigation and debate (Katz et al. 2008). Collaboration can also be seen as the purposeful "process of shared creation and shared discovery" that "requires the meaningful participation of all those involved" (Collis and Heeren 1993, pp. 36–37). Other definitions of collaboration also involve the mutual and coordinated efforts of participants toward problem solving as opposed to cooperative work that involves the division of labor and independent work toward solving a part of the problem (Roschelle and Teasley 1995). Similarly, Dillenbourg (1999) described cooperation as the process where partners divide the work, solve subtasks individually, and then bring together the partial results into the final output, whereas in collaboration, partners do the work "together."

Since the development of collaborative projects in the 1950s, technology use has always been central to school collaboration—from telephony in the 1950s and 1960s, to audio and video recording in the 1970s and fax and computer networks in the 1980s. Yet, the introduction of the internet and other digital communication technologies in the classroom in the 1990s is seen to have raised new challenges and has given impetus to the notion of what has been termed as "telecollaboration" or more recently "e-collaboration." In particular, it has been argued that:

> The hallmark of telecollaboration is the use of Internet communication tools (e.g. e-mail, chat, blogs, videoconferencing) to link linguistically and culturally disparate groups of language learners and teachers in institutionalised settings for the purpose of (bilingual) social interaction and project-based intercultural collaboration. (Belz 2007, p. 127)

As might be expected, telecollaboration has been celebrated for allowing both "synchronous" and "asynchronous" modes of student interaction—"synchronous" referring to technologies such as chat rooms or videoconferencing that allow online communication that occurs under real-time conditions between pairs or groups and "asynchronous" including emails, discussion forums, wikis, and blogs that allow delayed, non-real-time communication. For example, from the early 1990s, the arrival of the electronic mail was seen to offer opportunities for linking students, surpassing geographical boundaries, and replacing the use of regular mail that was considered "impractical" due to the time it took for classes to correspond and letters to reach their destination (Barr 1991). Thus, since the 1990s, the use of computer and web-based tools and applications to support inter-school communication and facilitate collaborative projects has continued to grow—welcomed by many educators as a ready means of providing increased possibilities for learning, communication, and collaboration. For example, the internet is often perceived as a "culturally and linguistically 'neutral' environment that provides learners of all different social, linguistic and cultural backgrounds with the same balanced 'playing field' on which they can interact and learn" (O'Dowd 2007b, p. 19).

Although web-based types of collaboration have long stimulated and enthused researchers and educators, it is in the past few years with the pro-liferation of social media that popular interest in online collaboration has bloomed (Forte and Bruckman 2009). For instance, the notion of "telecol-laboration 2.0" coined by Guth and Helm (2010) is used to expand upon "traditional" theories and practices of telecollaboration and is seen to mark the beginning of a gradual shift toward new pedagogies, approaches, and contexts as well as new tools and collaborative opportunities. Likewise, the new kinds of digital technologies are seen to create "exciting opportuni-ties for supporting collaborative learning online" as well as new pedagogical challenges (Laurillard 2009, p. 5). As such, a range of web-based collab-orative initiatives have emerged and will be presented in more detail in the following sections of this chapter. However, before looking more closely at the different types of intranational and international school collaboration that exist and before attempting to develop an understanding of the range of issues that underpin them, it is important to explore the different agendas and interests that lie behind the enthusiasm to set up and promote such programs.

Why Does School Collaboration Matter?

Web-based school collaboration has attracted the sustained attention of policy makers around the world and has begun to appear more prominently in the political agendas of many countries during the past decade. As such, the drive to insert collaborative initiatives into education has at large been led by individual governments, alliances between them, and in many cases by international bodies and organizations. For politicians and policy makers alike, participation in collaborative projects appears to provide a means of instilling a global dimension into the classroom; engaging in international cooperation; promoting global awareness and understanding; improving digital competence; supporting mobility and intercultural learning; enhanc-ing foreign language skills; sharing expertise and good practices, and many more. For instance, the aim of the previous Labour government in the

United Kingdom was to "engage in a programme of action between now and 2010 to enable every English school and college to establish a sustainable partnership with at least one equivalent institution in another country" (DfES 2004, p. 15). Similarly, US President Barack Obama has highlighted the need to expand educational exchange programs, "invest in online learning for teachers and children around the world; and create a new online network, so a young person in Kansas can communicate instantly with a young person in Cairo" (2009).

One of the most influential aspects of policy making is its role in promoting and funding such collaborative initiatives. To a great extent, governments and other international organizations have initiated and promoted collaborative programs, provided funding, built online platforms to host the projects, and offered technical support and teacher training. Overall, these official bodies have played an important part in making these initiatives widely known and easily accessed by schools and practitioners worldwide. The interest in such initiatives has significantly gathered pace during the last decade alongside the growing popularity of digital technologies and the rise of the social media. It is important to note that the collaborative and convivial nature of the new social media is seen to allow more creative modes of learning and enable students to connect to the real world beyond the classroom boundaries. At the same time, participation in online collaborative programs is associated with the improvement of students' "twenty-first-century" skills and competences that a knowledge economy requires.

As we shall see in more detail in chapter 2, the claims surrounding participation in collaborative initiatives also relate to the wider claims associated with the drive to insert computers in schools. Alongside the current enthusiasm with regard to the educational potential of digital technologies, a range of internal and external imperatives have made the implementation of social media tools within educational and collaborative settings more acute than ever before. These internal imperatives are associated with harnessing the potential of digital technologies to solve long-standing educational problems; supporting and enhancing teaching and learning; increasing flexibility and supporting e-learning and virtual communities; improving the organizational effectiveness of educational institutions; and widening access to education and participation (Selwyn 2011b). Furthermore, a range of "top-down" external imperatives for technology use in education can be found in the policy-making agendas of developed and developing countries alike. These relate to keeping up to date with technological changes and meeting the demands of the "knowledge economy" and the information society; providing sufficient levels of "human capital" and enhancing "employability"; and meeting the needs of the "digital native" students (ibid.). For instance, technology is often presented both as the primary driver of social and economic change and as central to the process of "upskilling" the future workforce (Buckingham 2007).

Notably, the convivial and collaborative nature of the new tools and the recent conditions of connectivity are seen as particularly suited to promote web-based school collaboration. As Davies and Merchant (2009, p. 107) argued, web 2.0 spaces can be seen as "an arena for learning through social participation" where students of different ages and cultural backgrounds can participate in an extended learning community, generate new content, and find new audiences for their writing. Moreover, the majority of these collaborative programs appears to allow for more flexibility, creativity, and innovation compared to more traditional teaching methods and resources. In addition, it is often argued that, with regard to technology use, schools are placed in a constant position of being "behind the times" compared to other sectors of society (Selwyn et al. 2010) while students are often portrayed as "digital natives" who expect social media to be woven into all aspects of their lives.

In these respects, promoting school collaboration and engaging with international partners on web-based projects is seen as more timely than ever, and collaborative practices have been gaining recognition as a key component of successful schools (Leonard and Leonard 2001). This enthusiasm to promote school collaboration has resulted in the creation of a range of initiatives at both intranational and international levels. These have taken a range of forms and shapes during their course of development and will be presented in more detail in the next sections.

A Typology of School Collaboration

Looking at the history of school collaboration brings to light the range of definitions and the lack of a collectively accepted typology as regards the type of available collaborative initiatives. School collaboration can take a range of forms and varied terms appear to have been employed in educational literature in order to describe the working relationships between schools. Within educational research, various practices are described as "collaboration," which emerges as a term that can be (mis)applied to a plethora of activities (Shinners 2001). Still, despite the large number of labels and terms adopted, careful examination of the various resources and existing initiatives allows us to identify some common characteristics and norms that can be used to inform the creation of a descriptive typology. Few commentators have, however, attempted to produce descriptive frameworks that encompass collaborative initiatives at both intranational and international levels.

At the intranational level, a typology of UK-based interschool collaborations was developed and five different models emerged (Atkinson et al. 2007): (i) expertise-based collaborations with the aim to share professional expertise and good practices (e.g., Specialist Schools, Beacon Schools, Diversity Pathfinders); (ii) cultural-based collaborations where the focus was on breaking down barriers associated with different cultures (e.g., independent-state school partnerships; interfaith and multicultural collaborations; international twinning); geographically based collaborations that linked schools within a particular area in order to serve particular needs or save on budget (e.g., federations, collegiates, and school clusters); commonality-based collaborations that linked schools with similar characteristics with the aim to address common problems or challenges (e.g., small rural primary school clusters/consortia), and, last, creativity/innovation-based collaborations with the focus being on innovation and developing new practices.

Thorough as this typology may be, it could be criticized for its rigidity and failure to fully capture the often-flexible nature of collaboration. It is more than often the case that collaborations are formed to serve multiple aims and bring about combined benefits; for example, breaking down cultural barriers, sharing good practice, and promoting creativity while also offering a means of making financial savings. As such, this chapter will endeavor to develop a conceptual typology of collaboration based on the level of school collaboration, ranging from intranational to international level, while it will also present in more detail the range of issues associated with web-based school collaboration.

The first parameter that is to be taken into consideration for the categorization of collaborative programs involves the geographical distance and boundaries that divide schools. On the one hand, intranational collaboration arises as a common model of linking schools that may be located within the same country but whose characteristics may vary in terms of rurality, religion, pupil need, or model of funding (i.e., distinction from urban to rural, denominational and nondenominational, special needs to mainstream, public to private sector). On the other hand, a broader model of collaboration involves initiatives organized at the international level that seek to surpass geographical borders and promote intercultural dialogue between schools that are spread across the world. International collaboration may encompass various models and approaches and can range from collaborative projects restricted within the European Union to initiatives that support linking at a global level.

Both intranational and international cooperations are also affected by parameters such as the depth and length of the collaborative relationship; the organizational structures or rules that have to be adopted so as to be in line with the agency or body that promotes the particular type of collaboration; the tools and resources used to promote and facilitate collaboration between students and teachers; the funding opportunities or the fees that may apply; the aims and objectives of the collaboration; and the level of flexibility allowed and the support provided by national bodies and local authorities. With these thoughts in mind, we can now go on to look at the recent history of school collaboration at both intranational and international levels.

The Recent History of Intranational Collaborations

The notion of intranational collaboration most commonly entails school federations, collegiates, and partnerships within a country, often emerging from local or state initiatives that aim at sustainability and school improvement, without, however, excluding other types of school linking. Since the mid-1990s, participation in "school networks" has been gaining in popularity and "many educational systems have experimented with networking and collaborative approaches to improvement" (Muijs et al. 2011, p. 1). As already highlighted, government agendas can often be key drivers for instigating and promoting partnerships of this nature. Indeed, government reports in the United Kingdom throughout the 2000s described collaboration between UK schools as a key strategy in raising standards (Rutherford and Jackson 2006).

Additionally, as Chapman et al. (2010) noted, the 2002 Education Act in England allowed governing bodies to amend their organization's structural configurations in order to support school-to-school collaboration with the aim of raising attainment, promoting inclusion, and stimulating innovation. In this sense, school networks were comprised of educators and principals from a range of schools that sought to share good practice, improve professional interaction, and help to "identify, analyse and solve pertinent problems impacting teaching and learning" (O'Hair and Veugelers 2005, p. 2). Similarly, the employment of various forms of collaboration such as clustering, federating, and forming networked learning communities has been identified as an alternative means of overcoming challenging situations and preventing the closure of small schools in rural areas (Jones 2006).

These mainly state-driven initiatives aim to promote the sharing of good practice, expertise, and resources and create richer educational opportunities for students; however, they do not involve true student collaboration per se. Consortia, federations, and collegiate academies appear to be mainly local authority or state-driven initiatives that build on the notion of collaboration. Such initiatives are often used as a means of addressing organizational and managerial issues of sustainability or ensuring school survival rather than creating links among the student population. Notwithstanding the educational benefits of this type of partnership, it is clear that the focus is not on collaboration per se but on making ends meet or cutting down on expenses.

A different type of intranational collaboration driven less by parameters such as sustainability and sharing of resources has been independent and maintained school partnerships. Here the main aim has been to break down barriers and enable schools to become involved in joint work in order to share expertise, raise educational standards, and create further teaching and learning opportunities (Ofsted 2005). Smaller-scale research in the field indicated that schools were approaching partnerships with enthusiasm and commitment and collaboration had succeeded in breaking down barriers (Turner 2004). A wider scale survey that investigated independent and maintained school partnerships in the United Kingdom highlighted cases when schools collaborated not only in terms of sharing facilities, but they also undertook joint projects related to curriculum and enrichment activities. Some of the reported benefits included increased communication, improvement in pupil achievement, and dissemination of good practice (Smith et al. 2003).

The attempt to tackle sectarian divides in various parts of the United Kingdom (most notably Northern Ireland and Scotland) has given rise to another model of collaboration between denominational and nondenominational schools with the aim to promote mutual understanding with respect to religious differences. For example, twinning between denominational and nondenominational schools in Scotland aimed to enrich pupils' experiences and provide them with the opportunity to meet together (Scottish Executive 2006). Furthermore, the "National Gateway" constituted a further example of a UK government–led initiative designed to promote school collaboration across England. Its aim was to encourage schools (particularly the ones serving a predominantly monocultural population) to form links and create opportunities for interaction in order to break down prejudice and foster cohesion across young people of different cultures, ethnic, religious or nonreligious, and socioeconomic groups (DCSF 2007).

Although the number of intranational initiatives in the United Kingdom appears to have proliferated in recent years, the impetus for school collaboration is not exclusively a British phenomenon, but examples of school collaboration can be found both inside and outside of Europe. Within Europe, the "Senior Secondary Education School Network," established in 1998, was described as a policy-focused Dutch initiative that sought to promote changes in the educational system, facilitate the sharing of good practice, and support communication (Veugelers and Zijlstra 2002; 2005). In the

United States there has also been a growth of "organic" school networks on the national level such as the practitioner-driven "League of Professional Schools" and the "Coalition of Essential Schools." Moreover, Smith and Wohlstetter (2006) attempted to gain insight into the different types of public–private partnerships that existed between charter schools and other organizations in the United States. Other examples of intranational networks focused on school improvement include the "Australian National Schools Network." Within a Canadian context, Rees and Woodward (1998) presented the case of twinned schools in Ontario and reported that although school twinning was a decision imposed by the central administration for economic reasons, school principals did identify certain advantages in connection with cost saving, prevention of closure, linking communities and greater resources, and opportunities for participation in events and activities. Finally, another case of school collaboration in Canada was the "Network of Performance (Based) Schools" (Halbert and Kaser 2002).

The Recent History of International Collaboration

As noted earlier, school collaboration can surpass the geographical boundaries of a single country and acquire an international dimension—especially in light of the developments in telecommunication technologies. In contrast to intranational collaborations reviewed previously, which appear to be driven mainly by state or local authority bodies and are quite often used as a vehicle for enhancing organizational capacity and overcoming burdens of practical or financial nature, international collaborations can be said to be more flexible, diverse, and student-centered, utilizing a wider range of tools and serving different objectives. Student collaboration and communication, the enhancement of cultural awareness, the creation of learning networks, the promotion of citizenship, and the improvement of information and communication technology (ICT) skills are some of the central aims that appear to lie at the heart of international collaborative initiatives.

As has already been highlighted, the literature on international collaboration is relatively slight in comparison to the abundance of the ongoing projects that have emerged in the last decade as a result of various governmental efforts. For instance, despite the proliferation of UK initiatives during recent years, very little systematic and in-depth research has been carried out and it is not possible to know for certain the number of international partnerships between UK schools and the rest of the world or the form they take (Doe 2007). As such, a conceptual typology to be adopted in this book has been created in order to reflect the type of organizations that are responsible for facilitating twinning across countries at an international level. First, the term "state-driven initiatives" will be adopted to describe the number of collaborative projects that have been introduced, promoted, and in some cases funded by official governmental bodies, policy makers, and international organizations. Second, the term "non-governmental organization (NGO) initiatives" will be assigned to twinning opportunities established and facilitated by charitable organizations and agencies or missionary delegations that promote collaboration at different levels and through a range of programs. Finally, the term "commercially driven initiatives" will be used to denote the commercially driven online platforms and programs that are used to facilitate school collaboration and are usually available for an annual fee. It should be noted that although the terms "school collaboration" and "web-based school collaboration" are used interchangeably, the majority of these initiatives employ the use of digital technologies to promote communication and interaction between participants. Furthermore, the URLs to the websites of the initiatives described in this chapter can be found in Appendix 1.

State-Driven Initiatives
Working with other schools at the international level and engaging in collaborative projects can take place within the framework of a range of state-driven initiatives. First, the "Comenius Programme," which is funded by the European Commission, aims to promote mobility and intercultural learning, enhance partnerships and teacher training, foster cultural awareness, and improve language learning and ICT skills among the European Union (EU) member states and other non-EU countries. In particular, the "Comenius School Partnerships" initiative seeks to promote collaboration at bilateral and multilateral levels, facilitating mobility and providing a grant so as to cover the expenses of student and teacher exchanges. Alternatively, "eTwinning" is seen as "a web-based social network of thousands of European schools, which can form partnerships to work on projects integrated in the curriculum of their pupils" (Breuer et al. 2009, p. 167). In line with the Comenius program is the "European Schoolnet," a network of 30 Ministries of Education in Europe and beyond. The European Schoolnet acts as a gateway to national and regional school networks and aims to provide insight into the educational use of digital technologies for policy makers as well as education professionals by fostering exchange at all levels of school education using innovative technologies (Vuorikari and Sarnow 2005).

In the United States, the state-driven aspiration to connect every school with another one around the world by 2016 has already been highlighted earlier in this chapter. To this end, a number of organizations that promote and facilitate school linking at the international level have come together under the umbrella of the "Connect All Schools" consortium. This interactive portal has been created in order to enable the building of new links and it hosts information on a number of collaborative initiatives. These range from pen pal programs such as the "School-to-School International" that promotes linking with schools in Africa, Asia, and the Caribbean to the "UClass" initiative, which provides safe online environments for students to collaborate. Furthermore, the GLOBE—Global Learning and Observations to Benefit the Environment—is another US state-driven program that focuses on science education and the environment and is active in more than a hundred countries worldwide. GLOBE's vision supports students, teachers, and scientists to collaborate on environmental projects and work in close partnership with the National Aeronautics and Space Administration (NASA), the National Oceanic and Atmospheric Administration, and the National Science Foundation.

In contrast to the explicit nature of these state-driven initiatives, there are a number of other collaborative programs that cannot be placed within strict boundaries as they have been the result of consortia between state and NGO synergy—illustrating the often diverse and nebulous nature of collaborative projects. Such an example is the "Global School Partnerships," a UK consortium established by a range of not-for-profit associations and funded by the Department for International Development (DFID). It aimed at promoting partnerships between schools in the United Kingdom and Africa, Asia, Latin America, and the Caribbean and central to the program's objectives was to broaden students' horizons and foster deeper knowledge and understanding of global development and cultural issues so as to provide them the skills and knowledge that will lead them to becoming active global citizens.

Similarly, the educational branch of the British Council also serves as a portal that provides information and access to a range of—mainly state-driven—school collaboration initiatives. Within the portal "Schools Online" teachers can look for partners all over the world and register for a range of international collaborative programs as well as training courses and educational resources. With the motto of "bring the world into your classroom" the British Council aims to help schools "give young people the opportunity to thrive in an increasingly global society" and equip them with "the outlook and skills they will need to live and work as citizens of the world" (British Council, n.d., p. 2). In particular, the "Connecting Classrooms" program provides educational institutions with students aged 3–18 years opportunities for collaboration with a range of countries from across the middle east, Sub-Saharan and North Africa, South Asia, Central and South America, and the United Kingdom. Similarly, the "Commonwealth Class" initiative, a joint effort of the BBC, the British Council, and the Commonwealth Secretariat, aims to enable schools to participate in online exchanges and work on collaborative projects in cross-Commonwealth teams.

NGO Initiatives

A large number of international collaboration initiatives do not derive from governmental or policy-making agencies but from charitable organizations and church-based delegations that seek to create links among schools worldwide so as to foster communication, raise cultural awareness, and at the same time provide support to schools of developing countries. For example, the Tony Blair Faith Foundations' web-based "Face to Faith initiative" aims to connect secondary school classrooms from around the world in order to support young people in reflecting on their own belief systems and those of others.

A long-standing US-initiated program at the international level is the "Global SchoolNet," a nonprofit education organization that was initially founded in 1984. It aims at helping teachers and K–12 students find learning partners across the world and engage in project learning exchanges in order to develop science, math, literacy, and communication skills; promote teamwork; and enhance multicultural understanding. Similarly, the "Flat Classroom Project," cofounded by two teachers in the United States and Australia, uses a range of social media tools to facilitate the creation of educational networks of teachers and students "for the purpose of sharing experiences in a focused and monitored environment" (Lindsay and Davis 2010, p. 14). Another long-standing initiative is the "Global Virtual Classroom" program, initially launched in 1996 and supported by the Give Something Back International Foundation (GSBI), a US-based nonprofit educational organization. Within its framework, primary and secondary school teachers and students from around the world can share good practices and interact as they collaboratively design a website on a topic of their choice.

"BBC World Class" is another initiative that aims to promote collaboration between schools in the United Kingdom and partners around the world. It acts as a portal that seeks to assist schools in their search of collaborative projects and provides a central resource of both state and NGO-driven partner organizations and initiatives—offering a range of resources and materials for schools, as well as successful examples of twinning and advice on how to acquire funding or organize exchange visits. The majority of these NGO-driven initiatives derive from charitable organizations and agencies that seek to establish links between schools in the United Kingdom and schools in developing countries in Africa, Asia, and elsewhere. These types of collaboration provide students the opportunity to share experience, develop global citizenship values, and be more sensitive toward issues on global justice and fair trade. As these initiatives seek to improve the teaching and learning conditions for the pupils in the developing countries, it is often the case that an annual contribution or fee is requested from the UK school in order to support its partner school.

Similarly, "Link Community Development" is a charity organization that aims at developing global citizenship values and cultural awareness between the linked schools and encouraging sustainable school development by facilitating partnerships between Africa, the United Kingdom, Ireland, and the United States. Likewise, the Australian-based "Global School Partners" project promotes linking between schools in Australia and Africa and creates an environment of support and learning between the schools. Other similar, but smaller-scale, charity organizations that facilitate linking with African schools are, for instance, "African Revival" and "AfriTwin." Additionally, other initiatives that offer opportunities to establish partnerships with schools in different parts of the world include "Japan-UK live," the "Arctic Voice," the "Atlantic Rising," the "Palestinian-German School Twinning Programme," "Link Ethiopia," and many more.

Commercially Driven Initiatives

In contrast to the state or NGO-initiated collaborative programs presented so far, a range of other commercial platforms also aim at facilitating international school collaboration but are only available for an annual fee. In brief, the UK-initiated "SuperClubsPLUS" is seen to offer a protected environment within which children can develop social skills and engage in creative behavior while teachers can develop national or international links with other schools (Pine 2006). Similarly, the "ePals Global Network" started as an online electronic pen pal service in 1996 and is said to enable K–12 classroom-to-classroom project sharing, language practice, and cross-cultural learning. The ePals Global Network claims to be the largest online community of K–12 learners, seeking to "truly bring digital age learning to life in classrooms" by enabling educators and students across 200 countries to safely connect, exchange ideas, and work together (ePals, n.d., p. 2).

The eTwinning Program: Taking a Closer Look

Having provided an overview of the plethora of collaborative initiatives that have emerged during the past decade, we can now go on to take a closer look at the eTwinning program, which formed the basis of collaboration for the schools that took part in the empirical study of this book. Born in 2004 and officially launched in 2005 as an initiative of the European Commission's eLearning program, eTwinning is intended to introduce a more European dimension in the classroom and raise students' cultural awareness. In March 2013, eTwinning was extended to schools in Armenia, Azerbaijan, Georgia, Moldova, and Ukraine, enabling these countries to join the existing network of schools. According to the official press release, eTwinning Plus has been initiated as part of the EU's Neighbourhood policy that aims to enhance dialogue with Easter partners and there are plans to roll out the scheme to Southern neighbourhood countries such as Tunisia. As noted, the budget for eTwinning Plus is € 834,000 with around half of this sum invested in developing the new online platform and carrying out coordination work while the remainder will be allocated to co-funding the partner support agencies in the above-mentioned countries (Europa 2013).

The internal and external imperatives described earlier in this chapter are seen to shape to a large extent the eTwinning program. Inherent in the organization and success of an eTwinning project is said to be the use of digital technologies. Digital technologies are viewed not only as the online platforms that will facilitate collaboration and interaction but are also seen as the pedagogical tools that will enhance teachers' and students' ICT competencies and will equip them with lifelong skills. The eTwinning program has attained a relatively high profile with European education. In particular, the large number of registered projects has often been celebrated in EU reports as an indication of success and the program itself has been widely promoted by organizations such as the British Council as the "Community of Schools in Europe" and a means of bringing Europe to school classrooms (British Council 2013). Meanwhile, a recent study published by the European Commission goes as far as to claim that "eTwinning 1.0 was born in 2005, but it took four years to realise that it was already 2.0 by nature. eTwinning was a teachers' social network before its time" (Scimeca 2010, p. 10).

The main eTwinning platform run and maintained by the Central Support Service is the eTwinning portal and is available in 25 languages. The portal comprises the main "meeting point" for teachers and provides online tools to find partners, share ideas, and set up projects. Publicly accessed areas include the "keep-up-to-date" section with interviews, publications, and press releases as well as the "progress" section with information on teacher-training workshops and online learning events. Alongside its informational role the portal hosts a range of ready-made "project kits" to assist and inspire teachers at the beginning of their projects as well as an open-access blog for sharing experiences and seeking advice. This information can be publicly accessed; however registered users are also able to access their personal online "desktop" where they can create and manage their profile, host information on their past and current projects, search for partners, and engage in discussions with other members of the eTwinning community.

Furthermore, as soon as an eTwinning project has been approved teachers are also given authorized access to "TwinSpace," a private online environment devoted to an individual project. It consists of the Project Activities section, the Staff Room, the Pupils Corner, the Chat, and a general guidelines section. TwinSpace is flexible in nature and the collaborating teachers can configure the particular tools they wish to use for their project. These range from blogs and wikis to the chat room and the discussion forum and they are all available on the TwinSpace platform. As such, TwinSpace has emerged as the official eTwinning virtual classroom where students can store and share content, communicate, and collaborate in a private and safe online environment (Miguela 2007). Indeed, the recent "facelift" and addition of tools such as blogs and wikis on the TwinSpace platform has been seen as facilitating a shift toward a more collaborative phase of eTwinning:

> It is impressive to see that eTwinning has adapted so readily to one of the deeper trends of social behavior nowadays: networking online in new configurations, thus creating new communities and new ways of relating. Yesterday's talk was technology and information, the time of eTwinning 1.0. Today, thanks to the symbology of Web 2.0, it is technology and society... "Social networks" are more than the buzzword of the moment; it is the "natural destiny" of the Internet... eTwinning's vocation is to provide a new grammar of relationships to the European teaching community. (De Kerckhove 2010, p. 7)

Web-Based School Collaboration: Issues and Empirical Findings

The remainder of this chapter now goes on to pay particular attention to empirical studies of web-based school collaboration. First we will examine some cases of online collaborative work that took place in the early 1990s and employed specific communication networks available at the time. Then we will look at the empirical findings reported from the study of collaborative projects that were based on digital technologies such as email, webpages, videoconferencing, and so on, as well as more recent tools such as wikis and blogs. Last, we will explore an array of issues that we need to be aware of when integrating web-based school collaboration into the classroom.

The Forerunners of Web-Based School Collaboration

The first reports of online collaborative work between learners in different schools appear in the early 1990s when internet access on a regular basis became possible (O'Dowd 2007a). Meadows's study (1992) of using Campus 2000 telecommunication system as an email provider to facilitate partnerships between teacher-training/higher education institutions and schools around the world marked one of the first instances of empirical research in this field. On the one hand, the study highlighted the enormous opportunities for "multicultural teaching and learning" and for forming direct links while on the other a range of difficulties associated with high cost, computer access, and lack of adequate training was reported (Meadows 1992, p. 123).

Another empirical study from the beginning of the 1990s focused on how communication networks and email could be adapted to foreign-language teaching in Finnish upper-secondary schools within the framework of collaboration with a range of schools from the United Kingdom to the United States (Tella 1991). The major inhibitors reported concerned: technical problems caused either by lack of experience in email use or infrastructure failure; high phone costs especially for the non-Finnish parties; differing timetables that prevented the use of a chat room; and extra work from all participating parties. Yet, Tella's study also reported positive outcomes such as increased motivation and creativity for teachers and pupils, as well as improvement of technology and communicative skills.

Web-Based School Collaboration in Practice

As we have already highlighted, although the practices that emerge from web-based school collaborations are rich and there is an abundance of ongoing programs worldwide, research in the area remains limited and fragmented. It is also common that empirical studies in the field often overemphasize the rhetoric aims of the initiatives rather than focusing on the actual course and outcomes of the projects in practice. As such, this section seeks to bring together the existing evidence in research findings and literature in order to construct a clearer picture of what we already actually know about current practices of school collaboration.

First, the potential of digital technologies to facilitate school collaboration at the intranational level was presented through the "Building E-Bridges Project," in the framework of which schools from two different UK counties were linked and students communicated through email with the aim to promote positive attitudes to difference within a diverse community, encourage interfaith dialogue, and create a potential forum for discussions and debates. Teachers valued the email project as it provided their students an opportunity to share aspects of their lives with their partners and learn from each other rather than from a textbook or an adult. The biggest obstacles they faced were related to technical difficulties and timetabling, while evidence from the email exchanges suggested that "teacher guidance or training in developing dialogues might have enabled the children to extend their discussions into more challenging and meaningful debate" (McKenna et al. 2008, p. 103).

At the international level, discussion forums were used to facilitate a collaborative project between schools in Ghana and the United Kingdom and the benefits included deepening students' understanding of issues such as human trafficking (DFID 2007). Other examples of web-based collaborative projects include the establishments of partnerships through email exchanges and videoconferencing between pupils in Scotland and Pakistan, which offered students' insight into the life and concerns of teenagers in different countries (Maitles and Gilchrist 2006). Similarly, the use of an online website enabled a British, a French, and an Italian school to exchange ideas and build partnerships (Barbosa et al. 2004). A different study explored the use of ICTs within the framework of the "Interlink" project between British and New Zealand schools. The study reported how undertaking online activities and engaging in email communication "enabled the children to develop more nuanced understandings of the similarities and differences between them...and construct a sameness across distance in their imaginative geographies" (Valentine and Holloway 2001, p. 390).

Similar examples can be drawn when looking at the various reports on the "Dissolving Boundaries" project, another initiative that has adopted an internet-mediated model of school collaboration. The project, first introduced in 1999, involved cross-national cooperation between schools at primary and post-primary levels and in the Special schools' sector in Northern Ireland and the Republic of Ireland with a special focus on the use of ICTs to form cross-educational linkages and build a virtual "community of practice" (Austin et al. 2006). The tools used to facilitate communication and collaboration between students during the first years that the project ran mainly consisted of email, asynchronous computer conferencing, and videoconferencing. Research evaluations from various stages of the project throughout its duration reported beneficial outcomes associated with students' motivation, self-confidence, and intercultural understanding as well as literacy, communication, and ICT skills (Austin 2006). A more recent report indicated that a total of 320 schools had taken part in the project since its launching in 1999 and highlighted that:

> The innovative work between linked schools, using a range of technology, has shown how frontiers of knowledge have been crossed in terms of linking subjects in the curriculum, in enterprise education, in terms of pupils' knowledge of others and of themselves and for teachers, in terms of their professional knowledge. (Austin et al. 2011)

A different web-based collaborative case involved two schools in Iraq and the United Kingdom respectively that employed the "Rafi.ki" online platform to discuss and plan their project. Despite some technical problems associated with slow internet connection at the Iraqi school, the project was successful in enabling students to make intercultural links and improve their ICT skills (Ward 2009, n.p.). Mobile technologies were adopted to facilitate the linking of a school in the United Kingdom with their partner schools in Uganda and Afghanistan when other tools failed due to difficulties with online connection and electricity supplies. This resulted in a series of exchanges ranging from snapshots of everyday life instances to videos with explanatory pop-up messages and enhanced students' intercultural understanding (Morrison 2012, n.p.).

Within the context of science education the potential of web-based collaborative projects was explored by the EU-based "Communicare Nelle Science" and "WebLabs" projects. In particular, the "Communicare Nelle Science" project involved the use of email and chat room discussions and the creation of project websites. As Barbosa et al. (2004) reported, the use of communication technology was central for the quality of the overall project and the collective knowledge and understanding that students developed. Similarly, the "WebLabs" project sought to "convey to young learners the real spirit of mathematics as a field in which they can not only generate, test, and play with ideas, but also share them with their peers from different countries" (Mor and Sendova 2003, p. 36). Through participation in the project students were encourage to develop personal skills and abilities, share their experience with their online partners, engage in team work, and be critical to the work published in the virtual environment (Sendova et al. 2004).

As regards eTwinning, the study of Coutinho and Rocha (2007) described the "Crossing the Borders" project that took place between a Portuguese and a Czech school and employed TwinSpace, a Moodle and a collaborative blog. Some of the reported outcomes were seen to be the optimization of students' autonomy, creativity and teamwork skills, as well as increased cultural awareness and development of citizenship, cooperation, and ICT skills (ibid.). Similarly, a different study reported that it is necessary for participants in collaborative projects such as eTwinning to be confident and skilled in using the new technologies for accessing, processing, and sharing online information through the appropriate computer software program (Öztok and Özdener 2007, p. 127). A more recent study of the eTwinning program highlighted how collaboration within schools often tended to take the form of "coordination" of teachers by the main eTwinner so as to participate in predetermined project activities within their classes. Moreover, direct interaction with pupils in partner schools was not common while email was the only form of online communication between pupils in most of the case-study schools. The study also reported that synchronous collaborative work by pupils in different countries was atypical and was often constrained by "timetabling, time differences and lack of appropriately robust ICT infrastructure" (European Commission 2013b, p. 7).

A range of other eTwinning projects has been featured in EU and other reports and publications as examples of good practices, such as the collaboration between UK and Afghan schools with the use of mobile phone technologies (Muir 2010) and the "Schoolovision" in which 30 schools across Europe created music video-clips for an online song contest (Hepburn 2010) while Freedman (2010) compiled an online book of 87 web-based projects from around the world. These cases, however, will not be presented in further detail since they do not form part of an in-depth research study but rather offer a simplistic overview of cherry-picked examples of collaborative projects.

Interestingly, research in the field of web-based collaboration within a higher education context appears to be richer and more in-depth. Some of these studies will be described in brief as they present findings, which are worthy of note particularly with regard to the adoption of social media. For example, the Skype and wiki-based "Padova-Dickinson exchange" between higher education students in Italy and the United States reported difficulties in receiving and offering peer feedback because of cultural differences. Additionally, the students took the initiative to establish alternative ways of communicating such as via Facebook in order to carry out the collaborative writing assignment (Guth and Marini-Maio 2010). Another example from a higher education context was a telecollaborative project between foreign-language students in Chile and the Netherlands that employed video-web communication tools. Among other positive outcomes the students highlighted the importance of videoconferencing, which contributed to overcoming anonymity and promoting proximity and familiarity. Overall, it was reported that technology made it possible to overcome geographical barriers, allowing learners from distant continents to break down their classroom walls and situate their language learning experience in a broader environment (Jauregi and Banados 2010).

Conversely, findings from the "Tridem Project" between British and American university students of French and native French speakers reported that on the one hand synchronous online communication allowed students to establish direct real-time contact; however, the use of blogs was seen to be more popular as it offered more time for reflection and freedom to work at individually convenient times at their own pace (Hauck and Lewis 2007). Other examples of web-based university collaboration included a USA–Japan Telecollaboration (Meguro and Bryant 2010), the "Intercultura Project" (Fratter and Helm 2010), an email exchange between foreign-language students in Spain and Ireland (Vinagre 2007), and many more (see O'Dowd 2007c; Guth and Helm 2010).

Issues of Safety and Connectivity

Besides making education more exciting and engaging for students, a further factor we need to consider is how to ensure the online safety of children when engaging with digital technologies. All these bodies and organizations that endorse the use of web-based collaboration appear to be particularly wary of the dangers arising from unconstrained internet interactions. One of the key considerations has been to ensure that student projects are materialized within a private and safe online environment. In order to ensure that student communication and collaboration take place in a protected online space, a range of online platforms has been created and is run within the framework of the state-driven and NGO initiatives presented earlier in this chapter. As such, a large number of these collaborative programs offer an online "space" where teachers and students can interact and work together with their partners. In line with the growing concern on safety issues seems to be the rising enthusiasm to embrace social media tools within an educational context. Thus, a range of tools such as blogs and wikis has been implemented in these online spaces alongside more traditional technologies such as email, discussion forums, and chat rooms.

For instance, "eLanguages" is an online collaborative platform that has been initiated by the British Council with the aim to enable teachers to create a virtual working environment for the students and facilitate international collaboration. It is available in various languages and can serve as a meeting point for partner schools—operating either as a "virtual classroom," a "portfolio," or a "showroom" according to the needs of each partnership. The "UK–German Connection" and "Schola-21," on the other hand, are at large focused on promoting the German culture. As such, the "UK–German Connection" seeks to foster contact and understanding between schools in these two countries through participation in "the voyage," an online portal. Similarly, "Schola-21" is a web-based collaborative platform where teachers can set up an online "project room" and individual pupils and groups can create their personal profile and get together "virtually" to exchange ideas and take part in collaborative projects with the use of email, forums, chat rooms, and the project room.

In the case where external tools are employed to facilitate collaboration it is crucial to ensure that students collaborate within a secure online space.

For instance, strict monitoring and security auditing took place to ensure that the Moodle virtual environment remained safe at all times within the framework of the "Dissolving Boundaries" project (Austin et al. 2006). Likewise, Eyre (2009) described his concerns about security issues with regard to students using social networking sites as opposed to the safe online environment that the "rafi.ki" platform was seen to offer. On the one hand, it resembled Facebook, facilitating students to communicate and share ideas with their partners but on the other its web-design tools allowed them to create profile and webpages to share without any worries over safety issues.

Overall, a large number of the collaborative programs described in the previous sections offer secure online spaces to host the projects and facilitate interaction between teachers and students. Even when collaboration takes places on external online platforms and tools, teachers need to address recurring concerns over the risks and dangers encountered in online worlds and discuss with their students' understandings of issues of online risk and sense of e-safety.

Notwithstanding the enthusiasm to embrace digital technologies, Barr (1991) contended that the implementation of sophisticated pieces of technology did not in itself guarantee sound educational outcomes. Additionally, Chapple (1991, in Campbell 2004) highlighted the importance of establishing well-defined objectives and clear expectations as well as ensuring that there is strong commitment between all partners of the collaborative project. Furthermore, we also need to consider that there are cases where the schools involved are located in developing countries that lack the adequate infrastructure to support the use of such tools. As such, it remains difficult to integrate digital technologies to countries that lack the connectivity (Beldarrain 2006). Moreover, it has been reported that there is great diversity among the schools within the UNESCO's Associated School Project Network, with only 47 percent of the 7,400 ASPnet schools having access to the internet, which was often simply access at a local internet cafe while other schools lacked electricity and other basic prerequisites to ICT use (Schweisfurth 2005). These teaching and learning conditions clearly create restrictions in terms of communication and exchanges between schools.

Despite perceived positive outcomes resulting from online collaboration and the examples of successful projects reported so far, some commentators have drawn attention to the range of issues associated with less successful collaborative efforts. For instance, O'Dowd and Ritter (2006) have argued that the literature in the field of telecollaborative exchanges shows that success is far from guaranteed. On the contrary, it is often the case that online collaborative projects end in "failed communication" resulting in low levels of participation, indifference, tension between participants, or negative evaluation of the partner group or its culture (ibid.). This "dysfunction" in online exchanges can be associated with a learner's level of "intercultural communicative competence" (ICC) and can also be attributed to "a complex, often confusing, array of factors related to the students and the sociocultural contexts in which they are operating, the organization and structure of the exchange, and the type of interaction which takes place between the groups in the online environments" (ibid., p. 624).

Why Look at Web-Based School Collaboration?

Having considered the long history of collaborative projects and the various forms and types these have taken over the years as well as the key issues arising from their academic evaluation, we now need to tackle the question of why it is important to further explore the issues underpinning school collaboration. As we have already highlighted, there has been a concerted push in recent years to encourage the implementation of collaborative initiatives in schools that has gone hand in hand with the general enthusiasm for the educational potential of the new digital tools that have emerged. As a result, the past decade has seen the launch of a range of collaborative programs worldwide. Yet, each initiative is launched with little attempt to analyze and evaluate those that precede it. Thus far, little consideration has been given to how these programs and technologies "fit" with ongoing school practices and the existing school curriculum.

As this implies, the internal and external imperatives associated with the use of digital technologies for school collaboration that were described earlier in this chapter suggest a rather deterministic approach and do not necessarily reflect the realities of classroom use. This in turn suggests that school realities are not wholly determined by the implementation of particular technologies but are also affected by social practices:

> Classrooms are steeped in cultural norms and practices, many of which have been constant for many decades. Using ICT doesn't necessarily change the norms and practices in the classroom unless the teacher or some other force establishes and guides new habits. (Loveless et al. 2001, pp. 73–74)

Indeed, it could be argued that, in the fast-changing field of education technology, the initial enthusiasm to embrace a particular tool usually fades away as soon as the next technology emerges on the horizon—resulting in little change in educational practices. Some critics have identified this endless "pursuit of the new" as a major reason why the promises of educational technology are rarely fully realized and have described this as a recurrent cycle of "exhilaration/scientific-credibility/disappointment/teacher-bashing" (Cuban 1986, pp. 5–6). In this sense, digital technologies are often seen to promise a great deal but deliver far less. The eagerness to celebrate the educational promises of the latest tool in the hope that it will reconfigure classroom practices has seldom chimed with the "wider picture" of the realities of technology use in actual school settings. As Sutherland and Sutch (2009, p. 30) described:

> Those of us who have been around since the early days of the introduction of computers into schools have observed how each new technological development, from Logo to multimedia, to the Internet to mobile technology to Web 2.0, has been heralded as being the final breakthrough that will make the difference to education. We have also observed that riding the wave of each technological breakthrough never begins to address the issues that face education.

These cycles or waves of "hype, hope and disappointment" (Gouseti 2010) have not allowed much space for more careful reflection and evaluation of the actual educational benefits and/or practical impediments surrounding the use of digital technologies in education. Additionally, academic commentators have long argued that these assumptions about the potential of digital technologies should be placed within the wider context of the "grammar of schooling" (see Tyack and Tobin 1994). This notion of the "grammar of schooling" is seen as "the set of organisational assumptions and practices that have grown up around the development of mass schooling" and are often seen to act as a major barrier to significant change in schools (Robertson and Dale 2009, p. 152).

From this perspective, although some changes have taken place within formal educational settings during the past decades particularly with regard to technological infrastructure, the social structures and powers of schools have, to some extent, remained intact. As a result, despite the generous investment in, and increased presence of the relevant infrastructure in schools, computers have been often found to be unused or underused (Zhao and Frank 2003). In light of the above, it is worth exploring whether the opportunities that digital technologies and, in particular social media, entail will prove worthwhile of the hype of web-based school collaboration. Thus, the question we now need to tackle is whether more fruitful conditions for school collaboration have been created that will take the transformation of education beyond this cycle of disappointment.

Conclusion

While by no means creating a definite or exhaustive list, this chapter has described a range of collaborative programs that have emerged over the past two decades and has explored some of the issues underpinning web-based school collaboration. In particular, it has shown that, although collaborative programs appear to have a long history across the past 50 years, the enthusiasm to embrace and promote new initiatives at national and international levels has grown considerably since the 1990s with the emergence of digital technologies. Furthermore, the number and range of these collaborative initiatives can be said to have benefited from increased governmental and policy-maker support as well as from increased funding opportunities and greater motivation and interest among the teachers. Still, this heightened importance to school collaboration belies the general lack of empirical research in the area, which, as this chapter has highlighted so far, does not allow for generalizations, particularly with regard to the successful implementation of the second generation of social media tools.

Having depicted in detail what we mean by web-based school collaboration and having described the imperatives and ranges of issues surrounding it, it is now worth taking some time to consider the key issues underpinning the educational use of digital technologies. For instance, digital technologies are seen to create collaborative and other teaching, learning opportunities that appear to be in line with the aims of the school twinning programs presented in this chapter. However, in order to materialize the potential of digital technologies into something more than aspirations, a range of other parameters need to be considered such as how the tools can be shaped along educational lines and collaborative practices.

In drawing together these observations, the following issues have been identified as worthy of investigation: (i) the notion that the use of digital technologies can lead to increased online student interaction, participation, and collaboration as well as creation and sharing of content; (ii) the notion that digital technologies can transform learning and equip students with twenty-first-century lifelong learning skills; (iii) the assumption that social media bear promises of instant connectivity and community building within and across the school classrooms; and (iv) the practical issues and technical implications that emerge with the implementation of social media in formal educational setting. With these in mind the next chapter sets out to explore how these issues are presented and addressed in the academic educational technology literature and explore their impact on web-based school collaboration.

CHAPTER 2

Digital Technologies in Education: New Tools for New Times?

Introduction

The prominence of digital technologies has been increasing steadily since the 2000s in many areas of society. A number of new internet tools have emerged, which can be said to differ substantially from the forms and the initial concept of the World Wide Web as it emerged into mainstream technology use in the 1990s. These new digital technologies appear to be especially connective and social in nature. As Haythornthwaite and Andrews argue (2011, p. 94) "what is new about current technologies is that they bring into institutions and organizations a suite of practices that originate in open, web-based interaction." Within educational communities the use of digital technologies in the classroom has been largely received with enthusiasm as it is seen to present educators with numerous opportunities for teaching, learning, and collaborating.

This chapter aims to introduce the main themes and issues that run through the book regarding the educational use of digital technologies. First, it briefly outlines the development of social media, describing the characteristics of the new tools and the conditions and imperatives that have facilitated the shift toward the more communicative, creative, and convivial nature of the new web era. Then, the chapter explores the role that these technologies can play in transforming the existing educational landscape and examines the educational claims made for social media use. It starts by considering the educational promises and fears over social media, in particular the "booster," "doomster," "anti-schoolers," and "critics" discourses that surround the use of educational technologies (Bigum and Kenway 1998). The focus then moves toward the educational theories that underpin the implementation of social media in education. In particular, the chapter reviews in brief theories of learning, theories of online communities of practice and knowledge-building networks, and other theories of individual and organization improvement in education. The third part of the chapter explores social media use in practice and presents an overview of findings from research studies on the educational implementation of digital technologies.

Taking a Historical Perspective on the Use of Digital Technologies in Education

The use of digital technologies to enhance and promote teaching and learning has had a long tradition in educational discourses—with successive waves of technology positioned as a "technical fix" that will solve a wide range of problems and will breathe new life into educational practices (Robins and Webster 1989). The educational expectations from current social media tools echo the claims of the information and communication technology (ICT) enthusiasts who foresaw the reinvention of teaching and learning with the introduction of new technologies throughout the 1980s and 1990s. Still, these tools were mainly successful in "delivering" existing forms of education in more efficient ways rather than prompting an exemplary transformation or reinvention of educational processes.

For instance, Cuban (1993, n.p.) compared the implementation of microcomputers in schools during the 1980s with the introduction of film and radio in the 1930s and instructional television in the 1950s and 1960s as regards the pattern of "blue sky promises of the new technology revolutionizing instruction learning." He argued that although the number of computers per student in schools had increased steadily during the 1980s, the use of computers was an expanding but still marginal activity—suggesting that scenarios of the "electronic schools" of the future were unlikely to materialize since educational technologists were prone to ignore or underestimate the influence and power of dominant institutional and cultural educational beliefs and practices. Similarly, Lankshear and Knobel (2006, p. 55) referred to the tendency of new technologies during the 1980s and 1990s to merely disguise conventional practices without bringing about substantial changes as an "old wine in new bottles" syndrome where "school literacy routines have a new technology tacked on here or there" without, however, bringing about any substantial change in traditional practices.

Yet, as the 2010s continue, it is again being argued that the nature of social media can allow for further reconsideration as to the possible use of technology in transforming education. In particular, social media have brought notions such as interaction, creation, sharing, participation, and collaboration to the forefront of digital technology use in formal and informal educational settings. Although older technologies were also seen to carry such promises, it has been argued that only with the use of social media these promises may actually become materialized in education on a widespread basis—not least because of their great appeal to young technology users. Davies and Merchant (2009), for instance, highlighted the shift toward a more participatory nature of a new educational era in internet use where web-based activity no longer involves mere information access but rather focuses on interaction and user-generated content creation.

Social media have not only attracted a significant core of online users, in particular among younger generations, but their emergence has also coincided with a number of wider infrastructural shifts that make the implementation of these new tools into formal educational settings less intimidating for teaching staff and institutions alike. For example, many social media tools are seen to be user-friendly and free-of-charge—qualities that along with the new conditions in terms of faster and cheaper internet connectivity and reduced hardware prices allow for their larger-scale implementation into school practices than ever before. As argued by McLoughlin and Lee (2008, p. 641) "in the emerging digital landscape of the Web 2.0 era, where social software tools like blogs, wikis and podcasts provide instant connectivity, promises of engagement and community building, there is a need to rethink models for teaching and learning."

Before identifying and exploring the key issues that surround the use of digital technologies in the classroom, it is useful to start with some basic questions and definitions. What exactly do we mean by the term "digital technologies"? How does it differ from the range of other terms used to refer to technology-related tools and applications? What are the characteristics of the new tools that distinguish them from their predecessors? Have the conditions that can facilitate technological innovation changed?

What Do We Mean by "Digital Technologies"?

From ICTs to web 2.0, social media, and the semantic web, a range of monikers have been used to refer to various types of computer-based systems and applications. Indeed all these different terms share common characteristics as they are all used to refer to computer hardware and software applications. Additionally, they are all inextricably linked with both the technical and social aspects of technology use. In attempting to conceptualize digital technologies, the present study adopts Lievrouw and Livingstone's (2006, p. 2) description of the social and technical aspects of technology who argue that there are three distinct and yet interconnected aspects to describe what technology is: "the artefacts and devices used to communicate or convey information; the activities and practices in which people engage to communicate or share information; and the social arrangements or organisational forms that develop around those devices and practices."

In this sense, this book adopts the term "digital technologies" to refer to the ever-changing complex of technological artifacts, tools, and applications that can be used to "produce, manipulate, store, communicate and disseminate information" (Selwyn 2011a, p. 6). Put simply, this can include computing hardware and software, personal computing devices such as smart phones, as well as internet-based applications such as email, weblogs, and others. However, the term is also used to describe what people do with these technologies as well as the contexts and social arrangements that surround their use. As such, digital technologies should not be viewed as merely technical devices that are adopted for online communication and collaboration. It is equally important to consider the teacher and student practices, the school context, as well as other institutional factors that can affect their implementation and use in formal educational settings.

The umbrella term of "digital technologies" has thus been adopted here to also include the so-called terms social media and web 2.0 technologies. Within an educational context, the notion of social media or web 2.0 has been often accepted as a catch-all term to describe a range of technological developments and a perceived shift in the way the web is used (Crook and Harrison 2008). In this sense, educational descriptions of social media have tended to concentrate on the evolution from passive consumption of information to more active interaction, creation, and sharing with the use of light-weight services that develop rapidly and allow users to make changes to content. As Haythornthwaite and Andrews describe (2011, p. 90):

> While web 1.0 has been about being seen, Web 2.0 is about being seen with and by others, and becoming part of a conversation and community. The focus is on *participation* in blogs, commentaries, wikis, Twitter, and YouTube, with broad access, contribution, retrieval, rating, classifying and evaluating. Web 2.0 operates on simultaneous updating, shared production, and a final product that is greater than the sum of the parts.

The various attempts to define and classify educational technologies highlight the "slippery" and fast-changing nature of these new tools. Indeed, if we are to accept that the notion of social media does not simply concern the constantly emerging technological applications but rather a wider ethos that evolves upon collaboration and openness then it is essential to look in more detail at the characteristics and conditions that differentiate them from their predecessors. Notwithstanding the affinities of social media and preceding generations of ICT tools, there are a number of characteristics that can be said to distinguish these newer forms of technologies from their predecessors and allow for reconsiderations as to the different opportunities they can create in an educational context. The next section will now go on to show how these new characteristics and conditions may justify the greater enthusiasm surrounding the emergence of social media.

The New Characteristics of Social Media

Despite the ongoing debates about the long-standing faith in the ability of digital technologies to transform schooling, the emergence of social media has generated new enthusiasm with regard to their educational potential. For instance, the use of the term web 2.0 seems to be useful "in drawing attention to new kinds of interactivity and describing a second wave of enthusiasm for the internet in the popular imagination" (Merchant 2009, p. 108). The tensions that have arisen over the impact of web 2.0 illustrate its multifaceted nature, denoting that web 2.0 can be used as an umbrella term to include not just the different tools but also the shift in the ethos behind the ways these technologies are used with a particular focus on notions such as collaboration and interconnectivity. From this perspective, it is worth taking some time to explore in more detail the properties of these new tools that differentiate them from their predecessors. For instance, what has made commentators go to such extremes to describe web 2.0 as a "social revolution" (Downes 2005)?

Difficult as it may be to determine what exactly marks the offset of the web 2.0 era, one can certainly identify qualities that distinguish it from the web use of the 1990s. It has been argued that the first version of the web that has been retrospectively termed as "web 1.0" was concerned primarily with broadcasting, accessing, and downloading information resources contributed by a smaller number of users—largely based on static webpages and a peer-to-peer network structure. This mode of internet use was about anonymous users browsing mainstream commercial websites, engaging in a two-way exchange of data and digital material or connecting through mailing lists and discussion forums. In contrast, web 2.0 is widely perceived to be constructed on the basis of the "three c's" notion of collaboration, contribution, and community (see Anderson 2007). As such, there has been a noticeable shift from the "one-to-many" mode of broadcasting content during the 1990s to the "many-to-many" notion of creating and sharing dynamic user-generated content between and within communities of internet users.

The metaphors of the "information superhighway" used to describe the one-to-many internet of the early 1990s or the parallel "cyberspace" world of the late 1990s that existed alongside the users' normal world are now seen to have been replaced by the notion of the "hyper-connected network" (Cavanagh 2007). The web of the early twenty-first century is portrayed as having entered a new, more social phase where networks and communities are created drawing on the notions of sharing and collaborating. Of course, many of the ostensibly new elements of web 2.0 originate in earlier incarnations of the web and, as such web 2.0 signifies the realization of some long-held potentials of the internet. The concept of virtual communities, for example, has long been used to describe a worldwide collection of like-minded users' emerging from the "intersection of humanity and technology" (Rheingold 1993, p. 57). Yet, only from the mid-2000s have networks and online communities acquired such a massive dimension and attracted a significant core of online participants.

The use of the term "web 2.0" is also seen to denote a recent shift from privacy to openness. The notion of openness constitutes a key characteristic of social media and applies not only to the public sharing of content of a more personal nature but it also embraces practices such as the use of open-source software and the free circulation and reuse of data (Anderson 2007). The notion of openness adhered to the philosophy of social media, however, draws on the preexisting "Hacker Ethic" defined by Levy as early as 1984 and the subsequent Open Source culture. Therefore, in many ways, Levy's vision appears to be becoming fully realized alongside the growth of social media with some of the fundamental principles of hacker ethic such as sharing, openness, decentralization, and free access to computers being in the limelight.

A further guiding characteristic in the ethos of the new tools is that of collecting, publishing, and sharing resources and ideas and collaborating online. Notions of sharing, decentralization, and democracy are seen to underpin the social media culture and create a ready platform for communities to distribute knowledge and ideas and promote a collaborative "we-think" ethos (Leadbeater 2008) or a "participatory culture" (Jenkins et al. 2006). Such notions of the "people-powered web" are underpinned by the idea that not only can people easily publish themselves but they can also discover and be discovered by other like-minded people and communicate or engage in debates and convey messages that can reach wider audiences than before. Thus, engagement with social media is seen not only to empower people to contribute to the richness of the web, but also to introduce the notion of a global online audience and promotes what is considered as "rhetoric of democratisation" (Beer and Burrows 2007).

This idea of democratization and openness seems to be associated not only with the nature of the technologies and the shift in types of engagement as outlined above but also to the sharing of content and private information—marking a shift in the values of privacy as social media users appear willing to disclose a range of personal information in their online profiles. As it is often the case, this information can be widely accessed by anyone with an internet connection and, although users may not seem to have any reservations with regard to the amount or the depth of personal data, they post online. This "mainstreaming of private information" (Beer and Burrows 2007, n.p.) has in turn led to range of concerns regarding online and offline safety and data protection as well as discussions on how to teach internet users and particularly children a better understanding of the public–private boundaries of online interfaces.

The New Conditions for Digital Technology Use

Of course it is important to consider not only the properties of social media that differentiate them from the preceding forms of internet tools but also the conditions that have facilitated this new technological innovation. To some extent this new form of web activity needs to be viewed in the light of "media and technology convergence" (Franklin and Van Harmelen 2007) and it has been affected by factors such as the cheaper and faster access to web services and the availability of wireless technologies and mobile internet that have led to new patterns of internet use. In contrast to the past, web services have greatly improved while internet access has become both faster and cheaper as the high-speed and relatively inexpensive broadband connection has widely replaced the dial-up connection of the 1990s, leading to expanded web access. Moreover, the majority of web 2.0 services are free and relatively easy to use and they provide the potential for synchronous communication. In addition, the number of broadband users has increased dramatically while public free Wi-Fi access points have proliferated and the use of mobile telephony for internet access has been gaining popularity. It has been argued that these conditions have facilitated ubiquitous connectivity and a new, "always on" pattern of internet use has emerged (Ito and Antin 2010). At the same time, the computer hardware prices have dropped while their technical characteristics have improved allowing for faster processing as well as greater data storage. These new conditions have resulted in increased internet use; easier and faster accessing, uploading, and downloading of content; as well as greater online engagement and interaction.

Alongside the substantial increase in the number of internet users and the average number of hours spent online, the web 2.0 era has also marked a shift from the traditional patterns of internet use. Crook (2008) notes two particular focal points that have determined recent internet developments, mainly the increasing number of web users and the new patterns of web trading that have emerged. To make it clearer more users and wider online engagement lead to the development of further internet services, whereas the change in trading relations has resulted in reduced commodity prices and more free services. The organic growth and massive use of most social software applications can be attributed to their free-of-charge nature while their success largely depends on network effects as the more users they attract the more viability they gain.

Additionally, within the last few years, the web browser has transformed into a universal platform that hosts a number of online applications and social software while webpages load in seconds and their design has become more versatile and attractive. The shift toward the browser as platform and the potential of online data storage translate into a hassle-free, more enjoyable web experience that in combination with ubiquitous connectivity enhances collaboration and the social participatory nature of web 2.0 (Crook et al. 2008a). The web has taken the form of an interactive and participatory leisure space and this shift toward online entertainment and communication has shaped the increasing number of users and their rising engagement with social media. Digital technologies have had particularly great appeal to the younger generations of internet users who have embraced the use of social media in their daily lives.

These new tools and conditions have to some extent reshaped expectations of technology use in schools and are significant in terms of their implications for educational provision and practice. For instance, educational institutions and teachers are expected to catch up with these technological developments and make changes so as to remain relevant in this fast-changing digital era. As Selwyn (2013, p. 64) notes, "the integration of digital technologies into education systems has been a growing feature of state education policymaking over the past three decades." With this thought in mind, it is worth exploring the role of policy makers and international organizations in shaping the ways that educational technologies are implemented around the world.

New Tools for New Schools? Imperatives for the Implementation of Digital Technologies in Education

It is without a doubt that the drive to implement the use of digital technologies in schools is at large influenced and led by a range of stakeholders, international bodies, and individual governments. Similar to the drive to insert collaborative initiatives in education, educational technologies have been promoted by politicians and policy makers alike for the past decades. For instance, the rise of microelectronics resulted in a range of national educational technology policies throughout the 1980s, which embraced the potential of technologies to revolutionize classroom instruction (Cuban 1986). Still, it was in the mid-1990s with the emergence of the internet into mainstream societal use that the field of educational technologies attracted the more sustained attention of policy makers at national and international levels (Selwyn 2011a). As such, over the past two decades, the influence of state policy making has been central to the ways that digital technologies have been implemented in formal educational settings. This has involved both an increase in funding with regard to technological resourcing of hardware, software, and network infrastructure as well as programs for teacher training and changes in the curriculum to accommodate the use of the new technologies.

In terms of infrastructure and availability, digital technologies now consist of a significant element of educational systems in most developed and developing countries around the world. National and international "ICT strategies" focus on ensuring that both computer hardware and internet connectivity are available in schools and significant amounts of funding are dedicated toward achieving this aim. The outcomes of these national efforts to support computer and internet access at schools often feature in a range of reports and statistical surveys. For instance, the recent "Survey of Schools: ICT in Education" carried out by the European Commission (2013) paints a very positive picture regarding available infrastructure at schools. As Wastiau et al. (2013) note, students and teachers have unprecedented access to educational technology, highlighting that there are around twice as many computers per hundred students in secondary schools than in 2006 while broadband is almost ubiquitous in all types of schools. Moreover, laptop computers and interactive whiteboards are also becoming pervasive in schools albeit to a lesser extent (European Commission 2013a). Additionally, substantial funding has been allocated to ensure that learning platform provision is available to schools. These learning platforms can encompass a range of technologies such as virtual learning environments, resource sharing technologies, and management information systems with the aim of supporting teaching staff, students, and less often, parents, to access learning resources, communicate and collaborate, as well as monitor, assess, and report on student progress (Jewitt et al. 2011).

Similarly, a national survey at school level conducted by the National Center for Educational Statistics in the United States reported that all public schools had one or more instructional computers with internet access with a student–computer ratio of 3.1 to 1. In addition, 97 percent of schools had one or more instructional computers located in classrooms and 58 percent of schools had laptops on carts (Gray et al. 2010). Various examples of allocating substantial educational funds toward equipping schools and students with technological equipment can be found in a range of more local contexts. For instance, the Common Core Technology project, initiated in 2013 in the Los Angeles Unified School District, aimed to invest $30 million to equip the students of 47 schools—a total of 655,000—with iPad tablets. This initiative endeavored to close the "digital divide" by ensuring fair access for all students to "21st century skills and technology" and preparing them for the Common Core State Standards and the state online testing system.

Likewise, a substantial amount of funding has been allocated through the Digital Education Revolution (DER) reform program in order to provide ICT access to public high-school students in Australia. In particular, with the financial aid of the National Secondary School Computer Fund, a one-to-one computer-to-student ratio has been achieved for students in years 9 to 12. More than 967,000 computers have been installed under the Computer Fund, exceeding the national target of 786,000. Moreover, the One Laptop Per Child Australia Project has been helping children who live in remote communities by providing them with purpose-built, high-quality laptops and educational software.

Aside from issues of technological provision and infrastructure, the use of digital technologies in the classroom has notably been included as a key component of educational agendas at national and international levels. It is important to recognize that the implementation of educational technologies into schooling has long been a significant element of the educational activities of the major Intergovernmental and supranational organizations. As Selwyn (2013, p. 46) argues:

> Intergovernmental organisations such as the World Bank, OECD and United Nations have all been prominent advocates of educational technology since the 1980s and have played a substantial collective role in initiating and influencing the implementation of educational technology around the world.

In particular, the promotion of educational technology has largely taken place through more specialized agencies and programs such as the United Nation's educational agency "UNESCO" or the Organisation for Economic Cooperation and Development (OECD)'s Program for International Student Assessment (PISA), and the European Union's (EU) "Education, Audiovisual and Culture Executive Agency" (EACEA). The educational technology agendas of these organizations seem to be a main driving force behind the effort to get more computers in schools. This is also reflected in the creation of various reports and publications that aim at advancing the use of educational technologies in schools, such as OECD's "*Connected Minds: Technology and Today's Learners*" or UN's "*Harnessing the Potential of ICT for Education.*" Similarly, the promotion of educational technology has been a significant aspect of the European Commission's work in the field. Considerable funding has been invested in conducting surveys on technology infrastructure and the benefits and impact of ICTs in schools. Moreover, through the "Lifelong Learning Programme" the EU has made systematic efforts to promote the use of digital technologies in the classroom and has pursued a number of educational technological schemes. More recently, within the framework of the "Europe 2020 Initiative" the Digital Agenda for Europe aims, among others, to enhance digital literacy, skills, and inclusion; tackle the digital divide; and support member states to mainstream eLearning for the modernization of education and training. The notion of "digital competence" features in the heart of many of these efforts and it involves the critical and confident use of ICTs to store, retrieve, create, and exchange information as well as communicate and collaborate online (European Commission 2007).

Inherent in all these initiatives and agendas is the belief that educational technologies can improve and even transform schooling. As Cuban (2009, n.p.) reasons, implementing digital technologies in schools aims at making "schools more efficient and productive that they currently are," transforming "teaching and learning into an engaging and active process connected to real life" and preparing "the current generation of young people for the future workplace." Indeed, contemporary digital technologies are often seen to play a key role in providing pedagogic structures and supporting radically different forms of learning than in the twentieth century. A range of perceived benefits and advantages is associated with technology use. These are seen to take a number of forms and include hopes for better learning, hopes for fairer learning, hopes of individualized and informalized learning, hopes for enhanced teaching and pedagogy, and hopes for enhanced management and organization of schooling (Selwyn 2011a).

In many respects, the collaborative, interactive, and participatory qualities of digital technologies have, on the one hand, resulted in growing enthusiasm among educators as to the potential of implementing them into school practice to support and enhance teaching and learning. Some commentators are predicting the imminent reconfiguration of education provision—foreseeing the era of "education 2.0" (see Rosenfeld 2007; Yamamoto and Karaman 2011). On the other hand, however, other commentators remain more skeptical as to the appropriateness of social media applications for formal learning while others have raised concerns about "the decline in social norms and standards exemplified by young people's social media use" (Ito et al. 2013, p. 29). As Selwyn argues (2008, p. 10):

> Both "booster" and "doomster" discourses have grown up around web 2.0, portraying its possible educational "effects" and "impacts" in decidedly overstated terms. At one extreme are enthusiastic hopes for a complete transformation of education systems, with some commentators extending the technology terminology of "2.0" through talk of a "rebooting" of teaching and learning. At the other, some commentators have used web 2.0 to generate moral panics about young people and the supposed death of education.

With these thoughts in mind, this chapter will now go on to describe these "booster" and "doomster" discourses (Bigum and Kenway 1998) as well as some other more considered approaches within these two extremes concerning the implementation of digital technologies within an educational framework. It will commence by considering the most enthusiastic discourses concerning the perceived potential of fully implementing such tools into education and thereby redesigning traditional models of teaching and learning. Conversely, consideration will be given to the skeptical conceptualizations of web 2.0 educational opportunities. As Thomas (2011, p. 1) notes "from Plato to Web 2.0, new technologies have always attracted both passionate advocates as well as an active dissenting tradition."

Educational Promises and Fears over Digital Technologies

The Educational Promises of Digital Technologies: The "Booster" Discourse

For many educationalists, digital technologies are seen as promising a significant reconfiguration of education provisions— conforming to what Buckingham (2007, p. 32) identifies as a trend in popular discussion toward "technological boosterism" where claims are made that attribute "enormous power to technology to equip, to empower and even to liberate young people." Indeed, Bigum and Kenway (1998, p. 378) argue that the most dominant group of commentators within educational technology discussions are the "boosters"—defined as "the unequivocal promoters of new information technologies in education." Their claims tend to focus on optimistic scenarios of how new technologies can be applied within an educational context to solve existing problems and transform schooling. As Selwyn (2011b, p. 21) points out, "the vast majority of popular and academic opinion could be said to hold an essentially optimistic view of the life-changing power of digital technology." Inherent in these discourses is the belief that technology can improve education and solve most if not all the problems that afflict schooling. Driven by a tangible excitement for the new, "boosters" view the growth and use of computer technology as inevitable—displaying very few doubts about the educational values of their idea for transformation.

As such, a number of educational commentators and digital entrepreneurs adhere to the increasingly popular perception that technologies have an inherent power to positively reconfigure education and modernize schools. Social media are, for example, said to spark an even greater revolution than that of their predecessors by encompassing the potential to transform the educational provision and learning (Brown and Adler 2008). Others perceive web 2.0 as the future of education that will overall have an even greater impact than the advent of the printing press (Hargadon 2008). This can be seen in the growing use of the 2.0 suffix in educational debates with terms such as education 2.0, (e)learning 2.0, school 2.0, curriculum 2.0, and classroom 2.0 coming to prominent use. In particular, the notion of "learning 2.0" has been defined as a new form of technology-enhanced learning that "goes beyond providing free access to traditional course materials and educational tools and creates a participatory architecture for supporting communities of learners" (Brown and Adler 2008, p. 28). In all these cases, digital technologies are seen to mark a shift toward a new more collaborative, interactive, creative, and participatory ethos in education as they are designed to facilitate dialogue, teamwork, and sharing. In particular, the "socialness" of the new technologies is seen to allow schooling "to break out of the paradigm of the monolithic learner into the more intricate and complex world of constructivist, active and situated pedagogies" (Poore 2013, p. 8).

These booster discourses are especially prominent in emerging guidance to educational practitioners with regard to the learning potential of social media. For example, the use of these new tools is seen to enhance and even transform instruction and student learning by engaging students' interest and motivation, developing critical-thinking and information-gathering skills, supporting cooperative work, and promoting interaction (Green et al. 2008). Along these lines, Richardson (2009) points out that the digital divide continues to grow between the ways young people learn and connect in their everyday life and the ways they engage into educational practices within the classroom. He views digital technologies as a means of transferring information, providing individualized learning, and facilitating active participation that can bring about transformational changes for teachers and students.

A sense of boosterism is also evident in the ways that education 2.0 or learning 2.0 have been associated with the characteristics of the new digital generation learners. A number of different terms and popularized accounts have emerged since the 2000s to describe this cohort of young people. Some of the most popular ones are the "digital natives" (Palfrey and Gaser 2008; Prensky 2001), the "Net Generation" (Tapscott 1998; 2009), the "iKids" (Prensky 2008), and the "Millennials" (Howe and Strauss 2000). These terms seem to evoke two popular assumptions regarding the characteristics of the new generation of young people. The first one is that they make no distinction between their online and offline lives as they begin their exposure to ICTs at very young age. The second assumption is that young people display ways of learning that have radically changed and they have dramatically different expectations with regard to their schooling. They are thought to be proficient and creative with computers and technology and very skilled at multitasking while they are used to the "always on" pattern of internet use as opposed to their educators who are often portrayed as "digital immigrants" (Prensky 2007).

It would be fair to conclude that a sense of boosterism pervades much of the current writing on digital technologies and education. Overall, the potential benefits of implementing social media in education are generally seen to relate to the flexible, participatory, collaborative, and interactive nature of these new tools that create new educational opportunities such as writing for a global audience, developing digital literacies and skills to accompany students through their lifelong learning, and facilitating synchronous student communication and collaboration (Beldarrain 2006; Godwin-Jones 2003) However, when looking beyond the assertion that these tools per se bear the power to increase skills or enhance schooling, these statements are often seen as overgeneralizations that are not presented in line with findings from empirical research.

The Educational Radicalisms of Digital Technologies: The "Anti-schoolers" Discourse

While the "booster" discourse presents digital technologies as means of transforming and reconfiguring education within its formal settings, an even more radical approach toward the educational use of technologies is presented by the "anti-schoolers." The "anti-schooler" discourse is predicated around the "demise of schooling"—presenting formal educational settings as a product of the industrial workplace that has now become past its sell-by date (Bigum and Kenway 1998, p. 381). What distinguishes this discourse from that of the "boosters" is that the anti-schoolers embrace the diminishment of schools rather than seeking ways to implement digital technologies into traditional settings and forms of schooling. For instance, Cooley and Johnston described (2000) how with the advent of computers, futurists foresaw a world of highly individualized education in which students take control of their own learning with the support of electronic learning resources and traditional teachers and classrooms become obsolete.

These anti-schooler discourses can be seen as stemming from the views of Ivan Illich (1971) who embraced the use of technologies to promote "learning webs" and criticized the inefficient nature of institutionalized education. This deschooling discourse gained credence throughout the 1970s and 1980s with authors such as Reimer (1971) who also criticized the institutional monopoly of education and proposed the disestablishment of the school system and its replacement with networks of educational objects, learning peers, or professional educators. As was later suggested, "learning is in and school is out" since technology-aided "hyperlearning" makes "the infrastructure of 'schooling' irrelevant and even obstructive" and, therefore, schools are bound to become obsolete in the future (Perelman 1993, pp. 19 and 63). The notion of replacing traditional methods of schooling with new technologies was also evident in Papert's (1993, 1996) vision of future schools. Among other suggestions, Papert proposed making traditional schooling a matter of parental preference and encouraging home schooling with the implementation of computerized technologies.

The recent shift toward education 2.0 and social media tools has proved a ready vehicle for the continuation of the "anti-schooler" discourse. For instance, Solomon and Shrum (2007) highlight the decreasing importance of schools as physical locations and suggest their possible replacement by virtual schools and online communities of learners where teachers act as "tree guides" or "information gurus," available to assist students in their learning journey. Other commentators propose the parting of schooling and learning and imagine schools as looser and more flexible public or private learning spaces (Collins and Halverson 2009). Schools are also criticized for being "out of kilter with the world children are growing up in" and for offering learning "cut off from real-world experiences" (Leadbeater 2008, p. 147). While not eschewing the concept of school altogether, Leadbeater does not regard schools as the most important places for learning, but instead he proposes that learning should be made available "all over, all the time, in a wide variety of settings" where students would be given more choice and more freedom, actively participating in the educational process (ibid., p. 149).

The Educational Fears over Social Media:
The "Doomsters" Discourse

Although persuasive, the above radically optimistic scenarios of an educational transformation with the use of social media are not unanimously
embraced across the education community. At the other extreme from the
"booster" and "anti-schooler" discourses stand a number of commentators
who refer in decidedly negative terms to the use of technologies both in and
out-of-school. These commentators talk of digital technologies as degrading
schooling and foresee the "death" of education because of the increasing use
and popularity of social media. As argued by Bigum and Kenway (1998,
p. 387) "if boosters are the blinkered romantics of scenario writing for high
technology in education then doomsters are the writers of tragedy." Broadly
conservative in nature, the doomster discourse evolves around fears about
the possible harm and damage caused by new technologies that can lead
to the deskilling of students in terms of traditional skills and literacies and
to the decline of the formal educational system in general.

Indeed, such "booster" and "doomster" scenarios have been advanced
since the advent of computers. As Buckingham (2007, p. 40) argues, "fan-
tasies of 'Edutopia' have been challenged by some equally fervent con-
demnation of technology in education." In contrast to the enthusiastic
educationalists who argue over the potential of social media to enhance
or reconfigure traditional schooling, the doomster scenarios that flourish anticipate the demise of education. Andrew Keen (2008, p. 143), for
example, criticizes social media for "creating a generation of cut-and-paste
burglars who view all content on the internet as common property" and who
are "downloading and using this stolen property to cheat their way through
school and university." Likewise, other critics view students' use of social
media tools as having a detrimental effect on their studies. For instance,
Brabazon (2007, p. 19) deplores web 2.0 tools as destabilizing authoritative
relationships between students and teachers—arguing that "2006 will be
remembered as a time when the mediocre, banal and self-confident discovered blogs...and grainy mobile phone footage of the embarrassing, humili-
ating and voyeuristic gained a new home—YouTube." Similarly, although
not a doomster herself, Jackie Marsh (2010) described how young children's
engagement with online games and virtual worlds has been associated with
numerous "doomsday" scenarios.

While these concerns relate to the social deterioration of educational
relationships, other educational commentators have described pessimistic
scenarios relating to the harmful results that the increasing use of digital
technologies can have on youth's physical and psychological development.

For instance, concerns have been raised with regard to the detrimental effect that engagement with social media has on children's cognitive and literacy skills, leading to short attention spans, limited capacity for sustained thought, greater stress, and loss of focus (Carr 2010; Greenfield 2009; Pea et al. 2012). A sense of doomsterism is also evident in recent commentaries that portray a disengaged generation of young people immersed in the use of new technologies that somehow harm their intellectual development. For example, Bauerlein (2008, p. 201) describes current generations of net-savvy youth as the "dumbest generation" characterized by a "vigorous, indiscriminate ignorance." He argues that rather than empowering and enriching knowledge and connectivity with the broader world, the use of new technologies has instead resulted in decreasing young people's knowledge of social, political, and historical issues. Additionally, this "dumbest generation" is said to have become adept at peer-to-peer interaction that focuses on popular culture and allows little or no space for the participation of older non-digital generations.

The Educational Challenges of Social Media: The "Critics" Discourse

As the previous sections have described, the history of educational technologies often appears to be characterized by "a debate between uncritical romantics and dismissive skeptics" (Thomas 2011, p. 2). The advent of social media, in particular, seems to have offered even more ground for extreme optimistic or pessimistic scenarios that foresee either the radical and imminent transformation or the demise of the traditional educational settings. However, both positions appear to "often exaggerate or downplay the impact of technology, and this leads to entrenched positions and polarization" (ibid.). Underlying many of these either optimistic or pessimistic accounts is the notion that technology will somehow cause change—for better or for worse. These arguments are often driven by a deterministic approach where technology is viewed as the major governing force that determines history (Williams 1994). Implicit in a technologically deterministic view is regarding digital technologies as something separate and independent of society, where "inventions can merely 'happen', and then society has to deal with the consequences of that happening and the new ways of life that follow" (Miller 2011, p. 3). As such technological determinism does not take into consideration the social relations and conditions that underpin the implementation and use of digital technologies in education, but instead positions technologies as the driving forces behind social change.

Conversely, one small but vocal group of commentators is seen to be more skeptical as to the potential benefits and affordances of new technologies for schooling, challenging the "taken-for-granted assumptions" of the boosters' discourse (Bigum and Kenway 1998, p. 383) and adopting more moderate views considering the issues that surround the successful (or not) implementation of social media in education. For these authors at least, the spirit of enthusiasm that currently surrounds discussions of educational technologies contrasts with a range of practical challenges and fears that emerge from the implementation of digital technologies in formal educational settings. Some critics argue that careful consideration should be given to issues of e-safety and privacy, especially when bearing in mind the recent shift in many users' values of privacy and disclosure of personal information online (Beer and Burrows 2007). Although it has been reported that young people seem to have a high degree of awareness of safety issues (Mediappro 2006), some critical commentators raise concerns over the need to limit the potential of students being at risk when using online tools and applications. Recurring concerns over safety issues are largely seen to focus on the danger of cyber bullying and "falling prey to predatory strangers online" (Crook et al. 2008a, p. 22). Additionally, other commentators express concerns over the protection of students' privacy in relation to the public nature of the internet and the need for teachers to minimize potential risks and embed e-safety in the school's teaching and learning practices (Hasebrink et al. 2008; Walker 2009).

Skepticism is also expressed when considering whether the so-called digital native or net generation tag can be applicable to the total student population or whether "digital divides" and differentiations still exist according to the socioeconomic status of the pupils and whether even the "net-generation" of learners make simplistic, superficial use of the new technologies or manage to engage in more in-depth practices. As Selwyn (2009, p. 76) points out, the users and audiences of social media "remain skewed towards young, male, well-educated, affluent Western users," arguing that "the most used social web tools are most often appropriated for the one-way passive consumption of content." Similar concerns as to the relation of the socioeconomic status with the access and use of new technologies are highlighted by Notten et al. (2009) in their cross-national study of the use of digital technologies by adolescents. As Bennett et al. (2008) also argue, evidence from empirical research suggests, that, while a large proportion of young people engage with new technologies in a skillful manner, another considerable proportion of young people do not have the skills or the adequate levels of access to technology as predicted by proponents of the digital native idea.

Notwithstanding the skepticism expressed as regards the possible implications and the essential precautions that need to be taken into consideration, these critics do not necessarily dismiss the potential of digital technologies for education but seek ways to make it as unproblematic as possible. For example, Owen et al. (2006) have highlighted the changing patterns of engagement with knowledge, identifying a shift in the current role of education as a means not only of acquiring knowledge but also of developing the skills to cope with societal changes and promoting lifelong learning. Thus, the perception that underlines the critics' discourse is that "web 2.0 social software and its conceptual underpinnings do not indicate a sharp break with the old but, rather, the gradual emergence of a new type of practice that is evolution rather than revolution" (Kamel Boulos and Wheelert 2007, p. 16).

Furthermore, it can be argued that the appropriation of digital technologies for school collaboration has been slow and this can be associated with a number of factors. Apart from the more obvious technical inhibitors relating to the technologies, connectivity, and infrastructure that were highlighted in chapter 1, a range of other themes and factors appear to underpin the success of web-based collaborative projects. According to Crook (2012, p. 77), collaboration and communication practices "do not exist independently of the socio-cultural structures" but there is a range of social actors and factors that can affect the implementation of digital technologies for school collaboration focusing on different levels of analysis: the "micro," "meso," and "macro" levels of description. As Kozma (2003, p.11) argues:

> Innovative pedagogic practices are embedded in a concentric set of contextual levels that effect and mediate change...At each level there are actors and factors that mediate change. According to the literature, the successful implementation of innovative practices depends not only on the characteristics of the innovation but also on factors such as classroom organisation and personal characteristics of the teachers and students (micro level), the school organisation and personal characteristics of administrators and community leaders (meso level), and national and state policies and international trends (macro level).

At a micro-level of analysis we should consider individuals' motivation and disposition to engage with digital technologies and collaborative projects; their participation and contribution throughout the project; the teachers' familiarity not only with the tools but also with alternative pedagogic approaches; the barriers all participants might face; their collaborative and pedagogic practices; their in- and out-of-school engagement and familiarity with digital technologies; and last, their relation with their partner team and the time and personal effort they invest in the project. Notwithstanding the importance of these micro-level concerns, there is also a need to consider the wider context of the educational institution where the projects were materialized. At the meso-level, thus, it is considered important to look at the local governance of education and in particular at the school, as a physical, organizational, and cultural space. For instance, it is worth taking time to explore how different school settings and cultures, technological infrastructures, and other meso-level actors such as the local authorities affected the implementation and eventual effectiveness of using educational technologies for online communication and collaboration. Finally, at the macro-level "government led initiatives, national policy, national curricula, assessment regimes define the broad conditions in which innovations are developed and negotiated, politically and culturally" (Perrotta 2011, p. 3). In this sense, one should develop an understanding of how the wider institutional organization of the collaborative programs can affect the projects' outcomes.

All in all, while informing much of the general educational reaction to social media, these booster and doomster discourses presented in the previous sections are intended to be polemic and often unsubstantiated in nature. Still, contrasting accounts of educational technology use are nothing new. Booster and doomster scenarios have been common in the history of educational technologies. However, in reflecting on the significance of digital technology use in schools we should also consider the more specific and carefully argued justifications that have emerged from educational commentators—not least the reason for digital technology implementation leading to tangible improvements in the provision of education and learning.

Educational Theories Underpinning the Educational Use of Digital Technologies

The idea that digital technologies can support, enhance, or even transform learning is obviously part of a bigger story. As we have already seen, one of the striking characteristics of accounts and analyses of educational technologies over the past decades is their attributed power with regard to transforming teaching and learning. Since the aim of the collaborative programs that were presented in chapter 1 is to promote intercultural understanding and web-based learning, it is important to look at how technology use is linked with supporting the act of learning in one form or another. In the case of collaborative projects, learning can take different forms ranging from discovering different countries and developing a cultural awareness to enhancing language skills and gaining subject-specific knowledge. A new wave of enthusiasm has been generated regarding the potential of digital technologies to facilitate learning; particular informal and collaborative forms of learning and a range of educational theories have emerged.

In particular, social constructivist theories, influenced by the Vygotskian school of thinking, are often seen adhered to educational technology discourses and a large number of academic commentators and educationalists have associated constructivist principles with the collaborative, participatory, and creative ethos of digital technologies. Other educational theories underlying social media implementation are related to the "communities of practice" and networked constructivist knowledge-building pedagogies, as well as discourses on democracy, creativity, social justice, and informal learning. Although many of the specific issues covered in these arguments differ, they all provide a justification for the increased use of digital technologies in formal educational settings. It therefore makes sense to review in brief some of the key educational theories that underpin the use of digital technologies for learning.

Social Constructivist and Constructionist Arguments for Digital Technology Use

The use of computing technologies to facilitate educational practices has often been viewed in line with social-constructivist theories (Duffy and Jonassen 1993). Although the roots of social constructivism stretch back to the beginning of the twentieth century, the progression from a teacher-centered, "chalk and talk" model of teaching to a more student-centered and participatory approach has frequently been linked with the more convivial and collaborative nature of digital technologies. As argued by Jonassen et al. (1995, n.p.), the constructivist mode of "active" learning can facilitate student interaction and participation in their surrounding environment so as to create "a personal view of the world" going beyond the mere transmission of information from "instructors' minds to students' notebooks." In this sense, constructivist environments are seen to be looser and more activity based while they provide learners opportunities to engage in knowledge construction through collaborative activities.

Because of the parallels between these descriptions on learning and the more collaborative nature of the news and applications, constructivism is being favored by most contemporary supporters of educational technologies (Buckingham 2007). Enthusiasm for digital technologies has, therefore, often been underpinned by constructivist theories. Indeed, it has been argued that "the emphasis on community and social networks in web 2.0

has a strong connection to theories of social constructivism," positioning web-based learning as both an independent and community embedded process with the role of the teacher being reconfigured as that of a "facilitator" who supports collaboration and guides learners "through their interaction with the learning material" (Sturm et al. 2009, p. 371–373). Additionally, "learning to learn" has become far more important than memorization of knowledge and there has been an increasing call to adjust pedagogy to these new circumstances (McLoughlin and Lee 2008).

The association of social media with social constructivism theories has also been highlighted by a number of other commentators and can be made across most types of social media tools. For instance, Richardson (2009) described weblogs as especially constructivist tools for learning while Du and Wagner (2005) argued that weblogs enhance the traditional learning log with collaborative elements. What is more, the collaborative nature of wikis is seen to create opportunities for reflective thinking and knowledge building, which are notions adhered to the social constructivist pedagogy (Parker and Chao 2007). Notwithstanding the oversimplified justifications underlying this argument, the wiki is often seen as "a powerful tool for constructivist learning environments because it facilitates collaboration" (Notari 2006, p. 131).

The educational qualities of social media have also been underpinned by the constructionist learning theory that views learning as resulting from the reconstruction rather than transmission of knowledge and argues that learning is most effective when it is part of an activity such as constructing a meaningful product (Papert 1986). Constructionism has been long associated with Seymour Papert and the use of the Logo language to teach mathematics; however, it is seen to have potential application in other educational fields. As argued by Forte and Bruckman (2007, p. 32) "constructionism carries with it an ideology of empowerment and choice" and students learn by being engaged in "open-ended, unstructured, playful but productive construction activities." Similarly, constructionism is said to tie in with the use of social media for the construction of public content, for instance, by creating a video presentation, a blog entry, or a set of wiki pages (Franklin and van Harmelen 2007).

Creating Online Communities of Practice and Knowledge-Building Networks

The opportunities for collaboration that digital technologies offer are also seen by some commentators to relate to sociocultural theories of learning such as "communities of practice" and "knowledge-building networks" theories. The term "communities of practice," first introduced by Lave and Wenger (1991), refers to the process of collective learning that takes place in realistic sociocultural contexts and activities through engagement in actions and interactions. This notion has subsequently been taken up within the educational technology literature. For instance, technology-based learning has been defined as a situated process where, through participation, members of online communities of practice adapt to shared knowledge and practices (Schaffert et al. 2006). In this sense, technologies such as wikis can be perceived as knowledge platforms that allow members of the community of practice to collaborate and share their knowledge with the group. For instance, Schwartz et al. (2004, n.p.) associated wikis with a number of fundamental properties of Wenger's communities of practice such as "a virtual presence, a variety of interactions, easy participation, valuable content, connections to a broader subject field, personal and community identity and interaction, democratic participation, and evolution over time."

Notions of "knowledge-building communities," developed by Scardamalia and Bereiter (1994), are also often used to justify contemporary technology use. In this sense, it has been argued that there is a need to restructure schools as communities where the construction of knowledge will be collectively supported and the role of educational technology will be to "replace classroom discourse patterns with those having more immediate and natural extensions to knowledge-building communities outside school walls" (ibid., p. 265). Such conceptualization of knowledge-building networks sees learning as an intentional collaborative activity where learners are responsible for their own learning goals and seek to achieve them by sharing and participating in the community (Grant 2009). The knowledge-building paradigm is said to take advantage of the potential of digital technologies as it encourages a less top-down form of learning that is based on small teams, sharing, content creation, and the use of digital technologies to access, create, share, and continually improve ideas (McLoughlin and Lee 2007). In particular, wiki tools are often associated with knowledge-building network theories (Forte and Bruckman 2007; Parker and Chao 2007).

The idea of learning as a collaborative and socially situated process also relates to the pedagogical approach of "computer supported collaborative learning." According to this approach, participants share and construct learning via interaction with each other and by using technology as their primary means of communication or as a common resource in online and classroom learning environments either synchronously or asynchronously (Stahl et al. 2006). The field of computer-supported collaborative learning has now attracted considerable interest due to the development of social media technologies, which can not only provide learners with access to knowledge outside of their immediate environment but can also facilitate online social interaction and learning engagement with collaborative activities.

A more recent educational paradigm is that of the "Connected Learning model." This is defined as "learning that is socially embedded, interest-driven, and oriented toward educational, economic, or political opportunity" (Ito et al. 2013, p. 6). In other words, connected learning takes place when a young person pursues a personal interest with the support of friends and adults, and can link this learning and interest to academic achievement, career possibilities, or civic engagement. The role of digital technologies is to: "(1) offer engaging formats for interactivity and self-expression, (2) lower barriers to access for knowledge and information, (3) provide social supports for learning through social media and online affinity groups, and (4) link a broader and more diverse range of culture, knowledge, and expertise to educational opportunity" (ibid.).

Theories of Individual and Organizational Improvement in Education

While there has been an ever-increasing tendency to embrace digital technologies as powerful means of creating knowledge and building collaborative communities, further consideration needs to be given to the extent to which these promises are actually being fulfilled within formal educational settings. In particular, consideration needs to be given to how digital technologies relate to the conditions under which learning is seen to take place, the perceived possibility of using such tools to personalize the learning experience, and their influence on making education a more inclusive process.

In this first sense, it could be argued that the use of digital technologies and the educational opportunities that emerge are often seen to be underpinned by theories of informal rather than formal learning. This reflects a number of changes to the definition of knowledge and learning that have taken place throughout the last 20 years or so—with a range of activities that do not take place under formal educational settings now often seen as educational in nature, even if not in the conventional understanding of the term. For instance, Buckingham (2007, p. 24) suggested that informal learning can take place in a range of in-school and out-of-school settings and it does not necessarily "have to involve 'formal' definitions, either of content or of the pedagogic relationships between teachers and learners." In this sense, it is important to acknowledge that informal learning can take place within a formal educational setting—but is less likely to. Regardless of location, digital technologies are often seen as platforms that can facilitate informal learning, allowing a range of educational activities to take place. As Redecker argues (2009, p. 41):

> Access to digital technologies enables learners to tailor their informal learning to their own interests, to access information of relevance to them, to communicate with people who can support their learning, and to share ideas and expertise within informal learning communities.

In contrast to the often conservative, static, and institutional nature of formal education, web-based informal learning communities are said to be more experimental, innovative, and provisional and "can evolve to respond to short-term needs and temporary interests" (Jenkins et al. 2006, p. 9). In particular, it has been argued that wiki tools can promote self-directed or informal learning within the school setting (Schaffert et al. 2006). Luckin et al. (2009) also reported instances of sophisticated engagement with social media that resulted in informal learning among UK secondary school students through the use of a variety of applications, including Wikipedia, YouTube, forums, virtual world programs, and social-network sites to access or contribute content and resources. Similarly, a large-scale US ethnographic study that documented young people's everyday engagements with new media in informal peer-based interaction settings reported that "some of the drivers of self-motivated learning come not from institutionalized 'authorities' in kids' lives setting standards and providing instruction, but from the kids observing and communicating with people engaged in the same interests, and in the same struggles for status and recognition that they are" (Ito and Antin 2010, p. 22).

The enthusiasm for the adoption of new digital technologies in formal educational contexts is also often underpinned by theories of creativity, which has been the focus of various educational policy developments and is often touted by educational commentators as a contemporary skill. As Loveless (2007, p. 5) argued, twenty-first-century education systems are now compelled to "adapt to the changes, aspirations and anxieties about the role of creativity in our wider society" with digital technologies seen as a means to "provoke teachers' thinking about the media, the organisation, and the knowledge and skills required to support learners' creative activities." The deployment of digital technologies to promote creativity in the classroom has significantly increased over the last few years and is now often seen as a key pedagogical quality of social media. For instance, Rudd et al. (2006b) asserted that digital technologies foster new forms of digital creativity in the classroom—giving students increased opportunities to create, share, and publish content online. This new form of digital creativity, however, entails the danger of predicating creative interaction and production upon the power of the technologies. It may be necessary to acknowledge, therefore, that the implementation of social media in school settings does not essentially guarantee effective engagement but there is a need to direct and support children's interactions in informed ways.

Aside from these advantages of informality and creativity, digital technologies are also seen by some educational commentators to lead to an increased equity of learning opportunities and outcomes by enhancing the promotion of inclusive practices and increasing social justice in education. Inclusive education is seen as a range of practices that focus on the individual needs of students and also promote an understanding of social equality. It has been argued that social media use in schools can support inclusive practices not only by motivating and engaging learners but also by allowing personalization of learning. The notion of personalization involves tailoring education to better match learners' needs and aspirations and providing more flexible access to information and resources and more ubiquitous opportunities for collaborative learning (Green et al. 2005, p. 20; Walker 2009).

For some commentators, then, these qualities extend into enhancing equalities of opportunity and outcome. For example, web-based learning is often associated with widening access and facilitating new approaches to learning so as to engage people who have not managed to achieve their full potential when using more traditional approaches (Grant 2008). Similarly, technology is often seen as a means of addressing the needs of marginalized groups by enhancing learning and equipping students with the skills and knowledge prerequisite to articulate their own voices (Light and Luckin 2008). The notion of allowing space for "learner voice" associated with theories of democratization or "learner democracy" is also seen to be consistent with the web 2.0 ethos of openness and democratic engagement. Offering learners opportunities to make their voices heard and listening to their concerns, interests, and needs can be facilitated by the collaborative, communicative, and community-building properties of social media (Rudd et al. 2006a).

Digital Technology Use in Practice

The rationales and arguments presented so far have been at large based on presumption and prediction rather that actual empirical evidence of digital technology use in school settings. Alongside the various discourses and theoretical perceptions that either overemphasize, criticize, or dismiss the educational opportunities and risks that emerge with the deployment of digital technologies in formal educational settings, it is important to overview the empirical findings of the existing research literature. While school use of digital technologies has been the focus of a number of educational policy agendas, little relevant large-scale and in-depth academic research has been conducted to date to highlight the impact and the educational benefits and/ or challenges of their actual implementation in schooling.

The academic literature that does exist on social media has largely described and suggested ways of implementing social media in the classroom and argued about the potential benefits with regard to student motivation and engagement, interactivity and collaboration, and wider educational outcomes. Similarly, large-scale surveys and studies have focused mainly on issues of school infrastructure and access, rather than on why and how social media are used in the classroom and with what educational results. This next section aims to bring together the emerging findings from both large-scale survey, interview, and observation-based studies on the use of digital technologies mainly in primary and secondary education in order to explore whether the enthusiasm or skepticism outlined so far in this chapter reflects the actual use of such tools in school settings.

In- and Out-of-School Use of Digital Technologies in Schools: Findings from Empirical Research

Social media and the internet have become a pervasive part of the lives of children and young people in most developed and developing countries around the world. Previous research has established that young people are generally high users of the internet and digital technologies (see Dutton et al. 2009; Ofcom 2011). Within an EU context, 75 percent of European children and young people were reported to be using the internet between the years 2006 and 2009 when the EU Kids Online study was conducted (Livingstone and Haddon 2009). Similarly, "social network sites, online games, video-sharing sites, and gadgets such as iPods and mobile phones are now fixtures of youth culture" in the United States (Ito and Antin 2010, p. 1). This increasing engagement of children and young people with digital technologies has been highlighted in a number of large-scale surveys that have reported greater use of social media tools for looking up information and for social and recreational activities, and to a lesser extent for educational purposes (Mediappro 2006; Notten et al. 2009). However, these surveys have focused mainly on adolescents' out-of-school access, use, and engagement with digital technologies. Despite the increase in the number of computers and infrastructure available at schools, little research has been conducted at national or international level with regard to the actual in-school use of digital technologies. As Wastiau et al. (2013) argue, although infrastructure is indeed a basic condition, it is not sufficient on its own for any technological use to happen, and neither does it indicate genuine engagement with the tools. Moreover, many people highlight the digital disconnect that is appearing between high-tech pupils and their more low-tech schools noting that

> Whether in the form of smartphones, laptops, or tablets, digital technologies may be increasingly ubiquitous in a person's social life but marginal in their daily educational experience once they enter a classroom. (Potter 2012, p. xii)

Therefore, it is of value to look at some of the recent studies that report on the actual use of digital technologies within formal educational contexts and ascertain not just how often the technologies are used in the classroom but also what they are actually used for.

A recent survey initiated by the European Commission (2013a), which explored issues of access, use, and attitudes toward digital technologies in schools across 31 countries, reported some interesting findings. First, although most teachers had been familiar with digital technologies for teaching and learning for some years, they still mainly used them to prepare their teaching. Conversely, very few used digital technologies to work with students during lessons—and still to a limited extent. Additionally, it was reported that teachers organize combined types of web-based activities only several times a month on average. Around 50 percent of students at grade 8 (aged 13–14 years) and grade 11 (aged 16–17 years) in general education used a desktop or a laptop during lessons at school at least weekly, but around 20 percent of the students at the same grades never or almost never used a computer during lessons. Moreover, students reported that digital resources such as exercise software, online tests and quizzes, and the like, were still very rarely used during lessons. Additionally, their web-based activities related to learning at home were more frequent compared to ICT activities at school. Students also declare a fairly high level of confidence to use the internet safely while they appeared to be less confident in their use of social media. It is worth noting that "students stating they have high access to and use of ICT at school AND at home also report higher confidence in their operational ICT skills, in their use of social media and in their ability to use the internet safely and responsibly, as well as more positive opinions about ICT's impact on their learning, compared to students reporting low access and use at school but high access and use at home" (European Commission 2013a, p. 11).

Also, pertinent to the in-school usage of social media are the findings of a series of studies commissioned by the then British government technology agency Becta. The first study looked at the use of technology by primary pupils in the education systems of England and Wales. It reported that school computer use typically included activities such as writing and drawing, information searching, using databases, and playing math and science educational games while school internet use concerned mainly schoolwork-related activities such as information and picture retrieval (Selwyn at al. 2010). It was also noted that creative and collaborative uses of social media were not especially prevalent either inside or outside school, "with passive consumption rather than active production the dominant mode of engagement" (ibid., p. 70).

A corresponding study also commissioned by Becta that focused on pupils who were aged between 11 and 16 years in English and Welsh schools reported higher level of access to and greater engagement with social media compared to the previous decade. Interestingly, the most prominent of user categories among the participants were "readers, gamers, file-sharers, communicators and newscasters" (Luckin et al. 2008). This suggests that although high level of engagement with web 2.0 technologies had been reported, learners did not seem to reach the level of "producers" and engage in more sophisticated web 2.0 activities, such as creating and publishing their own content for wider consumption. The study also underlined that the educational use of social media largely depended on the availability of these tools in the classroom and the rigidity or flexibility of the secondary school curriculum. Additionally, fears related to e-safety and policy constraints, such as school internet restrictions and firewalls, were reported to often impose barriers for the adoption of social media tools. The study drew attention to the fact that "learners spend, on average, more time working on school work on a computer outside school than at school itself" (ibid., p. 64). Overall, the study suggested that many examples of engaging and educationally worthwhile web 2.0 approaches were encountered; however, a range of implications are yet to be overcome. On the one hand, social media practices are seen to challenge traditional school structures and teachers are often cautious in their exploration and adoption of social media in their classroom. On the other hand, barriers relating to access, infrastructure, and bandwidth were found to have a significant influence on impeding social media use (ibid.).

Outside the school setting, a large-scale US ethnographic study documented young people's everyday engagements with new media in informal peer-based interaction settings and reported three types of user engagement. These included "hanging out," which mainly involves maintaining social connections; "messing around," which denotes a shift to more in-depth, "trial and error" exploration of and involvement with the technologies; and, finally, the state of "geeking out," which refers to high levels of specialized knowledge and a more frequent, intensive, and interest-driven mode of engaging with new media (Ito and Antin 2010). As the study highlighted, most young people use digital technologies and online networks to "hang out" and extend existing friendships and connect with peers in new ways. A smaller number of youth use online technologies to explore interests, find more specialized information, and join "interest-driven" networks while an even smaller number seek opportunities to improve technical skills, publicize and distribute their work online, and gain visibility and reputation (ibid.).

Conclusion

This chapter has outlined a range of issues associated with the educational use of digital technologies. In brief, digital technologies are seen to create more opportunities for teaching and learning while they have also caused moral panics about the demise of the youth and the death of education. As Larry Cuban (1986) observed over 20 years ago, the advent of each new technology in education is largely accompanied by a wave of enthusiasm as to the potential application for teaching and student learning. This enthusiasm, however, is seldom reinforced by robust research that provides evidence of the means to effectively implement these new tools, or else highlights the practical challenges and issues that emerge from their actual application. For instance, there has been growing frustration that there has been little solid evidence from research findings to support many of the claims and counterclaims currently surrounding social media (Facer and Selwyn 2010). As this chapter has shown, the current "booster" or "doomster" scenarios do not provide a sufficient or adequate framework for the effective educational use of these technologies in schools on a widespread or sustained basis. The beneficial outcomes of implementing social media to reconfigure education cannot merely rely on the presumed affordances of the tools.

Indeed, there is an array of influences and issues considered over the first two chapters of this book that can shape the implementation of digital technologies to transform education in general and school collaboration in particular. Notwithstanding the new conditions and the enthusiastic claims made by educational commentators and technologists alike with regard to the potential of educational technologies to enhance school collaborative practices, little quality and in-depth research has been so far conducted in the field of implementing digital technologies to facilitate school collaboration. As such, the need for a more sustained study on the realities of web-based collaborative projects could be argued to be pressing. In particular, a number of questions are identified as worthy of empirical investigation as to how educational technology is "working-out" in practice in each of the four schools that took part in this research study:

- How can the use of digital technologies create opportunities for online student interaction and collaboration?
- How do these opportunities "fit" into existing school practices?
- What are the drivers and inhibitors for engaging with a collaborative project for teachers?
- What are the drivers and inhibitors for engaging with a collaborative project for students?

With these thoughts in mind, the next chapters will go on to unpack the range of actors and factors that shape web-based school collaboration through an empirical investigation of four collaborative projects across Europe. It will explore the views and experiences of participants in these projects and will take a deeper look at the social, cultural, political, and economic aspects of web-based school collaboration. If we are to make sense of web-based collaboration and the practical issues surrounding its implementation in the classroom, we should try to step back from arguments over the merits of one tool over another and the overall "potential" of particular collaborative initiatives. In order to develop a deeper understanding of the realities of web-based school collaboration and be able to come up with useful proposals for the future, we need to pay close attention to the experiences of the actual participants—teachers and students themselves.

CHAPTER 3

Collaborative Experiences in Practice: Case Studies from the United Kingdom

Introduction

The focus of this chapter is on the practical implementation of digital technologies to facilitate school collaboration. In particular, the chapter sets out to present teachers' and students' hopes and experiences from their participation in collaborative projects. Drawing on empirical data from case studies of two collaborative projects initiated by schools in the United Kingdom and partnered with schools in Greece and Germany, respectively, this chapter presents a broad picture of the actual practices and challenges in a range of diverse secondary education classrooms.

In particular, the chapter is rich in providing a detailed account of teachers' and students' perspectives and expectations of web-based school collaboration as well as their actual engagement with the technologies throughout the duration of the projects. It succinctly captures the individual journeys of the participating teachers as well as the students' collaborative experiences with their partners. Furthermore, the chapter focuses on various issues ranging from the participants' initial drivers and expectations to the technical difficulties and other inhibitors they encountered throughout the academic year and endeavors to unpack the actors, factors, and practices that shaped participation. As such, the chapter sets out by presenting the two UK-based schools and the collaborative projects that formed part of this study and then goes on to discuss the range of issues that emerged during practical engagement with the collaborative activities and tools.

The "Ancient Sparta" Project

The School

The school was a mixed-gender, nondenominational, urban sixth form college with 1,100 students on roll, situated in the West Midlands near the center of a large town with a mixed industrial and commercial base. The school prided itself on maintaining links with other local educational establishments and the wider community as well as national organizations, volunteering programs and other youth schemes. With regard to digital technology use, the school offered a range of extracurricular training seminars while the school's Moodle Virtual Learning Environment was used by both students and staff and hosted information and resources for all courses as well as administrative documents and information. In terms of infrastructure, the school had a library and a computer center both equipped with computers with access to the internet.

The Collaborative Project

The eTwinning project commenced in the autumn 2009 with initially two Greek partner schools: an inner-city school in Athens and a small rural school in the north of Greece. Data collection was carried out during the academic year 2009–2010 and was organized in three consecutive visits. The focus of the project was Ancient Sparta and the aim was to get students acquainted with the Spartan culture and traditions by collecting, creating, and sharing material online. The main tool employed was TwinSpace, the official platform of eTwinning. Most of the TwinSpace tools such as the wiki, the blog, and the forum were used for the project, although in practice most activity took place on the wiki. The language used was English, a first language for all but one of the UK participating students and a second language for all the Greek students.

The UK Participants

Two classes from the UK school worked on the project within the framework of the course on "The Society and Politics of Ancient Sparta" ($n = 35$ students). The coordinating teacher, Lucy, was a newly qualified teacher of ancient history and this was her second year at the school. She described herself as fairly experienced and confident user of digital technologies. She had registered on eTwinning in September 2009 and during the academic year 2009–2010 she built a network of 33 teachers across a range of eTwinning countries. She took part in an online workshop on "Exploiting web 2.0—eTwinning and collaboration" through eTwinning's Learning Lab. She also attended the national eTwinning conference in the United Kingdom where she was awarded a quality label for the Sparta project and took part in some of the ongoing workshops there.

The Greek Partners

The idea for the project was originally conceived and initiated by Lucy who then looked for other partners through the eTwinning partner-finding forum. Initially, there were two Greek partner schools registered for the project. The first was a vocational upper high school located in Athens, which faced a range of disruptions such as students' sit-in and the swine flu epidemic and eventually withdrew from the project. The second partner school was a small, mixed-gender, nondenominational mainstream upper high school with just 90 students on roll located in a village in Northern Greece. In total, 2 classes of 30 students aged 15–16 years took part in the project. There was one computer lab, which was used by the eTwinning team on a weekly basis throughout the duration of the project. The school was not involved in any other collaborative project during the data collection school year.

Dimitra was a teacher of English in her late thirties and she had been working as a teacher since 2001 at various levels of state education. This was the first year she had become involved in eTwinning and she described it as a "totally exploratory" experience. Within a year after registering in eTwinning in September 2009 she had collated a contact list of 20 teachers and had taken part in eight projects. As a teacher of English, Dimitra had fluent command of the language; however, her information and communication technology (ICT) skills were less advanced, so she often requested Lucy's help and sometimes found the use of TwinSpace and the wiki problematic. However, as the academic year progressed her confidence in using digital technologies was enhanced and she even created a blog to share their collaborative and other extracurricular activities with her students.

The "German Project"

The School

The school was mixed-gender, nondenominational, and international located in a prosperous town southwest of London within the London commuter belt. The school had approximately 1,300 students from about 60 nationalities on roll, aged 2½ to 18 years attending all levels of education from early childhood to high school. It was a fee-paying school with a range of academic, athletic, and boarding facilities. The teachers and students who took part in the project were part of the middle school division, which as the head teacher described hosted "a diverse community both internationally and academically" with "about 45% Americans and about 55% different nationalities and about 60 nationalities within that group" ranging from students with learning needs to the bright and gifted ones as well as students who did not have English as their first language.

As regards ICT infrastructure, the school had an Apple computer lab open to students who wanted to work on class or homework projects while ICT skills were also integrated into core, arts, and elective courses. Apart from the computer lab, six laptop carts were available for use in the classroom. Among the range of extracurricular activities, various field trips were organized including exchange visits for students of French and Spanish as well as visits to art galleries, museums, environmental centers, and other points of interest in the United Kingdom and internationally. Other local and international programs that ran in the school included "Habitat for Humanity," "Model United Nations," and "Mission Antarctica," as well as ongoing projects in India, Zambia, Kenya, and Namibia.

The Collaborative Project

The project took place during the academic year 2009–2010, it was carried out exclusively outside the eTwinning platform and external tools were used. Data collection was organized in three consecutive visits throughout the school year. The focus of the project was to create a connecting link between a mixed-ability class of nine students aged 12–14 years of mixed ethnic backgrounds who studied German in the UK school and a class of students in Germany who studied English as a foreign language. The project did not have a specific topic or title but the aim was to familiarize students with each other and use both languages (English and German) for practicing and learning within a more authentic context. In particular, the main focus was to get students to talk about themselves and their hobbies, interests, and differences in culture.

The UK Participants

Isabel was an American teacher of German with more than ten years of teaching experience in general and international schools in Germany, Japan, and the United Kingdom. This was not her first eTwinning project but she had taken part in five other projects before. In terms of ICT skills, Isabel was very confident and she was perceived by her head teacher as particularly "computer savvy" and an "innovative teacher... involved with a number of different programs." On top of her teaching duties she was also an Apple Distinguished Educator, responsible for setting up the program in her school as well as the sixth-grade team leader and a warden at the school's boarding house.

The Partner School

The partner school was a very small private secondary school on the outskirts of Berlin with only 56 students enrolled at the time of the research. Eighteen students between 13 and 15 yeas of age were involved in the project as part of an extracurricular after-school activity. The German teacher, Marlene, had eight years of teaching experience in the subjects of Spanish and English as a foreign language and had taken part in another eTwinning project before.

Before going on to explore the drivers for participation from teachers' perspective, it should be noted that for reasons of clarity and economy, the teachers' first names and the monikers "Sparta" project and "German" project will be adopted throughout the chapter. It should also be noted that pseudonyms have been applied in all cases in order to ensure the participants' anonymity.

Drivers for Participation and Initial Expectations: Teachers' Perspectives

The teachers' initial decision to get involved in eTwinning was based around expectations of what the project would offer to their students as well as a curiosity to gain new experiences. As such, participation in eTwinning emerged as an organic and spontaneous initiative of the individual teachers and was not imposed by the school administration or other external actors. In particular, Lucy considered it as a means of escaping the everyday classroom routine:

> This is something that I wanted to do really because I've lived abroad for a lot of time and wanted to give them another perspective on things... last year when we taught ancient history, I just thought to an extent it was a very dry course... most of the coursework was reading source materials

and things like that and I just wanted to give it a go and see if I could kind of add it in... to the curriculum and get away with it. (Lucy, Midlands)

What appealed to Dimitra most was the opportunity it provided her students to use the English language by collaborating with another school and engaging in interdisciplinary activities. Similarly, key to both teachers' decision to get involved in the German collaborative project was their desire to create a connecting link with a school abroad and enhance pupils' foreign-language skills (German and English respectively). Isabel, in particular, viewed participation in eTwinning as offering authentic context for her pupils to practice the language they were learning and motivate them more but also as a means of promoting their European identity. Marlene also reasoned that the main reason for taking part in eTwinning was:

> To give my students the opportunity to use language for real communication purposes, and to get them in touch with young people their own age in other countries in Europe. (Marlene, Berlin)

In addition, both teachers of the German project expected that their classes' collaboration for the particular project would lead to an exchange visit or even the establishment of a more permanent type of partnership. Isabel's enthusiasm and expectations with regard to the potential of the project as well as the students' initial reactions and excitement are depicted in the excerpt below:

> I think they find it like awesome, like it's someone real they are communicating with and I think it just makes everything... it's authentic finally, like it's something real and it makes them try in different ways and it makes them I think much more inquisitive and it opens up all these other questions for them... I think it's really great, I think it's totally the way for them. (Isabel, London)

Another perceived benefit for Isabel was associated with the flexibility that participation in such a project offered in terms of organizing her mixed-ability classroom by allowing students to work on the project at their own level. At a personal level Isabel felt that participation in such eTwinning projects enhanced her professional profile despite the lack of other monetary benefits:

> It keeps me up to date with what's going on technology-like. I think that's really important, and especially I don't think I'm going to be here forever.

So, I always want to have things on my CV and be really current and know what's going on. (Isabel, London)

As such, it was mainly the personal curiosity of the teachers and the potential benefits for their students that triggered participation in eTwinning. Although they did not collaborate with other colleagues within their school, they all had the support of their head teacher who encouraged participation in such initiatives. Additionally, they had been given sufficient access to the school's computer lab and library. At an institutional level, Marlene commented on how the project reflected positively on her school:

Parents and visitors have learnt about the exchange and are pleased that the school has connections or relations with other schools outside Germany, as this helps students open their horizons. (Marlene, Berlin)

Furthermore, the head teacher of the Midlands school appeared to appreciate Lucy's extra work and acknowledged the impact of the project at school level. As can be seen from the excerpt below she was quite pleased that their school had been picked out as an example of good practice:

eTwinning is a fantastic initiative and that was Lucy's initiative. It wasn't driven by SMT or any manager in the college, Lucy just did that, which is fantastic. And now we find ourselves in an area of good practice because of Lucy which is excellent as well... I would like to think that staff would know that I'd welcome those kind of initiatives and Lucy's been on a course on her own time at the weekend, if you can take time off then you're welcome to it if you can manage it. (Head teacher, Midlands)

At macro-level, Lucy as a newcomer to eTwinning was offered a range of stimuli throughout the year that shaped her overall experience and activity. First, upon the completion of her first project she was "head-hunted" and contacted by the British Council and the BBC World Class and this resulted in a second short-term project. Then she was invited to the national eTwinning conference in the United Kingdom where she was awarded a quality label for the Sparta project and had the chance to take part in some of the ongoing workshops. In this sense, there appeared to be some "formal" appreciation of Lucy's effort and it can be argued that these drivers stemming from macro-level actors had an effect on the individual teacher at micro-level in terms of motivation as well as on the school at macro-level in terms of accreditation and profiling the institution as an example of "good practice."

Participation and Expectations: Pupils' Perspectives

The initiation of both projects was a teacher decision and student participation was compulsory since the projects were implemented in the Ancient History and foreign-language courses of the curriculum respectively. Only in the case of the Berlin school the project was designed to take place as an extracurricular activity. Class time was devoted at several occasions on the projects, while additional personal work was assigned as homework. Furthermore, both projects did not form part of the students' assessment and as a result motivation and engagement ranged:

> I guess it was more the fact that because we had to do it, it was a class thing and quite a lot of people didn't actually want to take part in it whereas some other people were more motivated that others. (Ada, 16, Midlands)

During the initial stages of the Sparta project the majority of students who took part were enthusiastic with the prospect of communicating and collaborating with a school abroad. The two PowerPoint presentations that were exchanged provided rich background knowledge about the schools' location and the surrounding areas as well as information on the participating students such as their names, interests, and hobbies and two group photographs of the classes. As Lucy described:

> They had absolutely no idea at all about Greece…so one of the most interesting things for them was having a look at the PowerPoint that was sent by the Greek students to us about their school and the surrounding area, and they were, like, "oh my God, they have an ostrich farm, oh look at that, look at the mountains and look at this" and it just really kind of sparked their interest! (Lucy, Midlands)

As such, a large number of students were eager to take part since the project offered the element of surprise and it was seen as an escape from the boredom of the daily classroom routine.

> I think because it was new to us the majority of our class liked the challenge of doing something different and new so although it was quite

strange to us we did quite enjoy, I mean, to do something different. (Ada, 16)

When we heard about it we just sort of, like, we thought that we would talk with this school in Greece and it did sound a lot more interesting. (Greg, 16)

We got really excited, we thought, "oh my God, we are going to be talking to Greeks in school", we never did. (Lauren, 17)

In this sense, the motivation for many students was not the result of computer use in the classroom but the prospect of communicating with a school in a foreign country. However, there were other students who expressed indifference or dismissed the idea from the very beginning:

It just wasn't my sort of thing. I wouldn't ever do something like that if it was my choice. (James, 16)

In the case of the German project, students were also initially excited with the prospect of interacting with other students abroad and their perceptions of the aims of the collaboration were largely associated with using German to communicate with their partner school and compare interests and cultures:

We send messages to the other school and they reply and we talk to them and we, like, notice how their culture is and our culture is and we really just...look at the values...how everything is in Germany and how everything works here in the UK. (Stevie, 13)

The Tools

The Sparta project was hosted on TwinSpace, the eTwinning's official project-hosting tool and no other external tools were employed. The eTwinning documentations described TwinSpace as a multilingual, virtual classroom, designed specifically for eTwinning projects that can be used as an online platform to host all the documents and activities of each project. In particular, TwinSpace consisted of the Project Activities section, the Staff Room, the Pupils Corner, a Chat, and a general guidelines section. The Project Activities tab allowed teachers to configure the structure of the project and add or delete "activities" to their TwinSpace according to their needs. They could also decide on the particular tools they would use for each activity, selecting among a forum, a file archive, an image gallery, a blog, or a wiki. Another said benefit of using TwinSpace was associated with e-safety and school filtering systems that can make the use of other external tools more challenging for teachers. As Lucy described:

> I think the eTwinning platform is OK, it's a little bit basic...but I think it does the job for what it needs to do. (Lucy, Midlands)

Once the teachers agreed to collaborate, the initial steps of setting up the project involved a bureaucratic process of submitting an application to the relevant eTwinning authority in each country, getting approval for the project and being allocated their own TwinSpace. Of course, the nature of the projects' TwinSpace use depended on teacher (re)configuration. For instance, once the Sparta project was launched, the teachers mainly used the TwinSpace blog to communicate, arrange any practicalities, seek help or advice, and keep in touch, whereas in the case of the German project, the teachers mainly communicated through email. Lucy was not only the project founder but also the more tech-savvy of the teachers and this was reflected in the use of the blog. For example, Dimitra at first seemed unfamiliar with blogging practices and rather than use the "comment" feature to reply to Lucy, she instead created new entries and used the blog to ask for Lucy's help on practical issues such as student registration and access to the TwinSpace site.

The "heart" of the Sparta TwinSpace and the "busiest" tab in terms of activity was the "home" page. There, one could find all the different subtopics the students worked on, explore the recent activity of others, post or reply to an introductory/welcoming message on the blog, go through the list of all the participants, and use the email tool or the calendar. Additionally, teachers could manage project members by inviting pupils or other teachers and visitors to join, and also change pupil passwords. The Chat tab opened in a separate window and had the very basic properties of a chat while the Guidelines tab redirected users to the main eTwinning site where detailed instructions and advice could be found. The students were divided in pairs or groups of threes and worked on the different subtopics related to Ancient Sparta.

In the case of the German project the original idea was conceived by Isabel with the aim of starting a collaboration with a German partner that would lead to an exchange visit in the future. The eTwinning platform was used only as a partner-finding tool and once the partnership was established Isabel set up a project wiki at Wikispaces, a free wiki hosting service. Isabel appeared to be particularly unenthusiastic at the idea of using TwinSpace for their project since her prior experience with using the platform had been negative. She acknowledged the value of the eTwinning platform in helping her make the connections with the partner teacher, but she paralleled it to Facebook. As the commented:

> It's like the big educators' Facebook, the big educators' meat market and dating site basically, you know, like you put your profile up, you find each other great and go to a private chat room and…you see how you go from there. But I don't think it's ever as successful unless you also couple it with something off the eTwinning site, like a wiki space or you know something from Blogger, whatever works better for your purposes. (Isabel, Greater London)

Isabel was the lead teacher of the project, responsible for creating the thematic categories, configuring the students' pages, and updating the wiki throughout the academic year. As Isabel reasoned, the potential of wikis to organize content thematically was what appealed to her most and affected her decision. Other perceived benefits of using the external wiki provider were associated with ease of use and the notification tool available.

> [Wikispaces is] so much easier, I mean I know there are not so many steps to get into the eTwinning but there's just enough to make it that much more cumbersome. Plus I can direct any information or any movement or any changes on the Wikispaces, it can be directly emailed to both me and the other teacher…and I just find that far more convenient. (Isabel, Greater London)

The wiki consisted of a list of the names of the nine students in the UK school and the thematic categories they worked on. These tabs were configured by Isabel and the students had to create their "home" pages with information about themselves while they also added content to the other wiki pages. The UK students were able to log on to the wiki and work on their own either during their lessons when time was devoted to the project or from home. However, no separate pages were created for the German students since they were not able to use the wiki individually for reasons that will be further explored in the following sections. The students in the UK school posted in German while their partners in Berlin posted in English. Additionally, the students across the two teams exchanged emails through their teachers' accounts and used other tools such as Microsoft Office to produce word documents on various topics. Last, other "analogue" tools were used for communication when paper greeting cards were sent to each other before the Christmas and Easter holidays.

The Journey: Implementation of the Project in Practice

This section will go on to describe the participants' experiences and practices as they engaged with the collaborative project and will bring together the various issues and challenges they encountered throughout the year—ranging from technical barriers to other more socially shaped inhibitors.

Technical Inhibitors

Access to ICTs was fairly unproblematic for all partners and was not reported as an inhibitor. In the case of the Greater London school, the classroom was equipped with ten iMac computers plus one more for the teacher, connected to an interactive whiteboard, allowing each of the nine students individual access. The students of the West Midlands school used the computers at the library or the computer lab and worked in pairs. In theory, once the teachers of the Sparta project registered their students and provided them with usernames and passwords, they could then access the platform either from school or home. In practice, however, this use of TwinSpace was not without problems since both teachers experienced technical difficulties with online registration and access to the platform, which resulted in the loss of valuable class time for solving practicalities, rather than working on the actual project or collaborating with the partner school. As Lucy explained:

> It looked like the perfect platform until it all started crashing!...I registered all the students and then only about five or six could actually get on so we had to de-register them and re-register them so we spent a lot of time doing that...Well, I just got at a stage where I said I'll just take them off and put them back on the system and it worked the second time round...Each time I emailed them [the National Support Service] but the bad thing about them is that they would get back to me about a month later and by then I had figured it out by myself. (Lucy, Midlands)

Another issue was that once the students received their passwords, they often forgot and/or lost them and the teachers would then have to repeat the process of taking them off the platform and re-registering them in order to get them a new password. For others, the password may have worked at school but not at home if the computer configuration settings differed. Additionally, some students complained that the TwinSpace website URL was too long and that this would deter them from accessing the platform—especially from home.

All these perceived and experienced technical difficulties often resulted in student frustration:

> *Mike (16)*: The account system didn't work.
> *Jude (16)*: And there were these really complex passwords.
> *Int*: Couldn't you change them?
> *Mike (16)*: No. Which was annoying. You had all these letters which was ridiculous to remember, it just made it more time consuming.
> *Int*: Did that put you off?
> *Mike (16)*: Yeah, especially at home because you think "I've no idea" and you want to kick the service system.

Similarly, a range of technical issues came up when Marlene attempted to register her students on the wiki. As Isabel described:

> They had a lot of trouble because of their specific IT configuration...only the teachers were able to get through, the kids haven't been able to use it, if they use the school's computers...I don't know exactly why but the kids are also not able to log on from home but I think the teacher is not particularly technologically savvy so she does not know how to enter the kids email addresses and she is not comfortable with sending me the whole list of the kids email addresses. (Isabel, Greater London)

Although Marlene did not discuss whether she would have been willing to share her pupils' email addresses with Isabel, she reported lack of support from her school's ICT team as an important inhibitor:

> I couldn't get my students to create their own page on the Wiki because of support problems with our system here, and the lack of help I got from the ICT team at my school because of lack of time and work overload on their part...Students couldn't log on their accounts and it was all done through my account, which was a nightmare. (Marlene, Berlin)

Similar problems were reported with regard to organizing an online video-conferencing session. Isabel described how the other teachers' inexperience prevented them from organizing a Skype session with the students:

> One of the problem is that when we do the trial I'm in my room, the same room that I teach in but the teachers there don't have access to the room they are teaching so they do the trial with the two of them like in the head teacher's office and then they just took all the equipment to their

classroom but of course that has to be completely reconfigured for that and they don't know how to do that so it was a disaster. (Isabel, Greater London)

Conversely, when Marlene was enquired on this she briefly stated that they "never tried using Skype." As the excerpts from the students' focus-group interviews below denoted, students gave similarly equivocal answers as to whether there were indeed any attempts to use Skype with the other school:

> Stuart (13): I remember once when we actually were supposed to actually try to Skype with them but, like, it never actually worked out...I thought it was going to be awesome to be able to skype with them!
>
> Marla (14): They said we were going to skype and then Miss [Isabel] forgot about it and didn't do it.
>
> Int: The boys told me you tried once but it didn't really work out.
>
> Marla (14): She never...we never actually saw the trial, she just said it didn't work out and we never did it anymore.

Wikis and Blogs: Students' (Un)familiarity with the Tools

Apart from these technical difficulties associated with accessing the collaborative platforms, another emerging issue was students' unfamiliarity with using a wiki tool. Their experience of using a wiki was restricted to reading articles on Wikipedia and only one student out of all the participants had edited a wiki entry. Similarly, although the students were more familiar with the concept of a blog, only a small minority had read a blog in the past and none of them had actually created a blog or contributed to one. However, the teachers appeared fairly confident that their students would be able to use the tools efficiently. For instance, Isabel reasoned that they soon acquired the adequate skills since they were familiar with using other digital technologies such as podcasts and blogs in the classroom.

> The first time they didn't know what to do or how it worked...the wiki is set up a little bit differently maybe than other websites they've been on but we just went through together once and then they were fine. It's very easy, it's pretty basic. (Isabel, Greater London)

Indeed, during the class observation visits the majority of students in both schools were successful in logging on to the online tools and working on the assigned task, that is, adding content to the wiki pages. However, during the interviews a large number of students described how they were confused at the beginning of the project regarding what their particular aims and tasks were. From a "scaffolded" pedagogic point of view, the teachers selected the topic, configured the wiki by creating the subcategories, and allocated these to the students. In the case of the Sparta project one team from each class would be working on an allocated subcategory such as "Spartan Society" or "Spartan Education." The students of the German project were responsible for creating an entry on themselves and their interests and also contributing to joint entries such as "films," "Christmas," and the like. The technical features of the tools were introduced to the students at the beginning of the projects; however, the teachers gave them the flexibility to decide how to organize the material themselves:

> I kind of have left it up to my students, the idea was kind of they could decide which way they wanted to organize it…with the idea that they would actually collaborate and work…they are having trouble trying to figure out where to put all the information to begin with they were just filling up the blog and I thought "oh stop" so I'm going to suggest to them that maybe they try using the wiki to actually do their different things and see if that works. (Lucy, Midlands)

This freedom and flexibility, however, was interpreted by the students as lack of organization and guidance, which did not chime with the everyday learning and working experiences they were accustomed to. As the excerpts below demonstrate, a large number of students did not welcome this unexpected and unfamiliar sense of freedom:

> There was no real direction to it, there was just "here's the website, work" so there was no being told what to do really. (Ned, 18, West Midlands)

> Yeah, it wasn't very structured, I think, there was a deadline but there wasn't really much structure. (Penny, 16, West Midlands)

Students' In- and Out-of-School Use of Digital Technologies

Before looking at the more specific findings associated with students' engagement with the wiki, it is worth examining their more general attitudes and practices related to the use of digital technologies in- and out-of school. The students from the London suburban classroom appeared familiar with using the iMacs during class observations. Instances of engagement with technologies included: the use of online translator sites; the use of Word to create a digital Christmas card; Google searches for Christmas images; taking pictures with Photo Booth and adding effects; and adding content to their wiki pages. Students tended to work individually on their iMacs and the only exception was that of two students who commented on each other's work although their practices can be viewed more as examples of "peer-support" rather than collaboration.

Isabel appeared to be quite flexible and allowed them to work at their own pace and select the tools of their choice. It was quite difficult to moni-tor each student or group individually since there were three groups of dif-ferent levels of German in the same class. The common practice was that, while she worked with each group on their German, the others would be assigned a different task either lesson or eTwinning related. However, this often resulted in insufficient monitoring and some of the students spent their time doing irrelevant things online and pretending to be working on the wiki. This is apparent in the case of one student who only claimed he was not able to log on to his page minutes before the lesson finished although he had spent more than 15 minutes aimlessly browsing other web-sites online.

All in all, in the case of the German project, students' engagement with digital technologies demonstrated a mundane rather than exemplary use of the tools while not all students engaged with the technologies and about a third of them chose to read a German book or magazine as opposed to updating the wiki. Other types of in-school engagement with digital tech-nologies reported in the student focus-group interviews involved use of the school's computer lab for the ICT subject every eight days and random use of ICTs in other lessons. Several pupils mentioned the sporadic in-school use of the Rosetta Stone, a computer software program for language learning. As regards the use of social media only two students were familiar with using a wiki before as part of their social studies lesson the year before; however, it was only used by the teacher to post information.

Out-of-school use of digital technologies appeared to be more frequent and involved a wider range of activities. The majority of students used home or personal computers almost on a daily basis or several times a week either for school-related assignments or recreational pursuits. The excerpt below is representative of the most common activities associated with students' ICT use at home:

Flora (14): I use it for like internet and social networking and music.
Marla (14): Yeah, I go on Facebook…eh…I use it for Word to set up things, I use it for research.

Janice (12): On the computer I usually just check my email or do like school work, like type up things.

All students reported using the computer and the internet for school homework, which mainly involved using Microsoft Word to type school assignments and more seldom looking up information. Rob (13) also mentioned that he would go online if "we have some quiz on maths or some things for science or to check something."

Recreational activities mainly consisted of using Facebook, playing games online, listening and/or downloading music, watching videos on YouTube, and communicating with friends and family. Facebook was the most commonly shared online activity for all students but one girl, Janice. She explained that not having a Facebook account was not her personal choice but was rather imposed by her parents—"My parents think, it's like, not good for me, they don't let me have it" (Janice, 12). As this was an international school and students' ethnic background was varied, the use of Facebook and other online social networking tools was largely associated with keeping in touch with their families abroad. Another use of Facebook reported by students was related to contacting classmates to enquire about homework although to a lesser degree compared to using it for everyday communication with friends and family. More elaborate uses of digital technologies involved using iTunes not only for listening and downloading music but also for digitalizing it by "uploading CDs and stuff" (Rob, 13) while commenting on YouTube videos posted by friends was another activity reported by a different group of students.

Similarly, the case study of the Sparta project did not reveal any type of exemplary in- or out-of-school digital technology use. Overall, the majority of the 35 UK students who took part used computers and the internet almost on a daily basis either for school homework or for recreational reasons while a smaller minority reported using the computer at home once a week or less either due to lack of internet access or because they preferred engaging in other offline activities. The excerpt below mirrors the majority of students' experiences as regards out-of-school computer use:

I use computers daily for school work and kind of enjoyment purposes and yeah, like, it can be something helpful where I can look what's happening at the cinema, it's a good way to contact friends and keep in touch with other people. (Kim, 17)

Recreational activities mainly consisted of using Facebook and/or MSN, listening to music and to a lesser extent downloading music and films, playing games, and accessing a range of websites either for news updates or for entertainment. As regards in-school use of digital technologies, apart from the eTwinning project, the students reported only using the computer lab as part of their ICT school subject. With regard to school work, students' sporadic use of digital technologies was restricted to "doing research," which largely involved using the Google search engine and Wikipedia to look up—and often copy—information, as well as typing homework on Word and creating PowerPoint presentations. Moreover, students reported that they often used the school's Moodle website to access resources and check their school email account.

Overall, only two students out of 35 reported more sophisticated uses of ICTs and the internet and a more in-depth engagement with online activities. James (16) had edited existing entries or "the odd article in Wikipedia" to use his words but he had not created any new entries from scratch, whereas Tristan (17) used his computer to "design stuff" related to his hobby, skating.

> I have a computer, I use mine for, like, design stuff, I go everyday and just design stuff and talk to people in a general sense. Mainly [I use] Photoshop and stuff like that and all sort of different programs to, like, design stuff. When I want to share it I put it on Facebook or I've got, like, a little skating website thing I put pictures on or I just use it a general kind of personal thing to put different stuff up. (Tristan, 17)

Although some students did find TwinSpace and the various tools rather difficult to use at first, the majority reported that with the support of Lucy they managed to overcome most of the technical problems and they "got the hang of it" (Rita, 17).

> I don't think I had any real difficulty, I picked it up pretty quickly, I mean I was just orientating myself around the website and once I had gotten got used to it, it was pretty simple to use really. (Andy, 17)

The students who felt confident to engage with the tools reported that they often found the operation of TwinSpace problematic while they described how the plethora of tools and tabs was often confusing and made navigation more complex.

> I think it was a bit too technical for, like, cause Lucy is talking about how you can add different files to it but none of us really did that, it

was too technical. It didn't need to be that technical! It would have been better if we just posted things and they posted things, we didn't need all these...extra files and extras...It was like a jigsaw. (Lauren, 17)

On the other hand, a minority of students admitted that they did not make great use of the wiki since they never really understood how it worked and they were not willing to experiment though "trial and error" like some of their classmates did:

I had no idea how to do that wiki thing, it was explained but I still didn't quite grasp it. (Henry, 17)

I just can't use it, I need help. (Penny, 16)

As regards the Greek team, participation was more limited and restricted to a smaller number of students. When Dimitra was initially asked about her students' ICT skills she commended:

The students don't have problems with using computers, they're always on Facebook [laughing]. Well, the students are all day online, they didn't have a problem with that, the problem was with the passwords. (Dimitra, Northern Greece)

However, extended and frequent engagement with social networking sites such as Facebook did not necessarily guarantee that students had the adequate skills to use more unfamiliar tools such as TwinSpace or the wiki effectively. This was enhanced by Dimitra's own limited experience, which resulted in inadequate student training and guidance from her part. As she described:

They did [face technical difficulties], well, I also faced technical difficulties, when I started in September or October and I came across the word wiki, I didn't know what a wiki was. Also, in these starter projects I did...they presented on each weekly task a different eTwinning tool so...I started becoming acquainted with what it is and how it works. But also the students themselves faced problems, like, "Miss, so where do we upload this now?", "where shall we click on?", "how do we do it?"...And because I still don't know how to use the wiki well, it was difficult to guide the students on that, how to work on that and so on. (Dimitra, Northern Greece)

Students' Engagement with the Project and Use of Tools

The result of these technical difficulties, lack of know-how, and limited teacher guidance was that students experimented with the tools and often posted randomly on the wiki and blog in the case of the Sparta project. Some of the teams used the wiki to create their history-related entries while they posted short introductions about themselves on their team's blog. The wiki was frequently perceived, thus, as the formal "educational" space where students uploaded text and images relating to their allocated subtopic. On the other hand, they used the blog in a more informal context either to introduce themselves, or to do some "housekeeping." There were cases where confusion prevailed since some students posted on the wiki and others on the blog and there was a lack of direction and communication among them. During one of the class observations, Lucy encouraged her students to use the wiki to create their team project and move everything from the blog or the uploaded files archive.

One of the most active students from the Midlands school, Megan (16), not only deleted the blog posts and created wiki entries but also encouraged her "team" to post more, gave them advice on how to do so on the wiki and informed the authors of the deleted blog posts. As she commented:

> I've been sort of the person in my group who's been organizing it, sort of putting subheadings for other people to add work to and it's good to sort of see the Greek sort of keep adding work there as well... I think I put myself forward and then we sort of keep adding things and just going along. (Megan, 16)

Additionally, this team's earlier blog posts highlight how students drew distinguishable barriers between formal school work for which they use black fonts on the wiki and other more informal blog posts where some of them experiment with colors and emoticons.

In the case of the German project, despite the fruitful technical conditions and the relatively good ICT skills of the students, online observations and analysis of the wiki showed that students used it sporadically and in rather mundane ways, failing to take advantage of its collaborative properties. Students mainly logged in during class time while accessing the wiki outside school was perceived as homework. Since they were not formally assigned to do so they expressed no personal curiosity to explore the wiki or post in their free time. Additionally, Marlene reported that her students had "a bit difficult to understand the wiki at the beginning [sic]" and that although they "were very enthusiastic at the beginning, as time went by motivation waned" (Marlene, Berlin).

Despite the range of functions and collaborative opportunities that the wiki tool offered, students used it at large to add or edit content on their profile pages. This was restricted to text-based entries and no images or video files were uploaded. Furthermore, the majority of the students' profiles were plain black-font texts and the few instances of a more exploratory wiki use were restricted to font color or typeface changes.

In addition, when creating the topic-related pages on Berlin and films rather than using the wiki for collaborative writing, word documents were uploaded on each page. The word documents were individually written by either the German or the UK students and were all uploaded on the wiki by Isabel. In this sense, the wiki was employed as a publishing tool or a content-sharing online space and the partner teams did not take advantage of any of the wiki properties whatsoever. As Isabel described:

> I actually uploaded those in the hope that she [Marlene] would be able to download them more easily and when she emailed me a bunch of things I also then uploaded those for her so that my students from home could access them…A lot of the documents have like specific things in them. (Isabel, Greater London)

There was a sense that although students did not report any problems in using the wiki to upload text, they were not aware of its other features. For instance, their teachers had never explained to them that they could also post pictures or videos if they wanted and they never became very interested in using the wiki. On the other hand, Isabel reasoned that students soon lost interest in using the wiki and enjoyed more the activities that involved writing and receiving paper cards from their partners:

> I think they probably enjoy it less [the online activities] than they did at the beginning. I think they thought it was really fantastic to be able to like be online and but I think now they are actually much more interested in having a real thing written by a real German like in their real German handwriting, that's far more interesting and a lot better contextualized. (Isabel, Greater London)

However, the underlying reasons for students' limited and sporadic use of the wiki are more multifaceted. Although no technical problems were reported and all students found accessing and using the wiki "easy," lack of guidance and assessment also contributed to their restricted participation. For example, as noted earlier in this chapter, during the class observations, Isabel's instructions were limited to "update your profile page," which left a student wondering to herself "what are we supposed to do?" Similarly, some students reported in the focus group interviews that lack of assessment sometimes resulted in limited motivation. Other students described how they preferred working on the wiki compared to sending postcards or writing letters while others described how lack of reciprocity and late replies led to disappointment.

> Probably I'd say I'd change writing postcards because posting can take like almost forever when it'd take probably, like, a few days [for the postcards] to get to them and then a few days for them to respond and then send us back, I'd say probably about a month after we've sent ours so it's, like, kind of communication failure. That happened, like say, Obama was elected, they sent that to us and say "did you see that Obama's elected" and we were like "that was about a month ago" so that kind of takes time. (Stuart, 13)

All in all, for both projects, the wiki pages never came to function as an online collaborative space that could be used throughout the academic year. Once the students created (or not) their assigned entries and the teachers stopped allocating classroom time for the project the wiki pages remained static, and the online space was treated by the students as a type of electronic folder.

Editing Others' Work

The common practice among most student pairs or groups in the case of the Sparta project was that they discussed their allocated subtopic and divided it in smaller sections for each team member to work on. Then they either logged on to TwinSpace individually and posted their work or they assigned one team member to upload it online, especially in the few cases where somebody faced access problems and could not log on to the platform. While this "proxy" use often felt to work well, there were a few cases of students who complained that they had taken on all the work themselves. Additionally, there were a few students who admitted that their contribution to the project mainly consisted of copying and pasting content on the wiki. These different approaches are highlighted in the following excerpts:

> We tried to do it in college so we could all fit there and do it together so one of us would be on one computer finding information, the other would be putting it in on the website. (Jenny, 17)

I did Persian wars with Robyn. We both did some pretty good work. But we just basically copied it, just put it up but it looked good, it looked proper good. We didn't have any Greek people. We were supposed to be part of two groups but they never showed. (Mike, 16)

While students felt comfortable to publish their work on TwinSpace and share it with their partners, very few edited their own team's or the other teams' wiki entries. This was, first, justified by their lack of experience in using a wiki and their unawareness of the editing properties of the tool. During the focus group interviews, it was clear that only a small minority of the English students was aware that they could work collaboratively on the wiki and edit each others' work in order to create a joint entry. The students mainly used the wiki as a webpage where they would only add work to, and in particular, they thought they could only post on the specific section they had been assigned:

Kim (17): Eh...you can only add work to it, to the section that you've been designated...

Int: Can't you comment?

Megan (16): We haven't been told that we can so we haven't sort of tried it.

Kim (17): We are kind of in the process to exploring it ourselves.

Very few students appeared aware of the editing properties of the wiki, and there were limited instances where students described how they had edited somebody else's work either in their team or in a different team. However, these were restricted to minor editing of spelling mistakes or moving pictures around:

I can't remember [what we edited] but I think it wasn't major things, it was, just like, spelling mistakes and, like, put a name on somewhere so we logged on it and edited other people's work and stuff. Actually it seems pretty bad now [laughing]. (Sheila, 16)

I edited one of the posts they put up actually, those were just a bunch of pictures and so I moved them from one place to another because they wouldn't...they weren't needed to everyone. (Tristan, 17)

The interviews revealed one interesting—but atypical—instance of editing. While a large number of students admitted that their main contribution to the project was copying and pasting information on the wiki from other online resources with or without editing the text beforehand, one student took advantage of the editing properties of the wiki to set this right.

> We did edit some text [laughing] cause they just copied and pasted everything so we were like "this is wrong" [laughing] so we just changed it. (Jackie, 17)

Another emerging issue was that once the students were informed in the interviews about the editing properties of the wiki tool, they appeared rather skeptical and reluctant to engage in such practices:

> I think I'd rather left other's work alone. (James, 16)
>
> Yeah, I wouldn't mess with someone else's work. (Helen, 17)
>
> I don't know, probably not [edit somebody's work]. I might point out to them rather than just changing it myself. (Jenny, 17)

The Greek teacher and students also mainly added content to the wiki and did not take advantage of the editing properties of the tool. Although Dimitra was aware of the editing feature she found the wiki particularly hard to use and she could not guide her students toward this direction. The excerpt below mirrored their rather chaotic and unstructured use of the different tools:

> No, there was no editing. As I said they didn't use the wiki exclusively, they also posted on the blog or the forum, we used it...how can I put it...we didn't have a plan in mind that "this had to be posted in this section, this has to be posted in the other section." The students posted wherever they could and wherever they figured out how to do it, or where I showed them how to do it. (Dimitra, Northern Greece)

Similarly, in the case of the German project, student wiki activity was restricted to adding content or editing their personal page. There were no instances of editing reported and the history activity indicated that even when students edited their profile page this mainly involved adding some new sentences on their hobbies or favorite music and films. As revealed in the focus group interviews the majority of students were unaware that they could edit pages other than their own. Still, they did not find the prospect of editing the work of others particularly appealing:

> *Janice (12)*: She wouldn't be able to edit my writing cause it's, like, my personal part of the wiki.

Int: She could actually, if she wanted.
Janice (12): She could change everything I wrote??
Flora (13)-Sarah(14): Oh, wow!
Sarah (14): We didn't know that.
Flora (14): Yeah, but I wouldn't really want to do it [edit other entries].
Marla (14): Yeah, it would just feel like "are you serious? You made these mistakes too."

With regard to commenting and interacting with each other on the wiki space, there was only one instance of commenting on a wiki post but more replies were posted in the discussion section on the wiki page on films. The majority of the messages posted on the discussion forum received just one or two replies and although there were a couple of instances of the UK students attempting to initiate a discussion by posting questions, no further reply was posted by the German students and communication ended there.

Thus, the practices that the students adopted when engaging with the wiki reflected the broader discourses of their formal education experiences where they were not used to working collaboratively to produce written context. As such the wiki was mostly used to gather factual information—resembling at large an online "notebook" of individually assorted content. Although the project was not assessed and the students were given complete freedom to work however they wanted, this clashed with the common practices that pervade school norms, and only a few students took advantage of it—though to a minimal degree. In the absence of clear guidelines, the students seemed to have imported the school practices they were familiar with.

Copying and Pasting: The Wikipedia Example

The majority of students who took part in the Sparta project used online resources to research their topic and a smaller number mentioned using library books, textbooks, or their personal notes. During the class observations the common practice was that the students made use of either the Google search machine or the website "about.com" to research their topic and used the top hit pages to get information for their written assignments. All in all, a large number of students imported familiar "copying and pasting" homework practices, particularly since the project was not assessed. Additionally, although Lucy felt disappointed with some of her students for not putting serious effort in their project work, she also expressed some degree of leniency toward Wikipedia and a degree of compromise since the project was not formally assessed.

> I don't like Wikipedia very much. We try to keep them away from things like Wikipedia but actually the stuff on Ancient Greece on Wikipedia is actually quite good, it's not too awfully incorrect so I don't mind as long as they are using other sources as well. (Lucy, Midlands)

Similarly, the Greek students mainly copied and pasted from online resources and Dimitra not only was aware of it but did not object as she had to cope with her students' language problems and she could not push them very hard for fear they would get discouraged and totally give up on the project.

> We did the same [copying and pasting] but our problem is that we don't understand everything that's on Wikipedia [chuckling], you see, that was an issue. (Dimitra, Northern Greece)

Students' perceptions of using Wikipedia and similar online resources appeared to be rather mixed. Their understanding of "research" at large involved internet searches to look up information for school-related assignments while the majority admitted using Wikipedia frequently, albeit with a feeling of guilt. The following interview excerpt reflected clashing student sentiments: on the one hand, they perceived Wikipedia as "unreliable," but on the other hand, they admitted being too lazy to do research and homework differently.

> *Helen (17)*: We are, like, told not to use Wikipedia.
> *James (16)*: Wikipedia is very suspect, if it's source checked and it's not citations then it's generally reliable but a lot of it is just from people's memories.
> *Int*: Do you agree with that?
> *Helen (17)*: I generally use it. And most people do.
> *James (16)*: It's reasonable as an overview of what you need to do rather than definitely use it as your ultimate source thing.
> *Int*: Then why did you copy and paste everything off it for the project?
> *James (16)*: Because I was lazy.

Conversely, a small minority of students was against copying and pasting and used books and other online resources, arguing that Wikipedia was not reliable:

> I always use the BBC history website cause it's written by expert professors and that and people actually know that on Wikipedia anyone can

edit information, so you don't know what you're getting and if it's accurate. (Lauryl, 16)

Overall, "copying and pasting" practices regarding Wikipedia mirrored students' general patterns of engaging with homework. In particular, three major practices can be identified: (i) copying and pasting in bulk without even removing the hyperlinks that redirect to the original webpage; (ii) copying and pasting after having removed hyperlinks and sometimes having "changed the difficult words" (Mike, 16); (iii) using websites for guidance and then writing up the wiki entry "in your own words" (Lauren, 17). This last practice might have involved either uploading text-only entries or adding pictures and being more creative. There were, however, very few instances of students taking the initiative and spontaneously creating something more resourceful than a text-only entry.

No instances of copying and pasting were reported in the German wiki project, neither was the use of websites such as Wikipedia mentioned in the focus-group interviews when students discussed how they engaged with ICTs for school work. One reason for this might have been that the various wiki topics were related to students' hobbies and interests and were, thus, of a more personal nature. Still, neither were there any instances of copying and pasting on the Word documents created by students on the topic of Berlin and films.

Collaboration and Communication: From Enthusiasm to Disappointment

Drawing on both class observation and interview data, there were very few, if any, instances of collaboration either between the partner schools or between the different teams across the two classes in the case of the Sparta project. In particular, during the class observations at the school's library the students sat around one or two computers and worked on the project together by taking turns. There was also a small minority of students who appeared totally uninterested and disengaged with their teammates and simply watched them working on the computer without making any contributions. As one student commented:

I've barely really looked at my group's work, I mean luckily we've split the work in the middle but there's still no communication, we'll do our bit, they'll do their bit and then we'll put it together and that'll be that. (Ned, 18)

The very few instances of small collaboration on the wiki consisted mainly of posting questions and checking out each other's work before adding more content. Students mainly associated communication and collaboration with synchronous online interaction such as chatting as opposed to using other tools such as a wiki. However, the teams were unable to use the chat due to time and curriculum impediments. Classes at the Greek school finished at 13:40 while Lucy's earliest class was scheduled for 11:15. When taking into consideration the two-hour time difference between Greece and the United Kingdom this meant that they could only be both online for maximum 20 minutes and this could only work with one out of the two participating classes. During one of the class observations the teachers had arranged their first online meeting; however, by the time Lucy took her students to the library and logged on to the platform the Greek students had left. As one student acknowledged:

> I think the idea is really good and it should have been fun but I think that because the Greek students were never on at the same time there was no real collaboration between the two so you couldn't really work with the other school. (Henry, 17)

Similarly, students' engagement with the wiki throughout the German project was rather sporadic and mediocre and no instances of collaborative writing were reported. Online collaboration or rather cooperation with their partner school was restricted to sharing documents and taking part in some very brief discussions on the forum. The common pattern of wiki use was that students logged on individually from their iMacs and updated their profile or other wiki pages. Communication at large took place through two means: first, the students wrote short letters about themselves that were then exchanged by the teachers through their personal email accounts; and, second by exchanging Christmas and Easter postcards. Reasons underlying the failure to use the wiki as a collaborative tool and take full advantage of its properties were associated with lack of guidance from the teachers' part since the students were unaware of most wiki features, and also the configuration problems of the German school that limited student access. Initial expectations to arrange videoconferencing sessions through Skype did not materialize. Since students expected more frequent communication, they were at large disappointed by the sense of "disconnectedness" they experienced:

> I like the fact that I have a pen pal from Germany so...that I found cool but then we barely ever...we did do stuff but, like, we didn't do it for very long, it would have been fun if we did it, like, every week or

something, once a week...we do not, like, do that often, we have a few letters and like every like third month or something. We haven't really done too much stuff. (Janice, 12)

Overall, lack of synchronous online interaction at large resulted in disappointment and student motivation and interest in the project waned, as their expectations were not met:

Int: What did you expect at first?
Lauren (17): To, like, actually talk to people.
Jackie (17): Yeah, and maybe like a bit of conversation or something.
Lauren (17): But we were never online at the same thing.
Henry (17): It was supposed to be this big thing and it ended being nothing really, just, posting stuff, every now and again.

Although online discussions through forums or blogs are often perceived to be more inclusive and not constrained by timetabling, they did not seem to be positively received by the students in any of the schools. Asynchronous interaction on the TwinSpace forum did not appeal to the majority of the participants in the Sparta project, since it seemed to fall outside their everyday out-of-school online social practices such as chatting and instant messaging. Migrating from their everyday use of MSN and Facebook to a discussion forum failed to motivate the majority of the students. This resulted in very low participation as these students described:

We've got a forum where we can post questions, many people, I mean they're a bit nervous to ask questions so each on their own aren't bothered about asking questions so it's just really participation is a bit low, we'd rather just get the work done, put it up there and then that's that. (Ned, 18)

Everyone was, like, really shy because no one had posted and you didn't want to be the first one. (Jackie, 17)

Some other students also commented on how using the chat was "easier" for them and also "it was instant, it was more like what you're used to if you can talk to them straight away, I think that was why [we didn't use the forum]" (Sheila, 16). Additionally, the lack of Greek response was another factor that put off the minority of the students who tried to start a discussion on the forum. Only 8 out of the 65 students used it resulting in merely two threads with 10 posts in total (1 Greek and 7 English students posted). The messages posted were brief and included general "hellos" and "how is everybody;"

however, the use of emoticons and various colors did denote an attempt to set a friendly tone and "break the ice." There was only one instance in the forum, which is interesting to look at because it revealed student initiative and falls outside the prevailing "why bother" attitude. When Megan from the UK school posted a message on the forum, encouraging her partners to "get a conversation going," a Greek student responded writing "YES but not here if you want!! Have you got facebook???" As this student exchange suggested, the forum was dismissed as an unsuitable means of starting a conversation and Facebook was proposed instead. Indeed, Megan (16) confirmed during an interview that:

> I was talking there the other day and a girl from Greece sort of asked me for Facebook and stuff like that so that we can talk and get to know each other and stuff so it's really good. Yeah, I think I've got two girls from Greece on Facebook and we kind of…we don't talk often but a random kind of "hello" and "how are you" I get sometimes from each other. (Megan, 16)

These students' initiative to take it a step further and migrate to Facebook, however, was the exception rather than the rule and nobody else followed their example. A "formal" migration to Facebook encouraged by the teachers might have motivated the students more and offered them an opportunity to interact using a tool they were familiar with. However, this option was dismissed by the teachers for internet safety and child protection reasons:

> The thing is, there are problems with the law over here for teachers and students, like, I have a Facebook page but I'm not allowed to be linked with any of my students on it cause of issues of child protection and things like that so it's a very kind of grey area. (Lucy, Midlands)

Notwithstanding these few instances of online interaction, the prevailing student mentality was that "everyone is waiting for somebody else to do the first thing" as Lucy described:

> They put posts up about themselves "I like doing this" but they haven't actually commented on "what do you do" and I think it's one of these things…once you get one of them to put a sensible question up the others will follow. You know what I mean? Everyone's waiting for someone else to do the first thing. (Lucy, Midlands)

Other Issues Affecting Communication and Collaboration

Partner reciprocity was also associated with language issues and the difficulties in maintaining proper and quality forms of interaction were highly dependent on the participants' foreign-language skills. On the one hand, key to some teachers' initial decision to get involved in eTwinning was their desire to create a link with a partner school and enhance the pupils' foreign-language skills. On the other, contributing posts in a foreign language was sometimes a cause for student discontent that resulted in limited participation. In the case of the Sparta project, language was a barrier for some Greek students and prevented them from contributing to the wiki and participating in the online discussions:

> When the topic is so specialized, such as Ancient history they don't really know the relevant vocabulary and we had to work on that. But also producing written text on a specific topic is quite demanding, I can't claim we didn't face such problems, we did. (Dimitra, Northern Greece)

The role of the shared language in limiting participation was also acknowledged by the UK students who, despite their good will to appreciate the Greek effort, expressed discontent with the poor quality of the written exchanges that did not meet their initial expectations:

> The whole language barrier didn't help much either because I expect, if I had to speak Greek I'd be like "I won't bother" so I suppose it's testament to them that at least they tried and they put on like "hey, I'm Chris, I like basketball" or something but it's just a bit dull to read six people say "hi, I'm home with my friend" or "Hello, I'm ... " (Mike, 16)

In the case of the German project, another inhibitor that affected to some extent the quality of communication between the two schools was that of age difference. Although the students were of almost the same age, there was a sense that even if their pen pal was just a year younger it made a difference to them and the students highlighted this in the focus-group interviews.

> *Marla (14)*: Well, we had different topics, like, what your favorite music was or what we liked to watch so they are a bit younger and some of the girls said we love watching...well, we love listening to Jonas Brothers [American pop boy band] and watching Hannah Montana [American Disney teen sitcom] which... [all chuckling]

Nicholas (13): And, like, my guy told me he *still* watches Sponge Bob and that's a bit of... [all chuckling and laughing]

Flora (14): Mine is also, like, a year younger, so she watches a lot of Disney channels and listens to a lot of Disney channels, so there wasn't really much response, as I don't watch Disney channels [in a bit of dismissive tone].

Another factor that needs to be considered is that the idea of writing to random students in a foreign language where communication breakdown issues were common was a cause for student discontent:

It's kind of, like... it's hard because it's random strangers just writing to them. You don't really know what to say sort of and in a different language, it's also quite... And mine said they "ate their brother" which I didn't really understand. (Sarah, 14)

The issue of assessment appeared to be also significant in terms of affecting engagement with the projects in both schools. On the one hand, lack of assessment or any other form of kudos for contributing to the project demotivated students. On the other hand, the pressures of dealing with formative and summative assessment regimes made participation even less attractive. As this student described:

We had exams in January so everyone was like "Hm shall I do some work on the not-assessed project or shall I actually do some work for the exams that will affect my future?" I think assessing is the way forward because if you just leave it unmonitored people won't do anything. But if you assess it at least a good majority of people will actually put some work in it. You always get the slackers of this world who don't do anything. (Mike, 16)

Similarly, another student who was rather frustrated about doing all the work herself, as her partner remained uninvolved, added:

Maybe it would have worked out a lot better if people actually did like more work cause I know quite a lot of people who didn't, quite a few people did, but it would have been good if it was like a set project and we had to do it for a mark and more people would have got involved and that wouldn't have happened but it still wouldn't have made it better because we didn't speak to them. (Lauren, 17)

Curriculum and time pressures were also seen by Lucy as inhibitors to creativity since in the end they did not have adequate time to invest for being more resourceful and innovative:

> The project had to be focused on what we were doing which meant there wasn't as much room for creativity and it was, like, really dull. (Lucy, Midlands)

Overall, during the last phase of focus-group interviews the most common suggestion for change was associated with making the project more interactive and using Skype for real-time videoconferencing:

> *Janice (12)*: It would be fun [chuckling] . . . Because you could actually see the person!
> *Flora (14)*: It would be cool! You could like communicate without a break.

All in all, the digital technologies employed for both projects did not guarantee that communication and collaboration would take place in class or from home. The opportunities for stimulating new forms of communication and collaborative practices appeared to be poorly fostered among these students and student motivation waned from the very beginning. This in turn suggests how important the role of the teacher can be in guiding the students, structuring the collaborative activities carefully, and facilitating their collaborative experiences.

Other Benefits Arising from the Collaborative Projects

As the students reflected in the focus-group interviews, after the initial disappointment due to the lack of interaction the wiki on Ancient Sparta was perceived as a "useful" and "helpful" tool for exam revision. In particular, they appeared to associate it with an online repository where they could access resources at their own space and time:

> It will be useful for revision because you know where your section is and even if you did not do a lot yourself you can look at what else the others did but for that sort of exchange side of it was kind of pointless really. (Greg, 16)

Interestingly, although the students described Wikipedia as untrustworthy, they did not express any concerns regarding the reliability of their own project, which had been created to a large extent by using online resources such as Wikipedia. Overall, the use of digital technologies for school collaboration did not appear to have made a strong impact regarding the improvement of the students' ICT skills in any of the schools. The students who had described themselves as confident ICT users did not report particular enhancement of their skills whereas some other students commented that they noticed some small improvement with regard to using some new tools:

> Probably improved a little bit…I hadn't blogged before, learning to do that was quite interesting. (Neil, 16)

In the case of the German project, communicating with the other school and exposing the students to the culture of a foreign country was to some extent successful. Despite the general feeling of lack of cohesiveness and consistency in their communication, by the end of the project, the majority of students had formed a vague idea of who their pen pals were, had exchanged pictures and, depending on the level of their personal engagement and interest, they had become familiar to a lesser or greater degree with their online partners. As one student eloquently put it when he was asked about their pen pals:

> I like mine. I have an idea of the guy I'm talking to, I know what he likes, I know what he watches on TV and I know what he doesn't like, I kind of know what food he likes. (Stevie, 13)

Furthermore, the teacher reported some teaching and learning benefits associated with students improving their vocabulary and to a lesser extent their grammar skills while one student described how writing for an authentic audience affected her learning and commented that "I believe yes [it has helped my German], I guess, like, someone's actually reading it, they have to be great but not like that much" (Sarah, 13).

Conclusion

This chapter has described and explored the eTwinning journey of two UK schools and their Greek and German partners respectively. In particular, it has endeavored to unpack the micro-level, teacher and student practices that underpin the use of digital technologies in formal educational settings and look at the wider factors that affect online school collaboration at meso- and macro-levels. On the one hand, the focus has been on the range of technical difficulties and other inhibitors as well as drivers for participation. On the other hand, emerging findings relating to the use of tools and other communication and collaboration issues have been presented and further analyzed. All in all, it could be said that participation in the project was viewed positively by the majority of students and all teachers. However, the use of digital technologies to facilitate online communicative and collaborative practices appeared to be shaped by a number of ongoing challenges, interests, and actors. These ranged from technical difficulties and time, curriculum, and language barriers to student unfamiliarity with collaborative tools and practices, unsatisfactory teacher guidance, and limited student motivation and participation.

CHAPTER 4

Collaborative Experiences in Practice: Case Studies from Greece

Introduction

Following from the previous analysis, this chapter presents the case studies of two Greek schools that participated in web-based collaborative projects and their partners in Denmark and Italy respectively. Drawing on a range of empirical data, it aims to gain insight into the views and experiences of the teachers and students who took part in school collaboration and explore how they perceived and experienced twinning with their partner school abroad. The chapter starts by presenting in more detail the two Greek schools and their partners as well as the topic and the aims of the collaborative projects. It then goes on to describe the participants' initial expectations, the range of inhibitors they faced during their collaborative journeys, and the actors and factors that shaped their participation.

It should be noted that the second case study presented in this chapter can be described as a rather unsuccessful endeavor. Only four students from the Greek school were registered but never accessed the platform and several attempts throughout the academic year toward configuring the wiki tool and working on the project remained fruitless due to a range of technical and other impediments. However, since the purpose of this book is to explore the issues and tensions surrounding the use of digital technologies for school collaboration—successful, or not—it was considered more than appropriate to include this failed example of wiki-based collaboration in order to unpack the range of actors and factors that affected its implementation. Besides, as Cole has argued (2009, p. 146), "currently, published

material relating to Wiki's used as teaching tools only seek to promote positive elements of use…Uniquely, presenting a failed case of Wiki use provides the educational community with an opportunity to learn from the
mistakes of others."

The "Reading Club" Project

The School

The school was a mixed-gender, nondenominational, urban upper high
school (Lyceum) with 435 students on roll located in a relatively affluent,
upper-middle-class area in the northern suburbs of Athens, Greece. There
were two computer rooms available but the project at large took place at
the school's library. The library room was a rather small—no more than
30 square meters—and crammed but welcoming space that was constantly
filled with students. When the project first began there was only one desktop PC available to students; however, later on during the academic year
2009–2010 this was replaced by two newer PCs.

The Collaborative Project

The project was designed to run for two consecutive school years and all
the collaborative activities had been embedded in the school's student reading club. The project was initially registered in December 2008 and was
closed in June 2010. Data collection was carried out during the second year
of the project and was organized in three consecutive visits throughout
2009–2010. All the reading club meetings were carried out as an extracurricular activity at the school's library. The 60 participating students were
divided into two groups and there were two after-school meetings held
every week. The theme of the project was the relations between the two
sexes and how love is portrayed in literature, philosophy, and psychology.
The students read books, presented them to their classmates, and discussed
them during the reading club meetings. Then they communicated their
discussions and analyses of the books to their partners online through the
TwinSpace tool. As such, the focus of the project was twofold since the
teacher's aim was to engage the students both with the reading club and
the collaborative project. Three partner schools were initially registered on
the platform, including one from Denmark, one from Romania, and one
from Greece. However, only Sofia from Greece and Sanne from Denmark
were actively engaged for the duration of the project and only the pupils
from the Greek and the Danish school were registered on the collaborative

platform. The Romanian teacher "did very little work at first and then they disappeared!" (Sofia, Athens suburban). The project also consisted of two exchange visits between the Greek and Danish students, one during each academic year.

The Greek Participants

Sofia, the Greek teacher who originally conceived the idea for the project was in her early fifties with more than 20 years of teaching experience in the private and state sector. She was a teacher of French, who was also studying library science and was responsible for running the school library. During the visits at the school and the class observations it was apparent that she was on very good terms with the students and that they thought quite highly of her. The library was a buzzing place, constantly filled with students who used the two available computers, did their homework, borrowed and returned books, or simply came to have a chat with Sofia.

This was the first eTwinning project for Sofia and as she commented "the other teacher from Denmark, she was also a novice, we were both a bit of greenhorns." With regard to her information and communication technology (ICT) skills she considered herself not very experienced with "little exposure to computers" but still relatively confident and did not hesitate to ask for help. Approximately 60 Greek students aged 15–17 years took part in the project from different classes. Although the number of students remained roughly the same, new students replaced some older ones who quit due to lack of time and assessment pressures as they were preparing for the state exams. As eTwinning was not implemented in a school subject but consisted part of the reading club, and thus, was not compulsory, student participation varied in frequency and range. However, there was a core of about 20 students who worked harder than the rest and remained engaged throughout the two-year duration of the project.

The Danish Partners

The Danish partner school was a secondary General School (Dansk Gymnasium) located in a rural/industrial area in the Jutland Peninsula in western Denmark. There were approximately 420 students on roll and in terms of ICTs the school boasted advanced infrastructure that included computer labs, laptops, and wireless internet throughout. Approximately 60 students aged 16–19 years took part and the project was implemented within their "Ancient culture" subject. Sanne, was a teacher of Russian, Latin, Ancient Greek, and Roman culture and had been teaching in secondary education since 1976. She had not taken part in eTwinning before but had participated in a Comenius project with a school in Italy ten years ago. She was in her early sixties and she was not very familiar with the use of computers.

The "My Studies" Project

The School

The school was a mixed-gender, nondenominational, urban vocational school with 213 students on roll located in a central area of Athens, Greece. The area was considered to be middle/working class and had attracted a large number of immigrants. The school offered specialization in the fields of Mechanical Engineering, Electrician, Information Science and Networks, Economics and Management, and Health and Welfare. It boasted a range of labs and facilities while eTwinning projects had also been organized in the past.

The aim of the teacher was to work on the project in either of the three computer labs or the school's library. However, the library room was rather small and uninviting and was not very often frequented by students. During an observation there the internet connection did not work, the librarian had to provide us with an extension cable in order to plug the computers into the power socket, and the desks hosting the two computers were so impractical that students had to struggle in order to type their notes. All in all, the library appeared to be a sterile, dark, and unfriendly place that was not frequented often by students.

The Collaborative Project

The project was designed to run for the school year 2009–2010 and there was no assigned time within the curriculum; so meetings were expected to take place on a weekly basis after the end of lessons. Data collection was carried out during 2009–2010 and took place over three consecutive visits. The meetings were not fixed but ranged throughout the year and so did the number of the participating students—this kept changing during each research visit with only a couple of students forming the core of the team. The aim of the project was to compare and discuss students' perceptions of their vocational education school and their aspirations for the future. The project idea was conceived by the Greek teacher, Eirini, and her Italian partner, Miriam. They had already collaborated before on two other eTwinning projects; so they were both fairly experienced and well acquainted with each other. Additionally, they had met face to face when the Italian team visited the Greek school during their first project in 2007.

The Greek Participants

Eirini, the Greek teacher, taught courses in the field of Health and Welfare. She was in her late forties, had long teaching experience in secondary education, and was fairly confident in her ICT skills. In 2007, she had created a blog that hosted information and updates with regard to the eTwinning projects she had been involved till then and she also made frequent use of "eclass," an online platform where teachers uploaded supplementary material for their students to access. Approximately ten students from different classes and levels aged 16–18 years took part in the project.

The Italian Partners

The Italian partner school was a vocational school with 900 students (mainly boys) on roll located in an urban area in the east coast of Sicily offering students specialization in dentistry, electronics, electricals, and thermal mechanics. As Miriam described "many of the students come from a low social background, they can be difficult to deal with at times so as a school we look to open their minds and give them a better start in life" (sic). With regard to the school's objectives, special emphasis was placed on promoting foreign language and ICT skills through participation in European Union (EU) projects.

Miriam had been teaching English in secondary education for 20 years. She had taken part in eTwinning before and had been previously involved in two other projects with Eirini. She had also been involved in other eTwinning and Comenius projects in the past and had visited Greece and France within the framework of these projects. The students who took part were aged 14–19 years and the project was mainly implemented into the English- and Italian-language lessons although sometimes they were asked to work on the project outside of their school time.

Drivers for Participation and Initial Expectations

The main motivation for Sofia to initiate an eTwinning project derived from her personal aspiration to bring students closer to books and was related to her capacity not as a teacher of French but at that time as the school's librarian. She argued that statistically very few students made substantial use of the library and she had thought that participation in a collaborative project would facilitate her in getting students more acquainted with books. Her personal inquisitiveness and openness to new things was, however, the main reason for discovering eTwinning and deciding to explore it further:

> It was also personal curiosity…I used to hear about eTwinning…We were informed from a "memo" that briefing meetings for teachers were taking place, I went to one of these, to a couple actually, and I really liked it…because in general I like new things, I like trying out new things (chuckling), I'm laughing because my husband tells me off "you are always into trying new things" (laughing). (Sofia, Athens suburban)

Additionally, her role as a librarian meant that she had felt increasingly disconnected from students as she had stopped teaching and she explained that she was looking for new, more flexible ways to approach students that would also allow them to form links with a school abroad. For Sanne, the Danish teacher, the key impetus was collaboration with a foreign school; however, her uncommon subject matter combined with the particularities of the curriculum did not allow for great flexibility:

> I have always been interested in working together with other countries—and when I heard of eTwinning, I found that it could be a very convenient way of finding partners with interests like mine. In reality it was a bit difficult to find at the same time both appropriate project ideas, which I could use in my program/ lessons, and pupils of the same age as mine. A problem for me is also, that my Latin pupils only have Latin 2–3 months—and that the Ancient culture is only a subject for pupils one year. This is why my students changed during the project. (Sanne, Denmark)

The Greek head teacher was supportive toward the school's participation in extracurricular activities and programs. He considered the library an "outlet" for students during their free periods or when they had been expelled from class, and believed that "Sofia is really good and creates the conditions to attract them to the library" (head teacher, Athens suburban). He argued that although the process of participating in eTwinning could be simpler, involvement in other extracurricular activities and projects was vital as he saw school not merely as a learning space but as a core for social interaction and engagement.

> I always support these sort of initiatives, I don't see upper high-school as just a space for knowledge, it's not just for tuition to pass the exams and

go to university...well, you see I want the school to take part in programs of intercultural exchanges. The school is not just a space for education, it's also a space for culture and for other activities...it's a social space. (Head teacher, Athens suburban)

At school level, both teachers acknowledged that although they did not collaborate with other colleagues, the support of the head teacher was vital in their decision to go ahead with the project. In addition, for Sofia the small financial support she received from the school was critical in carrying out the student exchange:

We have the full moral support [of the head teacher], the financial [support] to a great extent...if this cultural space in the school is to run, it's a matter of the head teacher. If he supports it, all's well. If he doesn't support it or he is indifferent, then you lose the mood yourself. (Sofia, Athens suburban)

In the case of the "my studies" project, the pedagogical opportunities of collaborative learning, the use of ICTs for communication and collaboration and the potential to meet students from foreign countries was what attracted Eirini to eTwinning initially. For Miriam, her Italian partner, the key impetus was creating links with a foreign school, using English and digital technologies for communication and experimenting with new methodologies. In particular, web-based school collaboration was seen by both teachers as a pedagogical resource capable of providing alternative ways of approaching teaching and learning:

Students can improve their language skills, computer and communication skills. They were involved in some good team work activity, which is crucial for everyday life. (Miriam, Sicily)

At a personal level, Miriam found participation in eTwinning meaningful and beneficial since it enhanced both her teaching methodology and improved her rapport with her students. Similarly, Eirini also reported that eTwinning had benefited her at a personal level and retrospectively, she felt more confident with regard to her English-language and ICT skills:

Personally I have improved my English skills, apart from meeting exceptional colleagues from other countries in the EU, I have improved both my language and ICT skills. (Eirini, Athens inner city)

At school level Eirini did not acknowledge any particular drivers that triggered her involvement with eTwinning apart from the moral support of the head teacher. In terms of infrastructure she was content with the school's computer labs and the help she had received from her colleagues in the past. The head teacher confirmed his supporting role toward participation in such collaborative projects; however, as he had only been appointed in that post in January 2010 he was not very familiar with Eirini's eTwinning activities. Still, having studied at a Swedish university himself and taken part the year before in an exchange trip in Finland at his previous school he viewed positively such experiences and also actively encouraged the use of ICTs. Similarly, Miriam not only had the support of her colleagues but had also received financial funding from the school so that they could carry out the visits in Greece and France during the previous projects:

> An Italian language teacher also helps a lot with the project. Other teachers cooperate if we need the students to work on the project. Also, the school helped financially. The funds from the school are used for school trips. (Miriam, Sicily)

With regard to benefits at school level, Eirini appeared to have mixed feelings and was more skeptical as to whether the moral reward deriving from a nomination for the eTwinning awards for their previous project was a sufficient enough motive. She mainly wished for a more tangible type of reward such as receiving funding to organize an exchange trip for her students. Conversely, Miriam did acknowledge school-related benefits mainly associated with gaining local popularity and feeling more integrated in the European community:

> We feel like we have become more of a part of the European community. We were in the local newspaper with past work so it is good for our reputation. (Miriam, Sicily)

At the macro-level, no stimuli for participation deriving from the eTwinning central authorities or the national Ministry of Education were reported by the majority of teachers. Miriam, however, described how she had received adequate support and training from the eTwinning national authorities:

> They organized various seminars and helped us to prepare for them. They were always ready to respond and help us. (Miriam, Sicily)

Participation and Expectations: Pupils' Perspectives

For many students the idea of school twinning seemed appealing at first and they were attracted to the prospect of collaborating with another class online, combined with the prospect of travelling abroad. In particular, in the case of the reading club project the prospect of the exchange visit was one of the main incentives for participation along with their love for reading books and their desire to get in touch with foreign pupils. As these students explained:

> *Thodoris (17)*: To be honest most of us came for the trip. But there were also some people who wanted to be involved with books because it interests them.
>
> *Natalia (17)*: Well, Ms Sofia suggested it, since we were thinking of talking with a school, we could meet them better so that we would see what would happen with the exchanges.
>
> *Marios (17)*: To get to know other students and to make new groups of friends.
>
> *Int*: So the excursion was one of the motives but not the only one.
>
> *Natalia (17)*: It was the pretext to start talking about it and register anyway.

Similarly, the expectations of the students who took part in the "my studies" project were related to becoming acquainted with other pupils abroad and learning about their everyday lives as well as going on an exchange visit:

> *Aris (16)*: Well, I think mainly this program has been created in order to get acquainted with other countries, depending on where we will go to, I don't know.
>
> *Nikos (16)*: So that we can speak with children from abroad, to learn about their school activities and how they do their classes.
>
> *Fotis (16)*: We learn new things. We might, like, go on a trip with the program.

The Tools

Both projects were hosted on TwinSpace; however, the use of platform differed between the two. In the case of the reading club project, because it was configured in 2008, it was locked-in to using the old TwinSpace platform, which took the form of a more traditional website and included a discussion forum and a chat tool. The Greek and Danish partners employed TwinSpace primarily as a means of uploading and sharing content in the different forum categories related to the books they read and the topics they discussed during the group meetings. Other tools employed by the teachers were their external email accounts so as to arrange practicalities about the project and the exchange visits. Additionally, a small number of students migrated to other social networking tools such as Facebook and MSN for informal contact with their partners after they met face to face during the exchange visits.

Likewise, the "my studies" project was hosted on TwinSpace, albeit the newer "refurbished" platform, which made the use of other tools such as a wiki and a blog possible. Eirini and Miriam also employed their external email account, Skype, and Facebook as a means of organizing the project and keeping in touch.

The Journey: Implementation of the Project in Practice

The "my studies" project did not take place within the framework of a particular taught subject at the Greek school but involved the participation of a small group of students and was set up as an extracurricular activity where learner participation was voluntary rather than coerced. My first class observation coincided with their first meeting and their registration and introduction to TwinSpace was underpinned by a range of technical difficulties. One of the major problems was that although the teacher followed the same steps in order to register all students and their names appeared on the list of "student members" they repeatedly attempted to log on to the platform but their efforts were unsuccessful. These technical problems persisted and combined with a range of other hurdles that will be analyzed in the next sections resulted in a let-down and eventually both teachers gave up on the project and stopped updating TwinSpace. Apart from a few "icebreaking" introductory messages on the wiki and the blog posted by the two teachers no other content was ever uploaded. Instead, most of the tabs such as the "Staff room" and the "Pupils corner" as well as the different sections under the "activities" remained without content.

The folder "Image Gallery" contained 16 photos uploaded by the Greek teacher. These were images of the school and the students working on the project at the computer lab, which were taken during one of my first class observations when the teacher was showing them the features of TwinSpace. Additionally, the wiki included just one welcoming message toward the Italian partners posted by the Greek teacher during the first stages of the project. Only two blog entries were posted by the two teachers respectively and described the activities of the two teams in the period November–December 2009, namely visiting and presenting their work at an exhibition in Italy and taking part in an online discussion organized by the Greek Minister of Education.

Interestingly, during the consequent research visits and via email communication throughout the year Eirini would be pointing out the difficulties they were facing without actually admitting defeat—each time she would turn a blind eye on the situation and would describe their future plans as if they were actually still going ahead with the project. In reality, the Italian students were never registered on the platform, there were no instances of communication or collaboration between the two teams, and no content relating to the topic was ever posted by the students or the teachers. During the second phase of the data collection in February, things proved even more chaotic and Eirini did not manage to organize a class observation or a second round of focus-group interviews with the students. Still, when interviewed she described how they were planning to go ahead:

One idea on what to do next is that each student will choose two or three professions he likes and present some pictures on a power point or a video, pictures or whatever each student wants on the profession he likes...We'll arrange a meeting after school and upload them. (Eirini, Athens inner city)

During the third phase of data collection and despite the total lack of activity on the collaborative platform, Eirini had arranged another class observation at the school's library. Only four students were present and they appeared totally unfamiliar with the platform while only one of them was registered on TwinSpace but had lost his password. The result was that throughout the observation the students worked on Microsoft Word and created a short text about themselves and their professional interests. As the students described, they had already written them before but their teacher had lost them and they had to rewrite them on the day of the observation. As the interview excerpt below demonstrates there was a sense of chaos and lack of organization implicitly attributed to the teacher:

Aris (16): Well, we were given some papers and we had to translate them from Greek to English.
Fotis (16): Did these get lost?
Aris (16): We were told that we would send these papers later on.
Int: What sort of papers?
Aris (16): Some questions.
Fotis (16): They were about our school...what we're into...What we enjoy at school mostly.

Sakis (16): Which subjects we find difficult…which we find easier and…

Fotis (16): We first wrote everything into Greek…and then in English.

All: We had everything ready and we had left it here.

Fotis (16): Then Ms Eirini took them…

Nikos (16): She lost them.

During that observation the students wrote a brief description of themselves, their school, and their future aspirations; however, these were never uploaded on TwinSpace. No other activity took place before the end of the summer term and this eTwinning project ended rather unfruitfully. During our last interview, Eirini on the one hand continued making future plans for the project but on the other hand she appeared to have realized that her initial expectations had not been met although she hardly acknowledged her personal responsibility regarding the outcome of the project:

> Well, the truth is we got caught up with preparing the Comenius…In the meantime because Miriam was away on meetings a lot of the time because she was involved in a Comenius before…she didn't respond much either. And I haven't spoken to her for a long time. It wasn't a good year. (Eirini, Athens suburban)

In the case of the reading club project integrating the collaboration in the reading club activities entailed both advantages and disadvantages for the Greek school. On the one hand, as it was an extracurricular activity the teacher had the flexibility to organize the project as she wished and there was no pressure in terms of devoted classroom time or exam preparation. On the other hand, this suggested that the students took part voluntarily after school on either Friday or Saturday afternoons and although a register was kept Sofia could not be very strict with attendance. Furthermore, the students were preparing for the national university entry exams and their workload was heavy, which made their attendance to the meetings and their online engagement even less regular. In addition, another drawback associated with the project running as an extracurricular activity was that the computer labs were locked and they were restricted to using the two computers available at the library. As this next excerpt illustrates, Sofia admitted that she did not wish to take the responsibility of using the school's computer labs when the ICT teacher was not present.

> Because many times the computers break down I don't want to ask for the key personally and to open the lab and be responsible for it…one of

the students may cause a problem...and I don't want that...here where I can control them and I know things a bit better...I keep them here...we have two computers, we struggle with these two...other libraries have more...we, because of lack of space we have a shortage in equipment. (Sofia, Athens suburban)

Indeed, when the majority of the students described their in-school use of ICTs, they admitted that they rarely used the labs outside their ICT classes. For the purpose of the collaborative project Sofia registered students on TwinSpace so that they could access the platform either from the library or from home. In reflecting whether this was a successful year after the start of the project Sofia reasoned:

All students have access even from home if they want. There are some students who use it more but most of them don't use it. What I mean is that if I don't...I have this problem...if you don't make them, if you don't tell them, "come here, log in" they won't do it, you have to assign it to them. (Sofia, Athens suburban)

Sofia did not find setting up TwinSpace particularly challenging although it took some time before the practicalities regarding students' access were resolved:

There were so many students, we had difficulties with their passwords, they forgot them and then I had to re-register them. The first phase was so tiring that I missed the chance to do a lot. But I think now, the second time, we'll do better, we'll be more focused. (Sofia, Athens suburban)

Conversely, Hanna was not able to register all her students and she found her experience with TwinSpace particularly disappointing if not frustrating:

I found the Ewinning tool very unsatisfactory to use—it became confusing, where new materials were uploaded—and this made the communication heavy and in some ways uninteresting. A point of discussion might have started some week before anybody found it and would give a reaction. (Sanne, Denmark)

The initial configuration of TwinSpace involved deciding on the different categories and setting up the relevant forum topics and file folders such as philosophy, psychology, prose, poetry, music, and so on. As Sofia described:

> I had a plan in my mind and I sent it to her [Sanne] and she made some corrections and she added some other things and we used the corrected version. So, the two of us communicated at first quite frequently before we set it up. (Sofia, Athens suburban)

More than a month after the project was launched and the TwinSpace had been configured there was a message posted by Sanne encouraging the students to edit their profile details so that it would be easier for everybody to get a sense of who was who. Interestingly, indicative of the initial excitement to engage with the project and to explore the various tools was the range of posts published in various online "spaces" available on the TwinSpace platform as well as the number of posts and comments that appeared throughout the first three months of the project and were considerably reduced over the next year, in particular with regard to the Danish participation.

Thus, in the beginning of the project the teachers and some students showed a more active engagement to post messages and upload content in the different "forum" categories as well as in the file "archives" and the "folders" without, however, demonstrating any particular coordination or coherence. Content ranged from book summaries and author biographies to photos and embedded YouTube videos with songs about love. This range in content combined with the very few comments was also suggestive of the lack of "common ground" as regards the books read and discussed. There was a general, shared topic, which focused on love represented in literature, philosophy, and psychology but this was too broad since no particular authors or literary genres were selected from the start to be read and analyzed by the participating partners. The Danish school was more focused on Ancient Greek writers while the Greek school was mostly orientated on contemporary literature and, as such, there were not many topics in common.

Another interesting point to consider was how all the teachers who took part in the two projects associated the use of the collaborative platform with the projects' activities only. Neither of them viewed TwinSpace as an appropriate platform to discuss the practicalities of their collaboration or exchange trip and they used external tools instead. For instance, Sofia highlighted how much easier it was to use her external email account compared to logging to TwinSpace:

> Of course the discussion about the trip was conducted through our personal email and not through eTwinning. All this correspondence about

the itinerary and what we'll do and all this, I don't think it really fits TwinSpace, there's no relevant space for such a thing, perhaps through our mail [the TwinSpace mail] but, see, we also used our personal email. At the end of the day all this accessing a different website, entering usernames and passwords is more complicated…well, more complicated, I mean it's not part of your daily routine. (Sofia, Athens suburban)

Students' Profiles on TwinSpace

It is now worth considering whether the students who took part in the reading club project edited their online profiles and what information they provided. Out of the 106 registered students 21 never accessed TwinSpace while 22 only logged in once. Although as we saw earlier the Danish teacher prompted the students to edit their profiles, only one student from Denmark did so, succinctly adding the comment "Add me as a friend on facebook :)." In terms of the Greek students, 24 students edited their profiles adding information about their age, family, hobbies, and interests. Only five girls provided more detailed information out of which four also uploaded a photo—one of these four also included her Facebook page link while another added a link for her account on MySpace. Interestingly, these five girls who created a more detailed and open profile were also the most active student members both in terms of frequency of posts as well in terms of range and amount of content they uploaded throughout the duration of the project.

Technical Inhibitors

A range of technical difficulties affected the course and outcome of these two projects. In particular, the limited functions of the TwinSpace platform, as well as the initial registration problems that both teams faced and the complexity of accessing TwinSpace combined with limited motivation discouraged sustained participation to the project. Additionally, throughout the duration of the project there were unresolved configuration problems that put off the students and as soon as their initial attempts to log in failed they lost interest. As these students described:

Accessing the eTwinning site resulted in lots of error messages on many computers. It was really difficult to log in from some computers, there was a problem, I don't know exactly what it was but some couldn't get access. It was purely a matter of computer because you could access it from my friend's computer, I don't know exactly what happened to be honest. (Athina, 16)

I think it's not very easy to use. Well, basically I tried to access it from home and it was a bit confusing to find what I was looking for. (Manolis, 16)

It's easy but boring. (Stathis, 16)

Other technical inhibitors were associated with students forgetting either their password or the long TwinSpace webpage link while another student described the technical difficulties of TwinSpace opening in a new pop-up window:

The point where you enter the password is a bit problematic though. Because a lot of times some computers select not to allow pop-up windows, they think it's dangerous and you have to remove this restriction and allow pop-ups or whatever. Sometimes, the password does not work, in general there are some problems in logging in, after that there is no problem. (Anna, 17)

As Sofia described, apart from the configuration and access difficulties, getting the students to work on the TwinSpace platform proved challenging—perhaps unsurprisingly since they were accustomed to other less complicated and more attractive modes of online interaction:

Students get discouraged immediately, they are used to accessing everything instantly, in a flash, once they see it's problematic they give up ... At the end of the day all this accessing a different website, entering usernames and passwords is more complicated ... well, by more complicated, I mean it's not part of your daily routine. (Sofia, Athens suburban)

Similarly, Sanne was also discouraged by the initial technical barriers that they had encountered and curtailed her students' use of site—leading to limited contribution partly to registration and access problems:

[The students found the use of TwinSpace] difficult—some could not use the platform—we never found out why ... I think that I will suggest some alternative platform and only use eTwinning for finding partners. (Sanne, Denmark)

In the case of the "my studies" project a range of technical difficulties emerged at the first stages of the project and affected its future course. During the first months and also throughout the year Eirini reported that she found the new TwinSpace particularly challenging to use and was not able to configure and use the wiki tool as she had initially expected. Although she was confident about her computer skills and had used blog and wiki tools in the past, she found using TwinSpace particularly confusing. With regard to her unfamiliarity with TwinSpace and when questioned whether she could attend an eTwinning training seminar or use the online guidelines for the new platform, Eirini highlighted two further issues: first, the guidelines were only available in English in those early stages and second, time and traveling limitations did not always make participation in seminars possible. Moreover, Eirini faced problems registering her students as was highlighted earlier while her partner, Miriam, was not able to log on to the new platform at all.

> The other problem we have, me and my partner, is that she can't log into her TwinSpace…In Italy at the moment the TwinSpace doesn't work, the teacher can't even access it and she will send me her work so that I will upload it using her username and password but that's not collaboration that's a torture. (Eirini, Athens inner city)

On the other hand, Miriam argued that Eirini was the one facing problems with TwinSpace and not her team and, when asked why they did not choose to migrate to the external wiki they were already familiar with, again she passed the responsibility on to her partner:

> *Miriam*: Our partner is having problems with the new eTwinning website, it is more difficult to use.
> *Int*: Why didn't you use the same external wiki again this year?
> *Miriam*: Because we haven't started on the project yet, we are still just at the discussing and planning period. Also, as mentioned before, Greece haven't (sic) quite worked out how to use the platform yet.

Still, the Italian students were never registered on the platform and the project remained at a "discussion and planning period" throughout the year. Both parties appeared to renounce responsibility and these initial technical hurdles were never overcome but they curtailed use of TwinSpace and discouraged any sustained participation to the project.

Time Issues

As already described, the reading club project materialized outside the school curriculum during two weekly meetings scheduled for the two groups of students respectively over the course of two academic years. As such, the time commitment was great both for the teacher and the pupils. Sofia acknowledged how challenging it was to motivate the students to regularly attend these meetings while it was even harder to convince them to devote time from home. Moreover, in terms of her personal time, she did not always manage to complete everything during her office hours at the library but she often had to work from home at the expense of her family life since the project took up more time that she had originally anticipated:

> It got really tiring last year, trying to coordinate the whole team and see what is everyone going to read and write and chase up all of them. It's so tiring that in the end you're exhausted and don't have the courage to do many other things. (Sofia, Athens suburban)

Danish participation was also affected by time constraints and the students were not overly motivated to devote their free time on the project. This was exacerbated by the fact the some of the students had part-time jobs. As the Danish teacher described:

> Some pupils work 15–30 hours a week after school—others only 4–8 hours. I personally find this a bad idea—and some pupils overdo this, so that they are not able to do their homework or are sleepy at school—and they can be expelled of school, if they get too bad marks because of their jobs. (Sanne, Denmark)

A range of time issues also contributed to the failure of the "my studies" project, which was designed to take place mainly outside the school curriculum. There were no fixed weekly meetings as in the case of the reading club project but Eirini's initial plan was to use other online tools to communicate with the students on a weekly basis and arrange face-to-face meetings less frequently. Reflecting on why the activities were not organized on a more systematic basis, Eirini reported how the project was compromised by the time constraints and also students' lack of motivation as well as curriculum restrictions:

> It was difficult because I was off on sick leave several times, we missed some classes, well that's about it. And, also, the students' indifference. I said I'm not going to do all the work myself this year. There are no motives for the children. There isn't the slightest motive for the students to work on these programs. I can't run them within class time either because the students are from different classes. (Eirini, Athens inner city)

Conversely, the students reported that they were willing to attend weekly meetings belying Eirini's argument with regard to their indifference and lack of commitment:

Int: How do you feel about the project so far?

Nikos (16): Good, it can't be bad meeting new kids and talking about a trip!...But we just didn't have time...Miss didn't have time to do things and get on [with the project].

Int: Would you be willing to stay after school?

All: Yeah.

Aris (16): We don't have anything else to do.

Int: So you wouldn't mind staying after school?

All: No, not all.

The sense of noncommitment and of perennially postponing meetings and activities and often looking for excuses is striking in the excerpt below when Eirini mentioned in the second interview in the middle of the school year that she had still not allocated tasks to the students:

I haven't assigned anything to them. I will assign this task to them to do at home and they'll bring it to me eventually and we'll upload it all together. Each will prepare his part in electronic format of course and we'll see if they will be able to translate it. (Eirini, Athens inner city)

With regard to the Italian participation Miriam also described how organizing the project and meeting deadlines was time-consuming both in terms of personal and class time while she also argued that an early start and sticking to rules was important for the final outcome:

It took a lot of personal time, we had to implement the project into class time so this took a lot of planning in order to meet deadlines...we need to follow some rules, the project has to start at the start of the school year and follow the school timetable. (Miriam, Sicily)

Students' In- and Out-of-School Use of Digital Technologies

Similar to the case studies presented in chapter 3, students' in- and out-of-school engagement with digital technologies was reported to be commonplace rather than particularly sophisticated. The majority of the Greek participants described in the focus-group interviews that they used computers and the internet regularly (almost on a daily basis or a few times a week) mainly for recreational activities, routine forms of communication, and less often for homework. Recreational activities consisted primarily of accessing Facebook and/or MSN, listening to music, and to a lesser extent downloading music and films, playing games, and browsing a range of websites for news and updates. More sophisticated uses of digital technologies reported by individual students involved downloading films and synchronizing subtitles (Markos, 16) and learning "how to play some songs on the guitar" (Antonis, 16). Using the computer and the internet for homework was largely associated with looking up information on Wikipedia or search engines such as Google and typing up assignments. In-school engagement with ICTs involved the use of TwinSpace for the needs of the collaborative project and using the school's computer lab in the framework of the ICT subject. The excerpt below is representative of the students' experiences with regard to both in- and out-of-school use of digital technologies:

> *Tania*: I have Facebook, I download songs, I watch films, that's about it.
> *Stathis*: We look up for information if we have a project, we chat with our friends on MSN...
> *Sakis*: We play Pro.
> *Int*: Do you get assignments from school that require computer use?
> *Sakis*: Rarely.
> *Stathis*: No, we get some, to look up words and information on some stuff.
> *Int*: Do you use the computer labs at school besides the ICT class?
> *All*: No.
>
> (Athens suburban, all students aged 16 years)

Student engagement with social networking sites such as Facebook was also noted during the data collection visits. This mainly consisted of visiting the school library during their breaks and free periods and using the computers available there. Logging on to Facebook was by far the most common activity. An example of a slightly more sophisticated computer use was observed during one of the visits when the internet connection was down. This involved editing a picture and saving it as a desktop image in order to make fun of the teachers and students in it.

Similarly, no exemplary in- and out-of-school engagement with ICTs was reported from the students of the "my studies" project. The majority of students reported using a computer and the internet regularly (almost on a daily basis or a few times a week) mainly for recreational activities and less often for homework. Recreational activities consisted primarily of accessing social networking sites such as Facebook, MySpace, and/or MSN, playing games, listening to music offline or on YouTube, and browsing a range of websites for news and updates. Only one girl reported not having internet access at home and not being familiar at all with using online applications and sites:

Costas (17): For internet games, for (software) programs, for email, eh and for school homework, to access the internet and look for information...

Nikos (16): I use it for Facebook, MSN, MySpace... and for school homework, eh, for games too, and to keep myself up to date, to listen to songs on YouTube, to check out Filathlos [online Greek sports newspaper], for all that...

Melina (16): I'm not into that, no, at home where I have a computer but I don't have internet access I only listen to music.

With relation to homework the majority of students largely saw the computer as a means of looking up information on Wikipedia or search engines such as Google and typing up assignments. Again, in-school engagement with digital technologies was only reported within the framework of ICT school subject and mainly involved learning how to use Microsoft Office applications such as Word, Excel, and PowerPoint. Interestingly, the same students, who appeared to be close friends outside the school setting, reported engaging in informal, out-of-school, peer-learning activities with regard to improving their ICT skills:

Aris (16): I do the same because more or less we use computers together with the guys.

Fotis (16): No, we started using the internet all together, like, at the same time... and whatever one knows, we all know... If one of us learns something we tell the other.

Students' Engagement with the Project and Use of Tools

This section will now go on to describe students' engagement with the collaborative project. Since, the "my studies" project did not involve any student participation, the focus will be solely on the reading club project. In this case, student use of the project platform was rather infrequent and commonplace particularly with regard to interaction and collaboration—especially when taking into consideration the two-year duration of the project and the great number of participants. Although there was a range of entries posted under the different sections and the site appeared rich in content, the number and frequency of comments were very limited while the quality of the posts was also dubious. The following excerpt from a focus-group interview is representative of how the students engaged with TwinSpace:

Aliki (16): We upload photographs, videos, usually songs that we write the translation, of course, if they're in Greek so that they can understand

them, poetry, articles, reviews, etc, summaries of stuff we had discussed on Fridays here…We log in both from here and from home, it
depends. Here it's more like an assignments, like, "can you do something with the summaries and upload them there"? At home, it's like,
how can I say it, if you are personally interested to upload something
in your free time…

Int: Do the Danish students do the same?

Aliki (16): I have the feeling that they do it less often, I'm not sure but
I believe so, their teacher mainly does the work. For example when I
have uploaded things I see that the responses, the comments, everything is made by the teacher not the students.

Although students were able to use the library's computer(s) during their
breaks and free periods, they did not log on to TwinSpace very frequently.
This happened on very few occasions either when Sofia had given them a
relevant assignment or on their own initiative to post YouTube videos of
love songs on the website. Over the two-year duration of the project, discussion and postings on the forum covered a range of topics. One of the most
popular TwinSpace sections was the "Forum Music" with 42 entries that
consisted of embedded YouTube videos accompanied in some cases by a
short description of the song and the lyrics in English and/or Greek.

Despite the popularity of this forum it should be noted that all entries
were posted by the Greek participants and there were very few comments.
More than two-thirds of these postings remained unanswered and out of
these 11 comments all but one involved correcting uploading mistakes such
as re-embedding the video or adding the songs' lyrics. There was only one
instance of commenting when Sanne asked for clarification on a song's title
that was provided some months later by Sofia. This highlights the problem
of lack of notification emails or really simple syndication (RSS) feeds. As
students reported the only way to check for comments and new posts was by
going through all past entries one by one.

Out of the total 132 posts on the forum only 54 were published by the
students and out of these only 6 were initiated by the Danish partners. The
majority of the 64 comments involved adding more information on the initial post by the same or a different author rather than instigating a productive
discussion. The most popular category after the "Music" one was the section on "Prose" where the students posted summaries of the books they had
read and discussed during the reading club meetings as well as the authors'
biographies. The thread with the most comments (eight) was on "Romeo
and Juliet;" however, discussion did not take off and only the Danish teacher

participated in the thread. Most of the postings noticeably emanated from a dedicated "core" of 10–15 Greek participants and the online presence of the 5 girls who edited their profiles was dominant with regular contributions to the forum.

With regard to the other sections of TwinSpace the general forum was only used in the beginning mainly for "housekeeping" posts while the "photo gallery" folder was used to publish pictures of "love in art" as well as pictures from the exchange trips and some student activities in the classroom. As the students and Sofia described, because they were using the old platform it was not possible to post pictures in the forum but only text and embedded videos while in the "photo gallery" the pictures could only be organized alphabetically and it was not possible to leave comments:

> The space for the images is elsewhere, there is a section called "art gallery" and we upload the pictures which are all mixed up and then we use the forum where you can comment on something whose image is somewhere else…you can't have text and images together—it's a thing that we miss, perhaps they have improved it in the new TwinSpace platform. (Sofia, Athens suburban)

Overall, the use of the TwinSpace platform reflected a one-way communication mode of merely transmitting information rather than engaging in dialogue. As already discussed, the majority of posts were uploaded by the Greek participants and only at the beginning did their Danish partners post a few comments while at the latest stages of the project during the second year there were almost no comments at all. Apart from technical and time inhibitors and lack of motivation this was also justified by the difficulty to find common ground with regard to the topics discussed as well as lack of interest in the choice of books. As one student described:

> We read some books in the club that weren't particularly…it's not just being modern but be interesting…[they] were sort of…completely irrelevant…you had never heard of them before, they were from a particular Greek era, so…ok there wasn't much interest…The Danish students read ancient tragedies, so they tried to penetrate in the Greek culture but in the wrong way…well, not in the wrong way but differently from us. We on the other hand, did not read Hans Christian Andersen, we did not try to approach their culture, Danish culture and literature, so in practice it's like uploading comments that the others can't read because they are not interested deep down. (Aliki, 16)

Copying and Pasting

Analysis of the TwinSpace content revealed that the majority of posts were published by the Greek students and teacher. The students mainly used online resources such as Wikipedia for authors' and poets' biographies while they also created more original posts of book summaries or translated poems into English. As Sofia reported with regard to how students engaged with the activities and researched their online entries:

> They looked for information on the internet, it's the easy way out, quite frequently when we were here we would consult a biographical dictionary from the library and we would comment on that but I'm under the impression that when they had to write about it they went online again to look for information, they didn't bother typing it [from the dictionary], they went for the easier and fastest solution. (Sofia, Athens suburban)

Although Sofia objected to the student practice of copying and pasting, she had to compromise since the project was not formally assessed but relied on the students' voluntary efforts. Additionally, she recognized the additional barrier of translating everything into a foreign language while the lack of participation and contribution on the behalf of their partners discouraged her students from putting in more effort. Furthermore, as some students commented copying and pasting from online resources mirrored their general practices of completing school assignments:

> We type in the topic of the assignment we have to do and we find information online. (Kelly, 16)

Language issues were often seen as a barrier toward participation and communication in the cases of the reading club project. Analyzing literary texts in a foreign language proved to some extent challenging to the students particularly those with more limited language skills. Moreover, some of the students described how by using a foreign language for their online interactions part of the meaning-making process was inevitably lost in translation:

> We only speak with them in English, just in English. Some of us who don't speak any English they have no contact whatsoever. There were some texts we did and everything was translated into English, perhaps some of them suffered from the translation from Greek to English. And perhaps some of meanings and the concepts of the texts were lost, which

we consider as very important but they just thought it was just a text they read. (Maria, 16, Athens suburban)

Collaboration and Communication: From Enthusiasm to Disappointment

Within the TwinSpace platform some communication took place at the discussion forums but at large the focus was on transmitting information and content rather than engaging in dialogue. As such there were no instances of collaboration between the two partner teams and no collaborative posts while commenting was sporadic and unexciting. The majority of students found the platform uninviting and unattractive and only a small core of more committed Greek participants logged in regularly to check for recent posts and upload new content. The two teachers used their personal email accounts to collaborate at the outset of the project in order to set up and configure their TwinSpace. At the later stages of the project, however, the Greek team experienced a sense of "abandonment" when their Danish partners stopped contributing and disappeared from TwinSpace. As Sofia described with regard to reciprocity:

> The first thing necessary for the project to work is reciprocity, well if you upload something and there isn't a single comment, even whether it was good or bad, just a simple comment, if you don't get a reply and there is no interaction eTwinning can't work. I expected that they would definitely respond but I feel abandoned now, you can't see them anywhere, nobody responds. (Sofia, Athens suburban)

However, some of the students found different—and more appealing to them—channels for communicating with their partners and developing online friendships. As highlighted in the excerpts below, after the Danish visit to Greece the pupils exchanged Facebook and/or MSN contact details and migrated there in order to keep in touch at more informal and personal level:

Eleni (16): They came to our school, we went out together.
Kelly (16): I chatted online.
Eleni (16): Oh, yes, through Facebook, MSN and all that. We kept in touch throughout winter... we talked about how things are, what we will do when we visit them and so on.
Int: What about TwinSpace?
Eirini (16): [laughing] We don't go there.
Kelly (16): Yes, we talk mainly through Facebook and MSN.

The teachers were aware of the use of other social networking sites by students and as Sofia described:

> They keep in touch but only through Facebook. They don't log on eTwinning, they haven't loved it, they don't feel it as their tool. (Sofia, Athens suburban)

Student migration to Facebook and/or MSN was restricted to the students who had met face-to-face during the exchange visits and did not cascade to the rest of the team. Additionally, no other tools for synchronous communication were employed since Sofia appeared hesitant and not confident enough to test her ICT skills to such an extent. Her insecurity was at large reflected in the following excerpt:

> We haven't tried [to use the chat] because I don't feel comfortable about this, I don't know if I can handle it properly. At home I have Skype and I use it to communicate with the other teacher but here I'll have to gather all the students and she'll have to gather her students and it would be great, it could be a determinant factor but I'm copping out...I don't know the technical difficulties we could face and it's something that I would need to have somebody by my side to do it...I have to bring my own laptop that has a camera, it's something we haven't tried, connect it to the internet. (Sofia, Athens suburban)

Limited Student Motivation

Student motivation and engagement constitutes one of the most critical factors that can shape the outcome of the project and determine its success. However, in the case of the "my studies" project it is particularly challenging to assess student motivation. Since the majority of the students were never even registered on the platform, lack of content cannot be attributed to limited student participation. On the one hand, the pupils who signed up for the collaborative project and took part in the focus-group interviews appeared enthusiastic and reported that they were willing to devote personal time for out-of-school participation in the activities. On the other hand, Eirini described how difficult it was to motivate students to take part and what a challenge it was engaging them in activities and making them work from home.

Similarly, student motivation was one of the most critical factors that shaped the outcome of the reading club project and despite the large number of registered students, participation was relatively low. Notwithstanding their original excitement when the students embarked on the project this faded away as the time progressed and they engaged with the different activities on the collaborative platform. In particular, they were discouraged by the way TwinSpace was structured compared to the "commercial" and more interactive websites they were accustomed to using:

> When they presented me with the idea of accessing a site where you talk with another nation on a particular topic for example literature, love and so on...YES, I expected it a bit different!...I expected it would be more in the form of the commercial sites...The whole issue of the account was something I expected it would be very different—what I mean is that it's really difficult to access the profile of the person who is posting...If you want to check out who left a comment on something you uploaded you have to go through the whole list. (Nadia, 16)

The number of more committed Greek students who remained engaged with the project's activities throughout its duration, hardly reached 20, while the numbers were even lower with regard to Danish participation. Sofia associated student engagement both with the sense of individual commitment each of her students demonstrated as well as with the lack of reciprocity on behalf of their Danish partners:

> If there was reciprocity from the Danish students, I think it would have worked much better. My students logged in and uploaded things but nobody responded, nobody replied and commented if they agreed or not, if what they posted was good or not so there was interaction and they gave up as well. Do you see what I mean? They got the sense it was one-way. (Sofia, Athens suburban)

As such, when the students realized that there was no mutual interaction even the more motivated participants lost interest and the number and frequency of posts decreased:

> Well, let me explain, it's a bit problematic [the project] because there is no particular reciprocation, it's a bit sad...what I mean is that when I first started eTwinning I devoted quite a lot of time but then I saw they don't respond back so this makes you feel that you don't want to be that involved. (Maria, 16)

> Not many students from Denmark used it either so there was no point in us logging in and talking to ourselves or uploading songs for us. (Giota, 15)

Motivation also diminished when it became apparent that the students in the two countries were reading different books and as such it was not possible for them to find common ground for discussion and exchange of comments. Lack of interactivity on the website also played a demotivating role. When the students were asked what they would do differently the majority commented on their desire to communicate "directly" with their partners:

> *Chris (16)*: Well, first of all there should be a live messenger like many other sites have, like Facebook, to have something [some tools] to communicate directly with the others.
>
> *Dimitris (16)*: To be able to send the messages directly that would be better and if possible later to get access with webcams.

The Danish "Drifting Away"

As discussed earlier, the reading club project was set to last for two consecutive school years and the first few months had been quite promising with frequent interaction between the two teachers and relatively regular posts published by students and teachers of both schools on the online platform. As Sofia described, initially the Danish teacher put a lot of time and effort toward the project and she was worried that her team would not be able to keep up with the pace the Danes had set and engage in equal terms. However, as time went by the Danish participation decreased and the other team experienced a sense of abandonment:

> Sanne put quite a lot time to it too, I'd say we both got quite involved...At first we exchanged some messages, she interacted more as a teacher but just for a while, then she started to...drift away...Well, I didn't chase her up [rather indignantly]. She should have done it herself [participated more], well, what could I have told her? "Post more"? (Sofia, Athens suburban)

Although Sofia did not find it appropriate to confront her partner or chase her up with regard to her personal and her team's limited and sporadic engagement and participation in the eTwinning project, she also highlighted some of the external inhibitors that might have caused this change:

> I get the feeling that Sanne didn't push them much, they were busy but she didn't motivate them to post, she let them quite loose...She told me that she had time issues in dealing with the curriculum because they didn't have separate meetings but she tried to engage them in eTwinning within regular classes so she didn't have extra time like we did. As a result because she realized she didn't have enough time to complete her syllabus

she kept neglecting eTwinning and they didn't do proper work, she didn't take it seriously, she wasn't that eager. (Sofia, Athens suburban)

On the other hand Sanne described how her students totally lacked motivation to work on the project on their own initiative and how she even had to persuade them to take part from the start:

> Although my pupils' subject in the eTwinning was Ancient culture, I was able to persuade them to participate and write in English—2 classes participated (16–19 years old)—one class begun the subject and the year after another class finished. They had to be pushed and persuaded to write—they did not do anything on their own initiative!...And they only wanted to work during lessons at school. (Sanne, Denmark)

Students' lack of motivation was, thus, one of the inhibitors that led to limited engagement with the project's online activities. However, a range of other factors also attributed to the general outcome of the project and will be analyzed in the next section.

Teaching and Learning Impact

The anticipated benefits of the reading club project were largely associated with communicating with another school and exposing the students to the culture of the other country with the ultimate aim of organizing the exchange visits. Enhancing students' language skills was also viewed as an additional benefit particularly for the minority who hosted and were respectively hosted by their Danish partners:

> I think the students have actually benefitted from the program...The fact that they had to do everything in English...this, I would consider the language the top benefit. The students who were hosted really benefitted because they had to speak [English], they spoke with the parents, the bothers and sisters so they were forced to speak because in general they are too shy to speak English [though] they have the fluency. (Sofia, Athens suburban)

Similarly, the students who took part in the exchange and also communicated with their parents through Facebook and MSN felt that their English skills had improved:

> *Kelly (16)*: At first I didn't speak at all because...well...I couldn't communicate with them, I found it difficult but then I started...

Eleni (16): We were also a bit shy…

Kelly (16): Yeah, we were shy… but then when we started talking I definitely saw an improvement in my English and I spent more time with them.

Eleni (16): Well, they speak English better than we do but… well… I was a bit shy to speak to them and I was stuck at the time but, like, when I met them and we became closer, I didn't have a problem.

With regard to ICTs the students did not report particular benefits since they found TwinSpace easy to navigate and did not feel they had learned anything new. Other perceived benefits were associated with attracting lower-ability students to the library and motivating them to read books. As Sofia explained:

> There is a percentage of around 20% who are good students, the rest, however, are average to bad. These students, I consider it a gain that they came… it may have been the first book they ever read and I hope not the last and that it's their first contact with books and the impression they have that books are somewhat depressing and bleak… there were some teachers here that told me "no way this kid will ever read a book, no way s/he will present anything" and then we were stunned because they liked it I think, they like being involved. (Sofia, Athens suburban)

Conclusion

To sum up, this chapter has endeavored to portray the collaborative journeys of two Greek schools and their partners in Denmark and Italy respectively. A range of drivers and inhibitors emerged from the analysis of the data associated not only with technical impediments but also with the wider personal agendas of the participating students and teachers as well as the educational structures and the micropolitics of the classroom and the broader concept of the school as an institution. In the first case, despite the range of technical and other barriers they encountered both teachers viewed their experience with the collaborative project positively while the two exchange trips were seen as the most beneficial and engaging aspect of the project, particularly since online collaboration through TwinSpace did not flourish. Contributing to the forum did not appeal to the majority of students and the lack of reciprocity on the Danish part resulted in the collaborative platform being used mainly as an online publishing space for one-way communication by a more committed core of students. However, other social networking sites such as Facebook or MSN were adopted by a small minority of students to keep in touch with their partners.

Conversely, the second project was rather unsuccessful despite the initial enthusiasm of the participants. The two major and more explicit inhibitors that can be identified were technical difficulties as well as time and curriculum pressures. However, apart from these more prosaic and matter-of-fact impediments, other more complex and multifaceted factors also affected the final result. At a deeper level of analysis one could argue that the two teachers never really committed to their decision to engage in the collaborative project and kept making excuses and renouncing responsibility. Since this was not their first project but they were fairly experienced and had used other tools in the past creating projects that were successful enough to be nominated for an eTwinning award they could have easily migrated to another tool and overcome the initial technical difficulties. As such technical and time impediments and also the wider personal agendas of the participating teachers appeared to affect the final outcome of the project.

CHAPTER 5

The Bigger Picture: Understanding Web-Based School Collaboration

Introduction

The past two chapters reviewed a range of evidence from the case study projects—highlighting and illustrating the many issues underpinning schools' engagement with the eTwinning initiative and revealing how a range of overlapping and interrelated factors can determine educational collaboration. In this chapter, a comparative approach to data analysis is taken that allows us to compare the data collected from the four diverse cases in terms of the study's research questions. Given the main objective of this study to investigate the similarities and differences underpinning digital technology use for school collaboration across a range of classrooms, there is now a need to compare the four previously discussed cases. At the start of this book it was highlighted how the collaborative and other teaching and learning opportunities afforded by digital technologies were seen to resonate with the collaborative aims and flexible nature of the eTwinning initiative. This chapter will go on to bring together, summarize, and compare the findings from all four case studies—exploring how digital technologies were appropriated in practice and presenting the types of school norms and modes that did not fit comfortably with these perceived opportunities. This will be achieved by engaging in a comparative analysis and will be structured around themes rather than individual participants or projects—highlighting a number of underpinning issues that recur throughout the data while answering the four research questions of this study established in chapter 2:

- How can the use of digital technologies create opportunities for online student interaction and collaboration?
- How do these opportunities "fit" into existing school practices?
- What are the drivers and inhibitors for engaging with a collaborative project for teachers?
- What are the drivers and inhibitors for engaging with a collaborative project for students?

Creating Opportunities for Online Student Interaction and Collaboration

The perceived benefits reported in the empirical data resulted largely from overall participation in the collaborative projects rather than from the sole use of particular digital technologies. Certainly, the tools that were employed contributed toward facilitating online interaction—allowing participants to overcome geographical barriers and providing an opportunity for communication in the absence of face-to-face interactions. Additionally, data analysis identified a number of perceived benefits that resulted from the overall collaborative journey as well as the engagement with particular tools and activities.

Engagement with the Project and Perceived Benefits and Opportunities

During the closing stages of the data collection when teachers and students were asked to reflect on their general experience, the majority of them perceived it as enjoyable or "fun" and reported that they would consider taking part in a collaborative project again the following year. These teachers and students who viewed their experience positively regarded participation in eTwinning as a break from their everyday classroom routines and welcomed the opportunity to approach everyday teaching and learning activities more creatively. Some students from the UK schools, for instance, highlighted how using digital technologies was more motivating and enjoyable compared to their usual daily classroom and homework patterns. Additionally, some of the teachers were already in the process of planning their next project either with the same or with new partners while the students who were eager to engage in another project the following year explicitly noted that their motivation would increase if the next project was more interactive.

For other participants, however, "fun" can also be interpreted as an experience that was perceived as nonthreatening and did not transform but neither did it interfere with their schooling routines. Meanwhile, in all cases, there was a minority of indifferent students who remained unimpressed with the project, did not see any particular benefits, and were not enthusiastic with the prospect of taking part in a collaborative project again. These students appeared to have been more cautious when it came to altering their schooling routines and the use of digital technologies did not prove a particularly powerful catalyst that transformed their learning experience. On the one hand, this was associated with poor information and communication technology (ICT) infrastructure such as in the case of the reading club project where some students criticized the computers and internet connection available at school as opposed to the more advanced technologies they could access at their home environment. On the other hand, in the case of the German project, where the students were accustomed to an ICT saturated classroom, engagement with technologies was not seen to offer added motivation.

Other opportunities emerging from the use of digital technologies in the cases of the Sparta and reading club projects were related to using the official eTwinning wiki and forum respectively as an online revision repository. The benefits accrued from such digital technology use can be described as unintentional "side benefits" since they did not consist part of the original aims of the projects. Interestingly, some of the students who took part in the Sparta project primarily perceived TwinSpace as an online repository for having revision material readily available. Last, some of the students in the reading club project reflected on how their foreign-language skills had slightly improved as a result of engaging in the project activities and overcoming their initial shyness—particularly when it came to face-to-face interactions during the exchange visits.

Issues of Collaboration and Cooperation

Although the collaborative projects and the tools employed created opportunities for social interaction and online collaboration, it was apparent across the four case studies how the different classroom contexts resulted in different communicative and collaborative experiences. Even so, understanding and evaluating instances of collaboration largely depended on defining how collaboration was interpreted by the project participants. In particular, for a large number of students, collaboration, both online and offline, was rather poorly understood and was perceived as the last stage of independent research. For instance, after conducting research independently, they saw collaboration as the process of sharing and integrating things online.

Furthermore, one could argue that the collaborative nature of the projects and the initial ambitions of the teachers were somewhat compromised by the day-to-day practicalities they faced in the classroom, such as time constraints and curriculum pressures. Additionally, a number of students reported that they were somewhat uncomfortable with the idea of editing the work of others. As such, there was little evidence of collaboration in the strong sense of socially constructed content across schools and teams or pairs of students and the accounts of how the students in both projects engaged with the wiki demonstrated that cooperative practices prevailed instead. Overall, the various web-based tools adopted in the projects were used more as an information conduit rather than a communication facilitator.

To some extent real-time online communication with the partner teams was arranged in the cases of the Sparta and the German projects. The teachers organized to use the TwinSpace chat and Skype respectively but technical impediments and time issues did not allow these efforts to materialize. At another level, asynchronous communication did take place to some degree on the forums and blogs in three out of the four case studies but remained sporadic and rather mundane. In the two wiki-based projects, no collaborative writing occurred and there were few instances of editing the other participants' work. On the one hand, the wiki was used for the German project as a platform for learners to get acquainted with their partners and the entries were focused on presenting themselves, their hobbies, favorite movies, and so on. On the other hand, the wiki topic in case study 1 was Ancient Sparta and student practices were at large restricted to either adding authentic content to the wiki or copying and pasting in bulk from online websites such as Wikipedia. After some initial introductory messages posted randomly on the forum and the blog, the students mainly worked on their assigned thematic categories—the knowledge content produced was limited to wiki entries published individually or in pairs, rather than shared group work between and across the two schools. Hence, when interviewed after the completion of the projects, the majority of students reported having only a superficial idea of who their partners in the other country had been.

In the case of the reading club project, after the first year of posting on the forum and having short-threaded discussions, the students met face-to-face when the Danish group visited Athens. Still, this did not result in increased engagement and further online collaboration but rather the opposite—the Danish students used TwinSpace during the second year of the project even more sporadically than before. This was partially justified because some of the participating students either graduated or dropped out of the project and were, to some degree, replaced by new students. Still, meeting in person marked a transition toward using other less institutionalized web-based tools to serve the students' communication needs—resulting in a core of students from both teams exchanging Facebook and/or MSN details and continuing to chat on a more informal basis there.

In a similar manner, the use of Facebook was suggested by a Greek student on the TwinSpace forum of the Sparta project as a more appropriate means of online communication. Nonetheless, only one student from the UK school responded and befriended her on Facebook and, thus, the use of Facebook did not cascade to the rest of the team. The teachers from both case studies were aware of their students' "migration" to other tools and did not object; however, they did not opt to formally adopt such tools for the projects. In the case of the Sparta project social networking sites were blocked on the school's computers while the teacher also highlighted what she saw as legal "grey area" associated with linking with her students on Facebook because of child protection issues.

The Need for Partner Reciprocity

Another emerging theme linked to (lack of) collaboration was associated with the partners' uneven engagement with the project since in all case studies one of the two partner teams was more committed than the other. Close analysis of the data highlighted that some of the teams uploaded more posts and made more contributions and comments while at the same time they were waiting for some kind of response by the other group—which at times never came or came too late, resulting in frustration and disappointment. For instance, in the case of the reading club project, students often felt discouraged and deterred from posting online what they had discussed in their reading club meetings. Since their partners were not reading or not commenting on their posts it seemed like they were merely talking to themselves and, thus, lacked motivation to update the TwinSpace and add new content.

In the case of the Sparta project it was the English students who were considered to be more committed compared to their Greek partners. Not only were some of their wiki contributions more extensive and substantial but a couple of students also attempted to initiate an informal discussion on the Pupil's Corner forum, which declined fairly quickly due to limited participation. In the focus-group interviews the English students often complained about lack of reciprocity and mutual effort from their partners that inevitably led to loss of interest and limited engagement from their side. Similarly, when looking at the German project the English students had a greater online wiki presence compared to their partners in Berlin even though both groups failed to use the wiki tool collaboratively. First, they were each allocated an individual wiki page where they posted information about themselves whereas their partners did not create separate wiki entries due to technical problems and limited computer access. Second, when the German team initiated a forum discussion on the topic of films and the UK students posted back responses, the German students did not reply back; so the conversation did not flourish.

Many of the teachers recognized that one of the main obstacles was lack of interest, motivation, and reciprocity from their partners. Although they had initially committed to taking part in the collaborative project and had set off with enthusiasm it was often the case that both teachers and students did not follow through. Lack of partner reciprocity resulted in turn in a lack of audience that would give project activities more meaning and relevance for the students and that would perhaps encourage more online systematic engagement. In this sense, since the projects had no public audience other than the eTwinned teams, authentic tasks and activities greatly depended on partner reciprocity. As this implies, if the students were to use the online publishing tools meaningfully to express their "voice," then addressing an audience who listened and responded was crucial for the successful outcome of the projects. The lack of a sense of community was exacerbated by the tendency of students to only sporadically contribute, leaving only a small minority of regular participants to add new content and take part in discussions on the online platforms.

Language Issues

The nature of partner reciprocity was also associated with language issues. In particular, the difficulties in maintaining proper and quality forms of interaction were highly dependent on the foreign-language skills of the participants. On the one hand, key to some teachers' initial decision to get involved in a collaborative project was their desire to create a connecting link with a partner school and enhance the pupils' foreign-language skills. On the other hand, contributing posts in a foreign language was in some cases a cause for student discontent that resulted in limited participation. In the case of the Sparta project, for example, communication in a foreign language was a barrier for some of the Greek students and prevented them from contributing to the wiki and participating in the online discussions. The issue of the language barrier was also acknowledged by the UK students who, despite their good will to appreciate the Greek effort, expressed some degree of discontent with the poor quality of the written exchanges that did not meet their initial expectations. Similarly, in the cases of the reading club project some of the students described how by using a foreign language for their online interactions part of the meaning-making process was inevitably lost in translation.

As such, the successful outcomes of these projects did not only depend on their motivation and willingness to engage in online activities but also on their level of linguistic skills and knowledge that was necessary for taking part in the collaborative task. In a sense, even in the cases where the students used, on their own accord, other social networking tools such as Facebook, there was a clear difference between the types of literacy required for informal online interaction and those required for other formal types of learning activities such as creating wiki posts.

How Do the Opportunities Created by Digital Technologies "Fit" into Existing School Practices?

The "Goodness of Fit" between Collaborative Programs and the Institutional Structures of the Schools

At first glance, the flexible nature of collaborative programs, and in our case eTwinning, appeared to allow for easy fit with the institutional structure of schools. There were few increased expectations or imposed time frames, no administrative control or compliance with external demands, and no pressure applied to teachers to produce tangible outcomes. Participation in a collaborative program was seen as the organic and spontaneous initiative of the teachers who had become voluntarily involved and had the opportunity to adapt their project to their students' and their own needs. This flexibility was largely reflected in the varied nature and focus of the different project activities. However, despite the lack of any external authoritarian mode, teachers' efforts appeared to be somewhat compromised by other institutional and organizational pressures, with time, curriculum, assessment, and space being reported as some of the major inhibiting influences.

One of the most significant issues raised in the interviews centered on the importance of individual and institutional time. These descriptions ranged from the teachers' difficulty of finding time within the curriculum to dedicate to the project to engaging the students to devote their personal time for after-school meetings or project assignments. In the case of the two UK schools, teachers took up "class time" and implemented the project in the framework of their taught subject; however, both teachers reported how the allocated "class time" was still limited. Meanwhile, in the case of the two Greek schools, the projects were not implemented in a taught subject but required the after-school voluntary participation of students from different classes and achieving this proved to be rather challenging for the teachers. In particular, time was reported to be a major impediment by both teachers, since a large number of the participating students were preparing for the state exams. Sofia (Athens suburban), for instance, acknowledged how if a "library period" was allocated within the curriculum, they could take advantage of that time and use it for the projects' activities. Similarly, Eirini (Athens inner-city) reported that engaging students in such projects that took place after school hours outside the school curriculum was rather challenging and highlighted the differences across educational sectors and the need for an allocated time slot within the curriculum so as to run collaborative projects smoothly.

Time impediments were also associated with the different holiday and exam schedules across schools as well as the time zone differences between countries. Additionally, the different time-slots allocated for collaborative activities within the timetable of the partner schools did not make real-time communication possible. Moreover, curriculum time pressures combined with summative assessment and the general constraints on the teachers' time did not allow them to dedicate as much time on the project or employ more innovative approaches as they had originally anticipated. Furthermore, some additional, unplanned hurdles such as student sit-ins and the swine flu epidemic in the Greek schools resulted in unintended dips and lapses in the cases of the Sparta and the reading club projects.

Within educational contexts another dimension that needs to be taken into consideration in the design of web-based activities is that of space. For example, during the observation visits, it became apparent how having an appropriate space such as a computer lab was important but not critical for the success of the project. In the case of the reading club the library where the project meetings took place was a welcoming space buzzing with students but, with just two computers crammed in the corner of the room, it was far from ideal for hosting a web-based collaborative project. Still, the warm disposition and the enthusiasm of the teacher were a catalyst for student motivation. During the observation visits the students would often work on editing posts on either of the two available computers while chatting with their teachers. Furthermore, the lack of a firewall that allowed students to access social networking sites such as Facebook during their breaks and free periods made the library space more inviting. It is worth noting how the informal–formal boundaries were blurred when a student was showing the teacher pictures of their Danish partners of Facebook. Conversely, as described in detail in the previous chapter, the library of the Athens inner-city school was an inadequate and ill-equipped space that could actually discourage the students from using the computers.

It is also worth considering of course, the case of the more "high-tech" London suburban school. Although the classroom was equipped with computers and the students did not have to relocate to a computer lab or share computers, access to technology did not seem to consist of an additional driver for success. In reality, although the students had individual access to a computer they often preferred to engage with more "analogue" activities such as reading a book, playing a board game in German, or drawing and decorating a Christmas card to send to their partners in Berlin. As such one could argue that having a more "flexible" space, free from the many other institutional pressures of schooling, as well as an inspirational teacher to look up to might provide more motivation for participation than a "high-tech" computer lab.

Besides these issues of "fit" with the temporal and spatial structures of school, another overriding reason for the "marginalization" of the collaborative projects in the minds of the students was lack of assessment. In particular, lack of assessment was seen in all cases as a demotivating factor rather than an opportunity to experiment with more creative and unconventional activities. Since contributing to the collaborative activities did not consist part of formative or summative assessment the teachers often found motivating their students to engage with the project to be particularly challenging especially during exam periods. For instance, when it was exam period at school, contributing to the project was viewed by the students who took part in the Sparta project as irrelevant and time-consuming. The pressure to perform in exams often resulted in viewing participation in collaborative activities as marginal and therefore the projects were often "left behind." All in all, although online environments presented collaborative opportunities, the enduring nature of school organization appeared to influence the outcome of all four projects across schools and countries to a far greater extent than initially anticipated.

The Role of the Overarching eTwinning Organization

The eTwinning organization was seen to serve a range of roles and teachers expressed mixed feelings with regard to how satisfied they were with the assistance and guidance they received from the National and Central Support Services. On the one hand, the eTwinning umbrella can be seen as providing an external catalyst for action—inspiring individual teachers to get involved and enabling them to find like-minded colleagues across Europe in order to set up their collaborative projects. Despite the lack of external funding for face-to-face student exchanges, the fact that eTwinning was formally recognized by national Ministries of Education and local authorities added value and kudos to the project activities both in the eyes of the teachers as well as in the eyes of the school senior managers. As such, the websites of all four schools hosted online information about their eTwinning projects that were often listed under the school's "enrichment activities" umbrella.

Furthermore, the official eTwinning platform provided teachers with a useful partner-finding tool making their search easier and less time consuming. All teachers reported that they used the eTwinning partner-finding forum and considered the process of looking for partners fairly straightforward. In particular, as discussed in chapter 3, Isabel, one of the leading teachers, described eTwinning as the "educators' meat market" equating it with Facebook in terms of individuals seeking partners and forming links. However, more experienced teachers such as Isabel were also more likely to approach eTwinning as a "stepping stone" and migrate to other external tools.

Once the different projects had been initiated and the first hurdles emerged, mixed reactions were reported by the teachers with regard to the quality and level of assistance provided by the National and Central Support services. In particular the teachers who opted to set up their project using TwinSpace rather than other external tools encountered difficulties in terms of registering their students and accessing the platform. As described in the previous empirical chapters, the teachers' requests for technical help to the National Support Services were often unfruitful since the replies they received either arrived too late or did not solve the problem. This resulted in losing valuable time and increased teacher frustration.

Varied feelings were also reported with regard to the nature and quality of the teacher training and other eTwinning-related activities and great disparities appeared to exist between the British and Greek participation. For example, both English lead teachers were invited to national and European eTwinning conferences respectively where they had the opportunity not only to meet other teachers but also to attend a range of workshops and in the case of Lucy be awarded with a quality level. Conversely, the Greek participants were never offered similar opportunities and Eirini considered receiving a quality award label for her previous eTwinning project somehow meaningless since it had not opened any other doors such as receiving funding for face-to-face meetings or participation in eTwinning events.

Last but not least, the school year 2009–2010 signaled the transition from the old and relatively rudimentary TwinSpace to a new, more "web 2.0-orientated" platform that among other features allowed the configuration of wikis and blogs. However, this transition resulted in leaving some teachers struggling to cope with using the more complicated tools on top of overcoming the registration and access problems. Although some training seminars were organized in Athens during the winter months of 2009, Eirini (Athens inner-city) commented on the inconsistent content and mixed level of participants as well as the distance barriers associated with the location of the past training events. Time and space difficulties associated with taking part in these teacher-training events were also highlighted by Lucy (Midlands) who opted for the online "Learning Events" instead—short, intense courses that took place on the eTwinning platform and involved participants across Europe.

What Are the Drivers and Inhibitors for Engaging with Collaborative Projects for Teachers?

Drivers for Participation

A first glance at the data of this study revealed that the teachers' perceptions of web-based school collaboration and digital technologies as well as their understandings of teaching and learning were varied. All teachers were committed to their work and their subject and although their level of experience ranged they were all appreciated by their school's senior management and were considered an asset to their institution. At the same time, their interest to explore and implement a collaborative initiative in their schooling routines was shaped by a range of drivers. In particular, all the teachers responsible for initiating and configuring these projects were on the whole enthusiastic and committed practitioners from a variety of educational backgrounds. Although their teaching experience and ICT skills ranged, they were all equally passionate about the potential of online collaborative practices when they instigated their students to take part in eTwinning.

At the same time all teachers were willing to devote personal time in order to set up and monitor the project. Two of the teachers (Sofia, Athens suburban, and Lucy, Midlands) had been taking part in professional development courses at University while the other two were experienced eTwinners and had set up a range of other eTwinning projects in the past. The two, younger in age, UK teachers were seen by their head teachers as particularly adept in incorporating new technologies in their teaching practices and appeared confident users of digital technologies. Additionally, both these UK teachers had previous teaching experience at schools abroad and they were keen to expand their students' horizons and expose them to a different culture. Similarly, although the two Greek teachers were less familiar with the use of digital technologies and their school's ICT infrastructure was not as advanced as that in the UK schools they were equally active and committed practitioners constantly pursuing opportunities for professional development and looking to provide their students impetus for extracurricular activities. The eTwinning initiative appeared to provide them with an external "catalyst" by offering them the opportunity to experiment with something outside the norm of the school practices and explore the use of other tools and activities. Sofia (Athens suburban), for example, described how her personal inquisitiveness to explore new things was an additional driver for participation in a collaborative program.

As such the personal enthusiasm and commitment of those dynamic teachers triggered and shaped their participation in eTwinning. However, their experience consisted of a "lone journey" rather than a collectively shared experience within their school. Although all head teachers appeared to be supportive and in some cases enthused with the teachers' initiative, their input to the project was minimal. Support took different forms and the most notable examples were funding some of the expenses for the exchange visits in the case of the Greek–Danish twinning project and allowing Isabel (London) to take time off to attend an eTwinning conference. Last, despite presenting their collaborative activities to in-school department meetings, none of the teachers attracted the interest of their colleagues. Conversely, lack of support from her school's ICT team was reported in the case of Marlene and was attributed to lack of time and work overload on their part. As a result, in all four case studies, collaborative activities were to some extent "hero-led" by motivated individuals as opposed to being "group-led" by a team of enthusiastic teachers from each school.

Positive outcomes for teachers were at large associated with their professional and personal development. Not only did they view their participation in a collaborative program such as eTwinning as an opportunity to explore different teaching paths but also they felt it reflected positively on their professional status. Some of the benefits included creating links with colleagues across Europe who shared the same values and visions, developing their ICT skills, and enhancing their confidence with relation to implementing new technologies in their classroom. Although there were no monetary benefits, the teachers felt more valued and their sense of self-worth within their school increased. Less experienced teachers such as Sofia (Athens suburban) described how her ICT skills had improved, while more experienced teachers viewed web-based school collaboration as a prospect to do something more creative that could lead to future professional opportunities. Last, another key aim for teachers was to open up their classroom boundaries and present students with an external audience and, in particular, provide the foreign-language learners with an opportunity to interact with peers within authentic situations.

Technical Inhibitors

The issue of adequate resources did not appear problematic and for the particular projects the ratio of pupils to computers was satisfactory with an average of two pupils per computer in most cases apart from the Athenian reading club project. Still, this did not necessarily result in effective use of digital technologies and throughout the four diverse case studies various technical constraints were identified by both teachers and learners. Depending on the participants' confidence level and breadth of ICT skills and also on the particular tools used for different projects a range of issues recurred. In particular, TwinSpace was used to host three of the projects and the teachers reported difficulties when registering the students on the platform. As a result the teachers lost valuable time registering, de-registering, and re-registering the students in an attempt to overcome the technical difficulties. Still, some students reported that they had been unable to access all sections of TwinSpace during the project. Another significant issue highlighted by Sofia (Athens suburban) was that some students were prone to losing their log-in details or forgetting the URL of the website. As a result, the teacher invested even more time to sort out such procedural practicalities. Other technical issues were associated with TwinSpace opening up in a pop-up window and thus often being blocked because of particular computer settings.

Trivial as all these technical issues may seem in isolation, they often led to teacher frustration and blighted their experience. In particular, when these technical difficulties were combined with other organizational and time pressures they resulted in limited student engagement or even failure to materialize the project. For instance, despite the initial enthusiasm about the potential of using a wiki, a certain degree of technical skills and confidence in using the wiki technology was also vital for the successful configuration of the tool. However, both Eirini (Athens inner-city) and Dimitra (Northern Greece) described how their lack of familiarity with the wiki tool compromised the project outcome. In the case of Dimitra (Northern Greece) this translated to failure to explore the wiki's potential or guide her students effectively; so the wiki was mainly used as an online content publishing tool. Similarly, Eirini (Athens inner-city) described her experience configuring the TwinSpace wiki perplexing and frustrating and the project did not materialize.

In the case of the Sparta and the reading club projects when the teachers appeared successful in overcoming these technical challenges, a large number of students were disheartened with the process as they were used to more straightforward and user-friendly online tools and applications. Additionally, the majority of students did not report finding TwinSpace particularly appealing aesthetically while they also highlighted a range of shortcomings. One significant issue raised in the interviews was the lack of notifications and the difficulty to search for topics and authors both in the old and the new TwinSpace. For instance, it was not possible to link registered users with the messages and comments they had posted. In the reading club project, where the old TwinSpace was used, both teacher and student participants reported having to go through each thread and forum category to check if a reply or comment had been posted while in the new TwinSpace there was a window indicating "recent activity." These technical difficulties and the ways they were resolved are presented in this section because not only did they inhibit the collaborative journey of all the teacher participants but they also mirrored their different outlooks on schooling and highlighted the importance of the teacher role in orchestrating the collaborative project and configuring the different technologies that were employed.

What Are the Drivers and Inhibitors for Engaging with Collaborative Practices for Students?

Across the four case studies different approaches toward web-based collaboration and various types of student engagement were apparent. Interestingly, these attitudes shared similarities and differences across all projects rather than across types of schools or countries. In the case of the Athens inner-city school, there was very little student engagement with the project and no use of TwinSpace since the majority were not even registered on the platform whereas in the other cases students engaged more readily in the projects' activities. The major drivers for participation reported by students in the focus-group interviews were associated with communicating and interacting with students of a foreign school and possibly taking part in an exchange visit. Thus, students often appeared to view participation in a collaborative program as an opportunity for informal interaction with peers rather than a means of collaborative learning. There was also little evidence to suggest that their motivation was technologically driven since only a smaller minority of students reported that the computer-based nature of the activities affected positively their engagement.

The Realities of Student Participation

Student participation was characterized by a split in the levels of engagement with some students resisting more while others were more eager to take part in online activities. Thus, for the purpose of this study, students may be grouped in four broad types depending on their level and depth of engagement with the tools and the activities with most prominent of user categories among the participants being the "leaders," the "explorers," the "users," and the "lurkers." The main characteristics of these different types of team members are discussed below while it should be noted that these categories are not mutually exclusive, for example, "leaders" can also be seen as "explorers." Additionally, since the Athens inner-city project never fully materialized and the students did not contribute to the wiki or TwinSpace they are excluded from this categorization.

Student Leaders

The term "leader" is intended to signify a higher level of student engagement with the projects' activities and appropriation of online technologies. In a sense, student leaders, like their teachers, emerged as engaged and dynamic champions although they consisted of the smallest group in the student sample. Typically these students not only contributed more compared to the other participants but they also appeared more engaged, took initiatives, and attempted to lead their team. In the case of the Sparta project, Megan (16) emerged as the most active of her group. As we saw in more detail in chapter 3, she deleted blog posts and replaced them with wiki entries, encouraged her team to post more, gave them advice on how to use the wiki and acknowledged the authors of the deleted blog posts. She was also the one who responded to the Greek student's message on the forum and befriended her on Facebook. Similarly, other leaders may not have been as active and dynamic as Megan but were distinct from the rest of the group in terms of their commitment and unremitting contribution to the projects' activities. In the case of the reading club project, an engaged core of about five students (predominantly girls) contributed to the forum by posting messages, comments, and pictures. These were the same girls who had also edited their profiles on TwinSpace by adding pictures, descriptions of themselves, and other contact details.

Student Explorers

The student explorers consisted yet again of a small minority of students who demonstrated a more creative and exploratory use of the collaborative tools and contributed in more resourceful ways. These students, although they did not show any leadership skills, were more open toward experimenting with the tools and their learning practices. For example, in the case of the reading club project, this involved embedding YouTube videos in the "Music" forum category as opposed to copying and pasting the link, which was a common practice for other students. In the case of the Sparta project the student explorers could be said to have displayed greater engagement with different tools and experimented to a small extent with the editing properties of the wiki. These were, however, restricted to minor editing of spelling mistakes or rearranging pictures with the exception of one student who disagreed with copying and pasting practices in her team and edited the whole entry. Other examples of a relatively more creative use of the technologies included uploading pictures or videos and formatting the text-based entries or experimenting with adding a caption to a photograph.

Student Users

The largest proportion of the students can be described as "users"—they employed the tools and contributed to the wikis and forums albeit rather unresourcefully. Their engagement was shaped at large by their wider ICT experiences and they did not appear willing to take risks and try things out, neither did they engage in more proactive tasks such as initiating discussions. Instead, they followed the teachers' instructions, asked for guidance when they faced difficulties, and posted entries that predominantly resembled plain-text Word documents—sticking to tried and tested practices they were familiar with. This was particularly notable in the two wiki-based projects, which were not successful in using the tools for collaborative writing. Additionally, in the case of the Sparta project, a large number of "student users" resorted to pasting content directly from the source rather than engaging with the topic and they did not perceive the wiki as supportive of their learning practices but as separate from their main body of work and difficult to access—stating in the interviews that if they could get away with copying and pasting practices for their school assignments they saw no point in trying harder for the unassessed project.

Apart from lack of student motivation and/or interest to put more time and effort in the project activities, there were also some other reasons underpinning the uninventive use of the online tools. For example, there were original entries in the Sparta project albeit rather limited and uncreative. Similarly, in the case of the German wiki no instances of copying and pasting were reported—still the majority of entries resembled a Word document lacking in photographs or any other type of content apart from text. Conversely, the students employed more creative practices in the Word documents including pictures, tables, and experimenting with fonts. This, to a large extent, was the result of lack of training and guidance by the teachers who presented students with the tools but did not explain their full potential such as editing each others' entries, posting pictures, videos, and links, and so on but took for granted that their students were familiar with using them. However, during the focus-group interviews only one student reported having used a wiki before while all the other students were unfamiliar with the wiki-based format.

Student Lurkers

This group consisted of a significant number of students who preferred to make no or very limited use of the online tools and resisted participation in any of the activities. For example, in the case of the reading club project, out of the 106 registered students (Greek and Danes) 21 never accessed the reading club TwinSpace while 22 only logged in once. Similarly, 24 students out of the 64 registered never logged on to TwinSpace in the case of the Sparta project. Out of these 24 the majority ($n = 18$) were from the Greek partner school. Because of the technical difficulties that had been encountered, these numbers cannot be taken at face value since a couple of UK students reported that they used their partners' log-in details as their account did not work.

As such, it appeared that a significant proportion of students were resisting the use of the technologies and displayed indifference while others expressed discomfort or discontent either because they thought they were not adequately skilled to use the tools or they lacked interest in the project whatsoever. There were varied attitudes underpinning user disengagement with the project and the online activities; however, this was at large linked to lack of motivation and interest. The students felt no need to participate since the projects did not constitute part of their formative or summative assessment and it was particularly challenging for the teachers to enhance engagement and stimulate motivation especially if the students were asked to dedicate time for the project outside school. Interestingly, in the student focus-group interviews very few students openly admitted that they had never contributed to the projects—quoting indifference, technical difficulties, forgetting their password, and lack of time and assessment as the main reasons for their disengagement. Additionally, as already described lack of reciprocity by the respective partners affected student motivation and involvement.

Still, apart from the other factors underpinning student disengagement both Lucy (Midlands) and Sofia (Athens suburban) highlighted the importance of the group's size. In retrospect, they both found that having a relatively large group of student participants did not necessarily lead to better and more productive outcomes. For example, in the case of Sofia (Athens suburban), this resulted in more workload in terms of registering them on the platform and also coordinating and guiding them. Even if the students had all volunteered for the reading club, she found it was a mistake taking them all ($n \approx 60$) on board for the eTwinning project and contented that having a core of about 15 more committed students would have been more productive and less stressful for her in terms of arranging the practicalities and monitoring their contribution. Last, both teachers reported that the particular core of more engaged pupils were more motivated and hardworking as well as more independent learners in their general learning practices.

The empirical evidence highlighted a range of problems with regard to the "digital native" narrative, particularly when looking for differences between generations—in our case the teacher and student participants. The notion of a "digital gap" appeared highly problematic, as there was no sharp generational break between teacher and student use of the project tools and platforms. For example, although Isabel (London) and Lucy (Midlands) were the youngest and most adept at configuring and using social software tools of the participants, other teachers such as Sofia (Athens suburban) and Dimitra (Northern Greece) were able to overcome the initial technical difficulties. Moreover, a small but not trivial number of students from the three completed projects reported in the focus-group interviews how they were unfamiliar with using digital technologies in their everyday lives. As such, they lacked the confidence to learn to use the adopted tools by "trial and error" like some of their classmates did and they often resorted to their teachers' technical help.

Another seemingly important issue was the mismatch that existed between teachers' expectations and students' actual collaborative practices and ICT skills. For instance, both Lucy (Midlands) and Isabel (London) overestimated the "digital native" abilities of their students. In a sense the teachers' desire to step back and allow the students to work independently and take responsibility for their work did not translate well in the more institutional classroom environment. Additionally, it seemed that the teachers did not provide adequate guidance and/or ideas to encourage pupils to use the tools more creatively. For instance, during the observations both teachers often asked the students to "log on the wiki and update/work on their section" without offering any other detailed instructions—taking for granted that after the initial introductory session the students would be able to use the wiki efficiently and engage in collaborative practices. As a result of this unfamiliar freedom and flexibility, some of the students in the German project seemed rather lost and looked at what the person sitting next to them was doing or simply pretended they were working on their wiki page but were browsing irrelevant websites. Last, although the majority of students reported in the interviews that using the wiki was quite straightforward and after some "trial and error" they faced little difficulties, still their engagement and contribution were curtailed by constraints such as their unfamiliarity with the editing and collaborative properties of the wiki tool.

Bringing Old Work Practices into "New" Contexts

Despite the initial enthusiasm of the teachers with regard to implementing new technologies such as wiki tools to facilitate communication and collaboration between their geographically dispersed teams all four case studies showed that, although implementing technology into contemporary classrooms was associated with some positive outcomes, it did not result in instantaneous and ground-breaking changes. Bridging the gap between traditional educational practices and the more radical nature of digital technologies, at large, resulted in the integration of the new into the preexisting rather than the other way round. As such, instead of using online technologies to experiment with new forms of collaborative writing and communication, students' actual engagement remained unadventurous and rather conservative. This should not come as a surprise when considering how participation in a web-based collaborative project was novel to the students and involved some degree of risk-taking. With the exception of a few more confident students who appeared more willing to contribute and lead their peers, the majority of participants were more hesitant to experiment with new practices.

In developing a realistic perspective of students' engagement with the collaborative projects, we need to look at how they used ICTs outside the school environment. In brief, the use of digital technologies for the majority of students at large involved frequent engagement with social software tools such as Facebook and MSN at home and sometimes even at school during their breaks and free periods. Other popular types of in- and out-of-school digital technology use included employing Microsoft Office applications and listening and/or downloading music and playing games. In a sense students appeared to appreciate digital technologies as a means of more easily supporting their studies in terms of looking for information (and frequently copying and pasting it) as well as contacting their classmates for school-related enquiries. Thus, although it can be argued that the use of digital technologies was certainly a part of everyday life for students, their specific types of engagement were rather unspectacular. Additionally, it should be noted that in-school use of digital technologies was dominated by the "copying and pasting" of material retrieved from online resources into text documents, PowerPoint presentations, as well as wiki entries and forum posts in the case of the eTwinning projects. When students were questioned about these practices they reported that this was not restricted to the projects' activities but was also common practice for school assignments. Thus, even when using new tools such as wikis for collaborative writing the students adopted a more conservative approach and they implemented their old practices into a new context rather than exploring and building on the potential of the new technologies.

Replicating classroom practices in the context of all the projects was prevalent also with regard to collaborative uses of the online tools and platforms with individual posting of content rather than collaborative writing being the dominant mode of engagement. Additionally, as highlighted in previous sections, all projects revealed an overall lack of idea development and commenting from the side of the authors. Even in the cases where initiating the project was marked by a stage of hype and enthusiasm and students posted more frequent and substantial contributions, soon this was replaced by indifference and a "why bother" attitude. Although students were not fully aware of the collaborative opportunities entailed by wiki tools and did not experiment in that aspect, when presented with the idea of editing entries, the majority did not appear confident or willing to try out such new practices, while others appeared to be more in favor of individual ownership as opposed to collective ownership.

However, it was not just students who brought old practices into "new" contexts but teachers also appeared to approach the technologies rather uncreatively. For instance, in the case of the German project, rather than creating wiki entries on the topics of "films" and "Berlin info" the teachers asked students to create Microsoft Office Word documents, which they then uploaded on the relevant wiki pages so that the students of the partner school could then download them. This was followed by a short discussion of students' favorite films on the forum through 30 different messages addressed to an individual UK student and focused on a particular film. On the one hand the configuration problems the German teacher faced did not allow her students to log in and post their own entries on the wiki; so uploading the Word documents was an easy solution. On the other hand despite the technical difficulties the German teacher's rather mundane as well as unpractical use of the forum indicated her lack of familiarity with online communicative and collaborative practices.

The Tendency to Migrate to Familiar Tools and Online Spaces

Findings from the Sparta and the reading club projects highlight how some of the students took the initiative to use more familiar online tools other than the ones their project was based on. Interestingly, in both cases, the majority of those students came from the groups of "leaders" and "explorers." In this sense it was the most committed and hard-working students who had already experimented with the eTwinning platform that decided that the features and the interface of the TwinSpace tools were "unfit" for their aims and migrated to Facebook and MSN. In the case of the Sparta project, the suggestion to use Facebook occurred on the "official" forum while in the case of the Greek–Danish partnership this was triggered mainly because of the exchange trip and face-to-face meetings.

In the focus-group interviews, students reported that it was not lack of privacy and the feeling that any communication on the eTwinning platform could be monitored by their teachers that instigated them to migrate to other online spaces. It was rather the ease of using tools they were familiar with and which were part of their daily "online routine" and allowed for real-time communication—as opposed to using the forum that did not really appeal to them, was foreign to their everyday practices, and required additional steps to log in and post messages. Furthermore, in the case of the reading club project it was the only means of keeping in touch with their partners since the Danes made minimal use of TwinSpace particularly during the second year. Last, it is also worth noting that migrating to Facebook did not affect those students' engagement with the project but the students who were committed from the start remained so throughout the school year.

The practice of migrating to more familiar online spaces also seems to tie in to the idea of overestimating students as digital natives. As highlighted in more detail in the two case study chapters, student use of digital technologies predominantly evolved around the use of social networking sites for communicating with family or friends. The use of other tools such as wikis for instance was restricted to reading and often directly copying content rather than contributing to existing or creating new entries. Students were not familiar with online collaborative writing practices; so in the absence of guidance or other models to draw on, it seems plausible that they decided to informally import the tools they were most accustomed to, that is, Facebook and MSN.

Conclusion

In conclusion, this chapter has explored the range of issues underpinning the effective implementation of digital technologies for school collaborative projects within the framework of the eTwinning initiative. The study of the motivators, the inhibitors, and any other factors associated with using digital technologies for online school collaboration involved the investigation of a range of issues associated with the social context of educational technology use. Given the increasing impact of implementing digital technologies in educational contexts, it is essential that the other nontechnical factors highlighted in this chapter should be taken into account when determining what underpins a successful collaborative project. The deep understanding of the often complex and rigid school norms derived from comparative case study approaches as embodied in this research study can assist in identifying key drivers and inhibitors and can also inform the study of resemblances and differences between dissimilar countries as well as school sectors and types. As such the next—and final—chapter of this book will go on to contextualize the findings of the present study in relation to the theoretical background as well as in the light of the empirical findings presented in similar studies contained in the literature review.

CHAPTER 6

Conclusions and Suggestions for Improving School Collaboration—Where Now?

Introduction

As the previous chapter highlighted, the path toward implementing digital technologies into successful school collaboration is a complex one. Looking beyond the enthusiasm as well as skepticism that surround the educational potential of social media, a range of issues can be identified that are associated with the use of digital technologies for school collaboration. For instance, it emerged that the particular contexts and conditions within which the different case study projects were enacted largely shaped the use of the technologies and the modes of collaboration. While the availability of a range of digital tools created similar opportunities for the participants, the actual student and teacher engagement with the technologies and their participation in the collaborative projects shared similarities but also differed to some extent.

Against this background, this final chapter aims to round off the book by looking beyond the hype of social media use and outlining the array of influences, interests, and issues that underpin the implementation of digital technology in collaborative educational settings. In particular, it endeavors to compare these understandings to the growing body of empirical work in this area as well as the theoretical underpinnings of educational use of digital technologies described in the opening chapters. Finally, the chapter concludes with a range of suggestions for practitioners, policy makers, and educators in the area of web-based school collaboration.

Linkages and Disconnections with Empirical Findings in the Existing Literature

It is first worth considering the various linkages and disconnections of the present study's findings with the previous literature as discussed in the first two chapters of this book—from the wider picture of digital technology use in education to more specific examples of engagement with particular tools and collaborative practices. As previously highlighted, the notion that digital technologies can transform schooling and, in particular, the assumption that social media bear promises of increased connectivity and collaborative learning within and across the school classrooms has been a popular one within academic discussions (Greenhow et al. 2009; McLoughlin and Lee 2007). In practice, however, the empirical findings of the present study painted a contradictory picture, offering very little evidence that any kind of reinvention and/or transformation of educational processes was taking place in any of the four case studies. Instead, the present study could be said to highlight a range of linkages and disconnections with past studies.

For example, previous research has established that young people are generally high users of the internet and digital technologies (see Dutton et al. 2009; Ofcom 2011) and this was certainly confirmed by the majority of the participants in our study. When looking for particular patterns, students' in-school and out-of-school engagement with digital technologies and the internet mirrored the findings of previous large-scale studies that identified chatting and communicating, listening to music and game playing, as well as looking for information and doing homework as popular activities of younger children (Selwyn et al. 2010) and adolescents (Eynon and Malmberg 2011; Luckin et al. 2008).

Still, despite the differences reported with regard to the various types and levels of online engagement, the majority of users were involved in passive consumption rather than active production of content. Although digital technologies were present in both the in-school and out-of-school lives of the students and while the majority were confident information and communication technology (ICT) users, there was little evidence to suggest that they were involved in intense learning and "geeking out" activities (Ito and Antin 2010) or that they conformed to the profile of the "digital natives" or "iKids" (Prensky 2008). Instead, as described in the previous chapter, the students who took part in this study can be more accurately grouped in four broad types of users depending on their level and depth of engagement with the tools and the activities: that is, "leaders," "explorers," "users," and "lurkers." These distinctions bear similarities with the profiles of internet users described in recent studies of adult ICT users, that is, the "peripherals," the "normatives," the "all-rounders," and the "active participators" from a survey of over a 1,000 young people in the United Kingdom (Eynon and Malmberg 2011) or the categorization of over 2,000 Australian college students as "power" users, "ordinary" users, "irregular" users, and "basic" users (Kennedy et al. 2010).

With regard to the adoption of specific tools and applications, various digital technologies were employed to host the four different case-study projects and facilitate online communication and collaboration. As already described, there were instances of what could be termed content creation and interaction between the students across the different schools in three out of four case studies. However, these "creative" activities consisted of students posting new content and to a lesser extent commenting on the work of others. Additionally, there were few instances of informal online interaction between a minority of students through "personal" spaces (rather than official school spaces) such as Facebook and MSN.

All these different types of engagement and interaction could be said to have enabled students to develop some understanding and cultural awareness with regard to their distanced partners supporting the claims of others (Barbosa et al. 2004; Coutinho and Rocha 2007; Valentine and Holloway 2001). Yet, although these examples of engagement with the digital technologies met to some extent the overarching aims of the collaborative projects, they did not appear to lead to any further instances of online collaboration between the students. Alluding to Roschelle and Teasley's (1995, p. 70) definition of collaboration as opposed to cooperation, it can be argued that the accounts and observations of student engagement with the projects and the tools in all cases suggested that cooperative practices prevailed at the expense of genuine collaboration. In this sense, the experience of collaborating for students took the form of "loosely knit" networks of "peers working independently rather than supporting a shared construction" (Crook 2012, p. 71).

Also, striking was students' apparent unfamiliarity with collaborative practices within their school contexts—not only in online environments but also in terms of working collaboratively face-to-face with their native classmates. Perhaps as a result of this unnaturalness of collaborative practice it appeared that the teachers' decisions to allow for more flexibility and freedom was often interpreted by students as indicating a lack of guidance and resulting in disorientation and limited student participation. These teacher and student attitudes were in accordance with Grant's (2009, p. 114) findings who reasoned that collaborative practices "did not transcend the socially and historically determined practices of the classroom." Instead, it is suggested that "rather than focusing on the design of technologies, or on removing barriers to achieving the perceived potential of technology, the total ecology of the classroom needs to be considered" (ibid., p. 115). These findings would seem to chime with those of other studies that have highlighted the key supporting role of teachers in modeling and facilitating any eventual collaborative practices and students' interaction (Loveless 2007; Lund and Smørdal 2006). Additionally, apart from the importance of the role of the teacher as a facilitator, O'Dowd (2007b, p. 21) has argued that "not only must online activity make sense in the particular learning context, but the communication tools must also be seen as appropriate by the learners for the particular task at hand."

From a technical perspective the majority of students in the present study did not appear to face any major difficulties when it came to familiarizing themselves with the use of social media tools such as blogs and wikis—echoing the findings of other studies that suggested that a large proportion of young people who "are more likely to come from media-rich homes, are more confident about their skills" (Helsper and Eynon 2010, p. 515). However, observation and interview data demonstrated that many students lacked the skills and "know-how" in terms of using these technologies for collaborative writing and were not able to take advantage of their more advanced and sophisticated features such as editing content, linking, and commenting. In reality, many students' engagement with this type of social media tools appeared to be unadventurous (if not conservative) and often replicated their typical classroom practices of working individually and uploading new or adding to existing content.

As Lin and Kelsey (2009) described from their own research, students who used the wiki for collaborative writing and learning were the exception rather than the norm among participants. This again suggests that instructors need to provide "highly supportive learning experiences" in order to train students how to use wikis from technical point of view and also to teach them how to work collaboratively both in the classroom and online. Additionally, the findings of the present study highlighted the importance of time and group size—echoing the findings of Naismith et al. (2011, p. 13) who argued that "time is needed to become familiar with technology and with working collaboratively—with more time and smaller groups, students may have become more confident in working collaboratively and editing each other's work." Moreover, as other similar studies have suggested, when working with less familiar tools such as wikis, for example, it is necessary to train teachers and students so that they can make full use of the various image, sound, and editing options (Ducate et al. 2011; Wheeler et al. 2008).

This issue of social media being used in a rather limited manner was in line with the findings of Lin and Kelsey (2009) and Engstrom and Jewett

(2005). Similar to what these researchers described, there was limited student engagement with the wiki technology, mainly restricted to adding content and creating new entries to the expense of editing and improving the contributions of others or commenting. In particular, student engagement with the tools was in accordance with the findings of Grant's (2009, p. 111) study of wiki use in secondary classrooms, which reported that "editing others' work did not align with the accepted shared practices of the class." Additionally, not all students welcomed the idea of their work being edited by others (Lund 2008) while others complained of uneven contribution to the collaborative activities of the project—suggesting that "social loafing is sometimes observed where the contribution rate for some students is disproportionate to others" (Wheeler et al. 2008, p. 990). Moreover, the findings from the present study were similar to studies on wiki use that reported high levels of overall participation but little evidence of collaboration—with, at best, a preference for "cosmetic" rather than substantial edits prevailing (Judd et al. 2010). Additionally, the students in the eTwinning cases could not be said to have immediately embraced "any notion of collective ownership or epistemology but continued a practice where the institutionally cultivated individual ownership persisted" (Lund and Smørdal 2006, p. 41).

There was also evidence from the study data that "web 1.0" practices were being imported in the "web 2.0 environment" such as uploading documents or copying and pasting in bulk from online resources. Rather than engaging in collaborative writing, the students (and teachers) appropriated the wiki tools into online repositories for "one-way dissemination" (Crook et al. 2008b, p. 129). Last, similar to Cloke's findings (2010, p. 377), the majority of introductory contributions by students on all projects used only "traditional text" and there was minimal use of hyperlinks, images, or videos.

While all the leading teachers in the four schools appeared enthused by the potential of ICT implementation to facilitate their collaborative activities, their level of confidence and commitment to using digital technologies varied across cases. For instance, some teachers appeared less confident and more cautious with using the different technologies and developed a more limited working competence with the various tools. In this sense, the present study echoed the findings of a survey of English schools that suggested that although access to and availability of technology has improved, teachers' confidence both in secondary and primary education has decreased compared the last couple of years (BESA 2009). In this sense, teachers' enthusiasm to embrace the use of new technologies can be seen to mirror what Perrotta (2011, p. 3) described as responding to the implicit pressures within contemporary schooling to "look innovative" while "struggl[ing] to comprehend the instructional and pedagogical purposes of technology use in their classrooms." Similarly, Merchant argued that teachers "have been encouraged, persuaded and trained to incorporate new technology, but this has often resulted in a bolt-on to standard classroom practice" and, as such, "there is a pressing need to develop models of classroom practice that illustrate the communicative potential of new technology" (2005, p. 59).

Thus, while conditions may have improved in terms of technological infrastructure over the past decade, a "cultural mismatch" appears to persist between the more radical potentials of digital technologies and the tendency for students and teachers to employ "familiar strategies for designing and completing assignments when collaboration proved challenging" (Forte and Bruckman 2007, p. 39). In particular, schools' imposed time frames combined with dominant assessment regimes and the pressure applied to teachers to produce tangible outcomes with regard to formal examinations was reflected in the limited time and effort that teachers and students were willing to (and often able to) devote to the project. As such, despite the flexible nature of the collaborative initiative, the end result was compromised by more dominant institutional and organizational pressures within the formal school systems that the projects materialized. Even the most enthusiastic and motivated of the teachers soon realized that they had to "go with the flow" of the enduring nature of school organization and be more realistic about what they could achieve within the limited time they had at hand.

Overall, the findings highlighted in this study suggest that digital technologies in and of themselves entail no transformative powers—instead it would seem that practical implementation can be affected by a range of socially shaped realities. As Crook (2012) argues, we should not think about the notion of web-based collaboration in a totalizing way. Any web-based collaborations are contextualized by settings such as the school and are therefore compromised by the nature of the offline settings. As such, "technology should not be understood to operate on a causal model; it does not have straightforward 'impact' in some simple, mechanical way on the practices that it encounters" (Oliver 2011, p. 381).

Linkages and Disconnections with Prevailing Commentary on Educational Technologies

Having commenced this book by contrasting the optimistic and pessimistic scenarios surrounding educational technologies there is a pressing need to now consolidate the two and develop a more realistic and socially grounded approach. As described in chapter 2, for many educationalists digital technologies are seen as containing an inherent power to reconfigure education and modernize schools. This enthusiasm is also echoed in the school collaboration literature where technology use has been central to recent forms of school "twinning" with a view to supporting greater "engagement and community building" (McLoughlin and Lee 2008, p. 641) and facilitating online interaction and breaking down geographical barriers (Forte and Bruckman 2009). A sense of "boosterism" also prevailed in the descriptions of the "digital natives" or "iKids" (Prensky 2008) as well as in the web 2.0 educational scenarios (see Green et al. 2008; Richardson 2009). At the other extreme, doomster scenarios continue to evolve around fears about the possible psychological, cognitive, or social harm that new technologies can cause to students (Greenfield in Wintour, 2009)—resulting, for instance, in the creation of the so-called dumbest generation (Bauerlein 2008).

Yet, throughout the case studies presented in this book it would seem that neither the optimistic nor the pessimist scenarios were substantiated by empirical findings. This book's portrayal of what actually took place within school settings suggests that digital technology use is more often a case of "business as usual." That this finding has not been evident in much of the initial research conducted on educational use of digital technologies is perhaps not surprising. A large number of initial large-scale surveys focused mainly on questions of access and infrastructure while smaller-scale research studies often addressed issues of a more technical nature. Therefore, since the current discussions surrounding digital technologies do not provide a sufficient or realistic framework for their implementation in education, and school collaboration in particular, there is value in summarizing the actual (rather than imagined) place and role of school collaboration in the twenty-first century.

To begin with, very little of the optimistic rhetoric in the literature resonates with this study's empirical findings of educational ICT engagement. Despite the initial enthusiasm in the current academic literature with regard to the teaching and learning potential of web 2.0 tools (Davies and Merchant 2009), in practice, no significant altering of educational processes seems to have taken place. Comparative findings across the four case studies demonstrated that although the number of computing devices per student in school has increased and no issues relating to lack of physical access were reported, the scenarios of "e-schooling" have so far not come true. Additionally, the perceived "always on" pattern of internet use (Ito and Antin 2010; Redecker 2009) was not apparent in the findings of this research study.

As such, although digital technologies may well carry promises for greater interaction and user-generated content creation among communities of users as opposed to passive consumption and broadcast forms of exchange, it would be an overstatement to argue that the so-called era of "education 2.0" (Rosen and Nelson 2008) has arrived. In particular, analysis of the data has highlighted a likely gulf between the rhetoric of social media use and the reality of actual in-school engagement with the technologies, illustrating that educators should be cautious about relying on these tools as solutions for educational transformation. Indeed, it can be argued that the idea that web 2.0 will take the notion of participation and collaboration to a totally new level (O'Reilly 2005) has not yet come true since the technologies continued to be used as publishing tools in the schools of this study.

In this sense, the attempts to integrate digital technologies in formal educational settings, and therefore, "to fit the new into the pre-existing" (Bigum and Rowan 2008, p. 247), seem to have repeated a pattern of compromise that has existed in schools for some decades now. It could be argued that the more radical nature of social media did not translate well into contemporary classroom practices, resulting in procedural and rather uncreative engagement with the digital technologies. This is not to say that this lack of success to translate web 2.0 potential into web 1.0 classrooms was the result of teacher cautiousness or resistance to adopting more innovative practices as other studies have highlighted (Crook and Harrison 2008). On the contrary, the teachers in this study appeared quite motivated to experiment with the new technologies since the particular choice of tools was not externally imposed but consisted of a personal decision. Still, it often seemed that a range of "old habits" prevailed in the case of both teachers and students, and often resulted in retaining a "one-to-many model of broadcast pedagogy" (Bigum and Rowan 2008, p. 250). This has to some extent also been associated with the enduring school contexts that are often too rigid to bypass. As Luckin et al. (2009) noted:

> The current contexts and cultures of schools often offer teachers limited scope to incorporate them [social media], with other requirements taking precedence, such as e-safety, privacy, hierarchical organisation and infrastructure, set bodies of knowledge, assessment, and a long-standing pedagogical tradition that favours the individual over the group, the text over other modalities, and the enclosed environment over the open.

In other words, it is clear that there was a gap between the current opportunities generated by digital technologies and their actual or possible implementation in an everyday classroom. It seems that "this structure of experience for Web 2.0 collaborations does not fit comfortably the designs for such practices in the context of school" (Crook 2012, p. 71). In particular, the collaborative qualities of the wikis in case studies 1 and 2 did not seem to lead to exemplary educational practices or suggest the creation of successful collaborative learning environments. In the three projects that materialized, students were found to import traditional school patterns of individual content construction and there was little or no differentiation between the use of web 1.0 and web 2.0 tools. For instance, these findings contradict the enthusiasm within academic literature regarding the interactive and flexible nature of wikis. In our cases wikis did not "lend themselves to collaborative activities" (Wang and Beasley 2008, p. 80). Neither did they consist of "an ideal framework for composing different time and place learning environments" (Larusson and Alterman 2009, p. 372) for students to "develop social ties" (Elgort et al. 2008; Wheeler et al. 2008, p. 990).

In fact, student and teacher use of the wiki tools could be said to have closely echoed Crook's (2012, p. 71) conclusion that "the medium is not seen in terms of a site for the negotiation of knowledge—more as a depository." Conversely, students' decision to host informal discussions around other tools such as MSN and Facebook perhaps reflects "the communication structure afforded by social networking sites where the sense of collaborating is captured by a more conversational flow" (ibid.). As such it could be concluded that tools such as wikis may well bear promises of greater conviviality and community building but in order for these promises to materialize there is a need to give more thought on how their use is shaped by students' familiarity with the communicative rather than collaborative opportunities of digital technologies as well as the current models of teaching and learning. Moreover, tensions resulting from lack of reciprocity from partner schools and students clearly influenced student engagement and the development of the projects. For instance, with regard to partner reciprocity the findings of the present study were in line with the findings of a higher education collaborative project that reported:

> As soon as students wrote in the wiki, they wanted to see reactions and feedback to their contributions and this did not always occur. It was demotivating to wait for days or even weeks for an indication that they had an audience beyond the instructor. (Cloke 2010, p. 382)

These tensions, also, chime with Rheingold's (2008, p. 99) observation of the importance of receiving feedback from an audience and how it is difficult to talk about a student voice "if nobody seems to be listening." Ducate et al. (p. 2011) have also highlighted how providing students with an audience other than their classmates can increase student motivation as well as accuracy when engaging with a particular task. Besides it has been argued that

> True collaboration is not a routine process, involves a shared need or motivation, and requires the meaningful participation of all those involved.

> The complementary skills of the participants are melded so that what results from the process of shared creation is more than what any of the individuals working alone could do. (Collis and Heeren 1993, p. 37)

As a result it can be concluded that implementing digital technologies within formal educational contexts, albeit within the framework of a rather flexible collaborative project, proved a rather compromised process. Despite the perceived educational opportunities of digital technologies and their relevance with theories of knowledge-building networks and communities of practice, there was little evidence from the present study to suggest that their use led to the creation of online communities of students across twinned schools or that the students formed online networks and effortlessly adapted to collaborative practices. As previously discussed, while there were distinct cases of students who displayed greater levels of engagement, these remained the exception rather than the rule. On the contrary, many students can be seen as proficient practitioners of the "grammar of schooling" (Tyack and Tobin 1994)—often unwilling to alter their classroom practice especially where adequate teacher guidance was lacking. As other commentators have pointed out, the role of the teacher in a web-based environment should not be restricted to providing students the tools and allowing them to take their own initiatives but "learners have to learn how to participate and collaborate, and teachers need to play a role in facilitating this process" (Grant 2009, p. 113).

Rethinking the Social Context of Web-Based School Collaboration

All of those issues and findings presented in the previous sections contribute to a growing realization that online school collaboration is socially shaped rather than technologically driven. Despite some assumptions to the contrary, it would seem that one size does not fit all and that digital tools do not provide a ready panacea for the successful implementation of collaborative projects. Context (or rather contexts) are a key factor in understanding the implementation of technologies in education and, therefore, online school collaboration is perhaps best understood when approached "from a social point of view rather than from a technicist one" (Haythornthwaite and Andrews 2011, p. 225). As other commentators have also contended (see Miller 2011; Selwyn 2011a), the findings of this study appear to confirm that technologically deterministic approaches fail to take into consideration the social conditions that underpin the educational use of technologies. Overall, it has been argued that:

Any online activity does not exist in a vacuum, but rather belongs in a particular sociocultural context and its success depends on a complex array of external factors including learners' needs, expectations and life-styles, institutional requirements and common online practices in a particular society. (O'Dowd 2007b, p. 21)

On the basis of this study's findings, it could be argued that school collaboration is greatly dependent upon "systemic" and "pedagogic" factors rather than issues of "technology" per se (Crook and Harrison 2008). On the one hand, these systemic reasons are associated with technical impediments such as unfamiliarity with the tools as well as registration and access problems. In this sense, technical issues did not relate to physical access to digital technologies and connectivity even in the cases of the less advantaged Greek schools. These findings bear similarities with other research studies that have described similar "inhibitors," issues, and tensions surrounding ICT implementation in the classroom (see Meadows 1992; Tella 1991; Valentine and Holloway 2001). On the other hand, a bigger challenge seems to be how to transform rigid pedagogic practices and succeed in incorporating the potential of new tools to well-established classroom patterns. These concerns tie in with the findings of Luckin et al. (2009) and the discussions about how the use of educational technologies during the past decade has not been successful with bringing about any substantial changes or a striking transformation of education. As Bigum and Rowan (2008, p. 247) reasoned:

The deployment of increasingly powerful computing and communication technologies has had a profound impact on the way the world now works. Curiously, though, institutions of formal education in the main appear to have been least altered... The logic is to fit the new into the pre-existing, to integrate... An integration mindset privileges existing ways of doing things. It reflects a view of linear, manageable change and, to date, has allowed teacher education and schools to keep up technical appearances.

The primary disconnect between the collaborative nature of the projects/tools and the practical realities that prevailed in all four case studies can be seen to have been forged by a range of socially shaped realities of schooling that are better understood in terms of Kozma's framework presented in chapter 2. In particular, the range of actors and factors that shaped the use of digital technologies and the outcome of the four collaborative projects ranged from the motivations and skills of individuals at the "micro"-level to the wider pressures of time, fit with curriculum, and assessment regimes at the "meso"-level as well as the overarching role of the eTwinning organization at the "macro"-level of analysis. Additionally, although at first glance these collaborations emerged as the product of individual enthusiastic teachers, a more substantial analysis revealed that they were also shaped by a range of internal and external imperatives (Selwyn 2011b) such as the need of both teachers and schools to "keep up" with the fast-changing field of educational technologies and embrace new and ever-evolving pedagogic forms.

Still, this research study showed that, despite the initial ambitions and expectations of the participants, a range of pragmatic problems shaped the final outcome of these efforts and resulted yet again in another cycle of "hype, hope and disappointment," which has characterized the implementation of education technology since the 1980s (Cuban 2001). Indeed, it can be argued that the current gulf between the rhetoric and the realities of ICT classroom implementation highlights how the assumptions about the potential of digital technologies should not be viewed outside the wider context of formal educational settings. The wider picture of using digital technologies for school collaboration presented in this study points toward the obvious disparities between the collaborative opportunities offered by the tools and the realities of how they were actually used in the classroom. In the light of all the above arguments, it is crucial to recognize the often-constraining nature of these different actors and factors that shape the implementation of digital technologies for school collaboration at different levels of analysis.

For instance, the issue of time as an inhibitor has recurred across the four case studies in a range of forms and has largely shaped the use of and engagement with digital technologies—echoing Lortie's (2002, p. xii) line of reasoning that "time is the most scare resource in schools." In particular, from an individual level, perspective lack of time was reported by both teachers and students as a major inhibitor resulting in ongoing day-to-day negotiations of how to fit the project activities in their busy everyday schedules. Lack of time was also associated with the rigid organization of the timetable within an ordinary school day. As Collins (1996, p. 61) reasoned:

> The structure and conception of school that evolved in the last century is quite incompatible with effective use of new technologies. The view of teaching as transmission of information from teachers to their students has little place for students using new technologies to accomplish meaningful tasks. The forty-five-minute period makes it difficult to accomplish anything substantial using technology.

In this sense, from an institutional perspective, these issues of time were related to other factors such as assessment regimes and curriculum pressures while the appropriation of digital technologies in schools also depended on "schools' reliance on rigid timetables and scheduling" (Selwyn 2011a, p. 28). Moreover, at the macro-level of analysis although the teachers were given the opportunity to take part in face-to-face or virtual training seminars organized by the Central or National eTwinning services, this was only possible during after-school hours at the expense of their personal free time. As Banaji et al. reasoned (2010, p. 6) from a recent study on Creativity and Innovation in Education in EU Member States "it seems that [technology-based] creativity and innovation are stifled by an overloaded curriculum, by lack of time for flow in the teaching and learning schedule, by other systemic barriers such as summative assessment and league tables"—highlighting how "all these practices need time and space out of scheduled time-tabling to engage in more creative and innovative activities."

Suggestions for Improving Web-Based School Collaboration—Where Now?

Rather than embracing an idealistic approach that focuses on forward-looking perspectives of what *could* happen once digital technologies are adopted to facilitate collaborative projects, it has emerged from this book that the academic study of web-based school collaboration certainly benefits from adopting a more realistic approach. Notwithstanding the importance of the opportunities afforded by the various tools to link partners across countries, the data suggested that it is the pedagogical practices and the social contexts surrounding the technology use that can "make" or "break" collaboration. Digital technologies should no longer be seen as a driver of change within themselves since it is clear that they have not had the anticipated impact on facilitating and enhancing collaborative practices. Instead, there needs to be a shift from focusing solely on hardware and technologies to also thinking of the contexts and pedagogic relationships surrounding their implementation. As Buckingham (2007, p. 173) argues:

> The value of digital technology . . . depends to a large extent on the *pedagogic* relationships that are established around it—for example, on how students are given access to the skills and competencies they need, how far they can control the process, and how far they can enter into a dialogue with their peers and teachers. It also depends, more broadly, on the *social* contexts that surround it—on the motivations of the students who use it, on the ways in which cultural production relates to other aspects of their lives, on the audience for their productions and so on.

With these thoughts in mind, I would like to make some more specific suggestions for the future that could address and perhaps resolve some of the crucial issues associated with web-based school collaboration. These suggestions are not rigid and their adoption and implementation will—and should—inevitably vary from country to country and school to school. They are directed mainly toward improving the collaborative experiences for participating teachers and students by listening and responding to their needs. In brief, I would like to make the case for encouraging the loosening of rigid school structures and classroom practices, developing collaborative literacy, and reconfiguring the students' and teachers' role. The next sections, thus, round off the book by using the findings of this research study to suggest proposals for change that could see schools as more thriving, collaborative spaces.

Reconfiguring School Structures

A recent study on the use of ICTs across schools in Europe showed that digital technologies were used more frequently by students and teachers when they were based in "digitally supportive schools," the percentage of which reached a mere 25–30 across the EU schools covered in the survey (Wastiau et al. 2013, p. 18). The notion of the "digitally supportive school" was not defined solely in terms of computer infrastructure but also referred to existing policies about the integration of digital technologies in teaching and learning; the use of a range of incentives such as fewer teaching hours, competitions and prizes, and others, to reward teachers using ICTs; and the implementation of support measures such as professional development and the provision of ICT coordinators.

In order to create more digitally supportive schools, we need to adjust and loosen the rigid structures of formal school settings and make more time and space for creative and collaborative practices within the busy everyday realities of a typical school day. Since a lot of the issues relating to unsatisfactory implementation of digital technologies for school collaboration are associated with the lack of "goodness of fit" between the aims of the projects and the school structures, it is necessary to make changes toward "loosening up" the rigid nature of schooling as well as encouraging a "loose use" of ICTs (Selwyn et al. 2010).

As we saw in detail in the previous chapter, one of the most prominent organizational constraints for most—if not all—of the projects was related to issues of time. In particular, time emerged as one of the most significant barriers, along with curriculum pressures, assessment regimes, and an overall nonconductive school environment. Largely, teachers had to work around the varying pressures of the school calendar year and the curriculum in order to find mutually convenient times in the school day for students to meet as a team and also "meet" online with their partners abroad. In hindsight, teachers had underestimated the amount of time needed for organizing the project and often had to resort to working from home in their personal time.

It is not surprising, thus, that the "loosening up" of the school structures should at large be directed toward making more time available for participation in collaborative projects. This would involve providing teachers with additional time outside of the daily demands and routines of teaching in order to familiarize themselves with the collaborative tools, find appropriate project partners, register the students on the platform, and so on. Furthermore, efforts could be directed toward embedding collaborative initiatives more effectively into the school curriculum by making it more flexible, in order to provide more creative opportunities for technology use. As Potter (2010, n.p.) observes:

> We need to connect with the lives of learners in a curriculum based around the "what" and the "how" of the media that we make, share, consume, interpret and exhibit in lived culture…What we need is a curriculum that understands the agency of children and young people as a factor in their successful learning.

Adjusting the curriculum to create more time to engage with collaborative practices will allow teachers and students flexibility to experiment and familiarize themselves with more informal, interactive, and collaborative types of in-school technology use—leading perhaps to fewer practices of importing of "web 1.0" habits in "web 2.0" online environments. More time could in turn create more frequent and sustained opportunities to engage in communicative and collaborative interactions so that the participants can develop trust, experience a sense of belonging, familiarize themselves more with their partners, and perhaps even build a more sustainable online community of peers outside their school boundaries.

Allowing for more time and making the curriculum more flexible, however, requires deeper, long-term structural changes at both meso- and macro-levels and can only be initiated by national ministries and implemented though national policies. Consideration should be given to creating more flexible conditions for participation in web-based collaborative projects and bridging the gap between the rhetoric of collaborative initiatives and the realities of the educational systems within which they need to be situated and materialized. There is a pressing need to develop a better understanding of the range of issues and tensions that surround the institutional implementation of online school collaboration in order to reconfigure and adjust school structures and relationships accordingly. Overall, unless some altering of the school system occurs, such barriers to collaboration will undoubtedly persist whatever initiatives and collaborative platforms are developed in the future.

A final point for consideration is that technology use inside school remains at large controlled and regulated by their teachers and the school authorities. This clashes with the more interactive and open nature of collaborative initiatives, which might benefit from a more flexible approach to technology use. Notwithstanding the concerns often raised about e-safety and allowing student-to-student communication, unmediated by the teachers, this can constrain pupil autonomy and sap their motivation and interest in taking part in collaborative projects. Therefore, we also need to consider some kind of "loosening up" of school rules and regulations regarding ICT use and access in order to allow for more flexibility regarding student interactions. As Selwyn et al. (2010, p. 160) recommended, effort should be made to develop "cultures of trust" between students and schools regarding digital technology use and "pupils and teachers should be allowed to explore the leeway that exists for school rules to be relaxed or even ignored at certain times or in certain situations." By developing "cultures of trust" between teachers and students, we can also allow for more direct, pupil-to-pupil interaction that, due to organizational and time constraints in arranging synchronous online meetings, can take place outside the school space during the students' free time.

Reconfiguring Classroom Practices

This study highlighted that even in the most high-tech classrooms the tools were not sufficient to lead an online transformation or meet the unrealistic expectations of what a collaborative project should achieve if the relevant pedagogies were absent. As Burns and Bodrogini (2011, p. 188) noted "tools themselves do not make a community. Instructional design is critical in maximizing the creative and communicative potential of web 2.0 applications." It is important to realize that a technology-centered approach to education is never going to be successful. When technology makes a difference in any field, it is more to do with the input of committed and competent individuals and organizations rather then transformational power of the tool itself. Technology tends to amplify the existing dynamic of things, rather than change things. For instance, it is clear from this study that taking part in a collaborative project will not intuitively enhance student communication and collaboration online or in the classroom. The same way that opening a Facebook account will not make you more connected unless you start building on some kind of existing social network. As Ito (2012, n.p.) reasons:

> The power of digital networks is in the ability to connect learners and teachers across space and institutional boundaries, to build linkages between school, home and community, and to make information and learning resources highly accessible and personalized. Our challenge is in guiding more young people to take advantage of these opportunities.

In this sense, students lie in the core of all collaborative projects and their engagement with the activities is largely dependent on their everyday educational and technological experiences and the guidance they receive from their teachers in the classroom. As Buckingham (2007, p. 179) reasoned, "the school could and should be playing a much more positive role in providing both critical perspectives on technology and creative opportunities to use it." In reality, the emphasis on assessment regimes and test scores as a way of measuring both school and individual teacher performance has eliminated real collaboration and creativity in the classroom. Of course, in the absence of examples of good practice and previous collaborative experiences within the context of the classroom, it is not surprising that collaboration is often unsuccessful and that the online activity of the students predominantly mirrors established classroom practices. Instead, there is a need to create more meaningful collaborative learning experiences for students on a more regular basis in order to create more active and enganged learners. If students are used to a chalk and talk, top-down approach in their daily classroom routines how can one expect them to engage successfully in collaborative practices online?

It practice, young people's visions of collaboration are at large based on their existing educational experiences, and using technologies or working collaboratively online at large does not form a part of their classroom routine. It also seems that students use social media outside the classroom largely to communicate with their existing networks of family and friends. As such, more attention needs to be devoted toward looking at how students can broaden their repertoire of collaborative practices and gradually adapt to the idea of building links and communicating with another classroom abroad. For instance, in terms of addressing the barrier of "talking to random strangers" online and encouraging the shyer students to overcome their nervousness, it is worth taking some time to consider how to familiarize students with their partners by engaging them in various types of "ice-braking" activities beforehand.

Furthermore, given the clear disparity between what students actually use digital technologies for and what they are expected to use them for in the framework of the collaborative project, it would seem sensible that efforts should be made to bridge the gap between the two. This does not mean giving students the freedom to use computers in the schools in the same ways as they use them at home but it is suggested that, to begin with, classroom use of ICTs should fit better with the needs and experiences of the pupils. At the same time teachers should introduce, encourage, and guide students toward more creative and collaborative uses of digital technologies above and beyond passive consumption of online content and copying and pasting practices. Participation in flexible and open collaborative projects should offer pupils opportunities for interdisciplinary learning, exploration and play, resourcefulness and reflection, and allow them to take risks and make mistakes in a nonthreatening environment.

In this sense, we should remain wary of simplistic assumptions and loud claims with regard to how net-savvy students actually are and how technology-saturated their everyday activities are. For computers to be used effectively in the classroom a mere emphasis on technical skills is not sufficient. Instead, learners also need to develop a critical understanding of computing in its social context and be allowed to select their own activities as opposed to a more constrained teacher-directed use. At the same time, clearer, confident, and more structured guidance from the teachers might enhance student engagement and lead to more creative practices. There is a need to familiarize students with tools that they are unaccustomed to and at the same time forge collaborative pedagogies during face-to-face interactions. As Dooly et al. (2008, p. 82) argued, "training the students is *more than just getting them used to the technical aspects*; it is also getting them to *reflect on their roles and responsibilities* in the interaction-taking place in the ICT format." Once students become familiar both with the tools and the collaborative practices, the transition to the online environment could be smoother. In order, however, to promote such a collaborative-centered design in the classroom adequate teacher training and support is required that will embrace not just the technical issues of using the technologies but also the pedagogies associated with collaborative environments:

> There is a strong need for pedagogic training which empowers teachers with the required ICT skills to help their students become digitally competent on the one hand, and for guiding students towards more exploratory and creative interaction with ICT tools on the other hand. (Cachia et al. 2010, p. 7)

A further suggestion is related to the use of digital technologies for informal learning. What can informal uses of technology teach us? As Ito et al. (2013)

argue, informal learning is at large interest-driven since a person usually pursues a personal interest or passion. Still, although young people, in principle, can follow their interests online in any way they wish the majority "take the fairly basic steps (such as checking Wikipedia for schoolwork, watching clips on YouTube, or playing single-person games) [while] fewer undertake the more complex, social, or creative activities that techno-optimists have hoped for them" climbing a fairly predictable "ladder of opportunities" (ibid., p. 25). Thus, the majority of students need more support, guidance, and mentoring in the classroom in order to use technologies in more meaningful, creative, and collaborative ways.

Developing Collaborative Literacy

Arguments in favor of the need to promote critical digital literacy at schools feature frequently in the work of media educators and educational technologists. The definition of media or digital literacy includes the ability to access online information, understand, analyze, and evaluate content as well as the ability to process this information in order to create your own content (Buckingham 2007). Although the notion of digital literacy appears to be threefold most academic discussions tend to place the emphasis solely on accessing information. Notwithstanding the importance of developing research skills, schools should be places that also develop students' "collaborative literacy" skills.

As we have seen, the idea that the implementation of technologies in collaborative projects will somehow transform online practices is rather overstated and born out of technological determinism. A perceived shift toward more creative and collaborative school partnerships is possible but is greatly dependent upon the participants' experiences and "collaborative literacy" skills. As Gee (2012, p. 38) contends, "in our technologically driven society, literacy is changing dramatically. What appears to be crucial for success now are abilities to engage in lifelong learning, innovation, technological and technical learning, understanding complexity and complex systems, and being able to collaborate (e.g., on workplace teams) with others."

Collaborative literacy can be simply defined as the skill to work jointly with others either face-to-face and/or online to create and produce something. This entails creating situations where students can engage in teamwork and interaction, either synchronous or asynchronous, give and receive feedback and guidance, edit the work of others, and disseminate the content produced to a broader public, that is, the classroom. Teamwork can initially take place face-to-face so that students become accustomed to collaborative practices in the classroom before starting to familiarize themselves with online collaboration and adopt the use of particular digital tools. In order to avoid confusion and disappointment, teachers need to create opportunities and supporting structures for students to practice these skills before embarking on a collaborative project for the first time. In a web-based collaborative environment, such as the eTwinning platform, enhancing collaborative practices can be realized through seeing students as a source of knowledge, guiding them and supporting them during their collaborative activities, encouraging them to leave feedback and edit the work of others, and facilitating online interaction with partners.

In practice, it is worth noting that although students may appear to enjoy teamwork in terms of discussing issues in groups, sharing ideas and learning from others, they are more cautious when it comes to collaborative writing and in particular commenting on and editing the work of others. The sense of ownership appears to interfere with educational collaborative practices and students are at large seen to prefer to cultivate a practice of individual accountability and ownership. In particular, as Caspi and Blau (2011, p. 283) argue "collaborative writing may evoke conflict between individuals' feeling of contribution and their sense of ownership toward the collective outcomes." Thus, the notion of collaborative literacy also entails enhancing the students' ability to distribute the responsibility for production of jointly written material, be confident to edit and comment on each other's writing, and accept the criticism of others. In particular, collaborative literacy should aim toward bridging the mismatch between the collective practices presupposed by multiauthored collaborative writing and the individual ownership of writing cultivated in formal educational settings, which is associated with assessment regimes.

The notion of collaborative literacy is also linked to that of online safety, which remains of paramount importance for schools. Although many schools have met parental concerns by blocking potentially risky websites, students need to actively learn about safety and become able to manage issues of risk during their everyday use of collaborative platforms and other social media tools. Collaborative literacy needs to be combined with lessons on e-safety so that students can develop an understanding of what constitutes appropriate use and content when using digital technologies. As Potter notes (2012, p. 180), "new opportunities for access and expression also carry risk and this is best addressed and brought into the open. Spaces in which children can openly discuss their concerns and learn for themselves how to manage risk will potentially have the greatest effect."

Against the above, developing e-safety protocols without curtailing the informal learning potential of digital technologies can be quite challenging. It is important to open up a dialogue among schools, teachers, parents, and students in order to develop clear guidelines and provide guidance about what is meant by "appropriate" access to and use of digital technologies. In brief, there seem to be three possible areas of change that include reorientating the theme and tone of the official discussions on e-safety, improving students' critical literacy skills, and establishing a meaningful and sustained dialogue among students, teachers, and parents about safety and risk when using digital technologies (Cranmer et al. 2009).

In addition, as Davies and Merchant (2009, p. 106) argue, "simply signing students up to a service is not enough!" Partnerships and learning through participation are more likely to flourish if we also acknowledge the importance of "purpose" and "planning." The notion of purpose is used to refer to the need to develop clear goals and engage students in something that is both authentic and relevant to their interests while careful planning allows for creativity and takes into account students' existing knowledge and experience. In addition, having coproducers—participants who are able to comment, give feedback, and generate their own content—and not just a receptive but passive audience can enhance the collaborative experiences of the learners. From this perspective finding age-appropriate partners and a mutually appealing topic for collaboration as well as planning the activities carefully might lead to more fruitful collaborative outcomes.

Last, there is a pressing need to introduce collaborative literacy from the earliest years of schooling. Many collaborative projects take place as an off-timetable activity or as a small part of very few lessons while the "project" itself does not get revisited once it is completed. However, it is only through recursive and repetitive engagement with collaborative activities across the school year that students will be able to enhance their collaborative literacy skills and successful partnerships will be built. Web-based school collaboration needs to be an integral component of schooling and not be restricted to "special occasions" since sporadic and low-level engagement will have little impact on altering rigid school habits and practices.

All these points suggest that gaining understanding of the notion of collaborative literacy and implementing it into the students' everyday classroom practices might be a slow, iterative, and time-consuming process. With these thoughts in mind, it appears that we need to think more carefully about supporting and guiding students through their collaborative journeys. The use of digital technologies for school collaboration involves not just familiarizing them with the technical aspects of the adopted technologies but more importantly considering the pedagogical changes that need to accompany technological innovations.

Reconfiguring the Students' Role

To date, the majority of collaborative initiatives have been more teacher-focused than pupil-focused. Despite *student* collaboration forming the basis of the programs, it is teachers who are at the center of most planning and pedagogical decisions. In particular, teachers hold the monopoly on the setting up of the projects while students have less involvement in decision making and minimal input to choices regarding the selection of project partners, topics, and tools. This indicates a restricted level of student empowerment and can to some extent justify their often-limited engagement with the project activities. Educators and policy makers alike should be cautious that in order to address the disconnectedness between different expectations and (lack of) motivation and reciprocity within and across teams, there is a fundamental need to consider the views and needs of those who are actually expected to engage in collaborative practices. As such, students need to play a more active role in the decision-making process before setting up the project and also during the collaborative process itself.

In particular, it is important to acknowledge the interests of the learners and work to resonate educational and collaborative practices with these experiences. By asking students to participate more actively and meaningfully in the decision-making process, we are giving them the opportunity to place their own stamp on the projects and we are putting them at the heart of their educational experience. In order to really put students at the center of school collaboration, it would also be necessary to engage them in the development of a collaborative platform, such as TwinSpace, and encourage them to take part in a wider discussion with regard to the collaborative practices that could be adopted in the future. This, in turn, might lead to the creation of communities that can be tailored to the shape of the students' interests and the pace of their learning. Additionally, establishing a dialogue and encouraging student participation in discussions about e-safety issues could allow schools to reshape their policies in ways which are more meaningful and relevant to the pupils and therefore stand more chance of success.

Still, making the collaborative projects more relevant to the students' interest and loosening restrictions regarding internet and computer use does not guarantee that *all* the students will be equally motivated and intrigued. It is worth taking into consideration studies that often report that students show little excitement about ICT uses related to formal education and/or school collaboration. By including learners in the picture and giving them the opportunity to express their voice and play a more active role in the selection and the setting up of the adopted tools, their overall engagement with the project might be enhanced but this will not ensure that *all* learners will be equally motivated. We should also bear in mind that there might be a small minority of students who do not enjoy engaging in web-based activities. As Selwyn (2002, p. 74) argued, "the political assumption that all children are naturally predicated towards using computers has been reinforced by academic literature on educational technology." In this sense, a "loosening up" of the collaborative project itself might be necessary so as to include other types of activities recommended by the learners such as exchanging postcards or handwritten letters or using other funnels of communication more meaningful to the particular students involved.

One last issue that merits consideration is how to enhance students' competences and confidence in using digital technologies. It is without a doubt that students' engagement with digital technologies is at large dictated by their level of skill and experience. Although some learners appear willing to expand and improve their ICT skills through trial and error, others are less confident to experiment in such ways and need cleared guidance and training. In this respect, it is crucial to ensure that all students have the skills required to use the collaborative tools unhindered by operational barriers. In particular, students need to be competent not only in their operational and social media skills but they should also able to use the internet responsibly and safely. Notwithstanding the importance of ICT skills, we should also acknowledge the significance of the teachers' role in enhancing students' digital competences and exploiting the full potential of digital technologies.

Reconfiguring the Teachers' Role

Teachers clearly have an important role to play in enhancing students' competencies and skills, encouraging student participation as well as planning and orchestrating their collaborative journey. Although the notion of "learner autonomy" is popular in academic discussions on the educational potential of new technologies, this should not mislead us into undermining the role of the teachers' in managing the collaborative experience of the students. As argued by Selwyn et al. (2008, p. 25), "collaborations need to be orchestrated if they are to be more than mere coordinations. The exposure of publication can be stressful as well as empowering. Confidence in reading the representational richness of the internet demands fluency in new literacies, which calls for careful tutoring."

In this sense, teachers need to understand that the ability to engage into collaborative practices independently is something that students need to be guided into acquiring. Despite the popular stereotyping of the "digital native" teachers should be aware that outside school, their students may have different levels of access to digital technologies and also different levels of familiarity with the various tools. As Buckingham contended (2007, p. 169), "it would be quite romantic to assume that they all have some kind of automatic expertise with technology, or that they will necessarily be able to learn to use it easily and quickly." Additionally, teachers should come to realize that whether or not the potential of the tools they adopt for the collaborative projects is materialized is not simply a matter of technology but a question of pedagogy. In this respect, the potential benefits of web-based collaboration will not be realized unless the teachers are successful in orchestrating the collaborative efforts of their students.

As such, there is a clear need to reconfigure the teachers' role and equip them with both the technical know-how in terms of using digital technologies confidently and creatively but also the pedagogical skills to support and guide their students effectively and coordinate online collaborative projects efficiently. For instance, a recent study has shown that "digitally confident and supportive teachers" not only have great confidence in their "own digital competence (operational and social media skills) and in their ability to use the internet safely and responsibly" but also they can influence their students positively and improve their digital competence (Wastiau et al. 2013, p. 19).

For this proposal to work it is important not only to guarantee access to technologies within the school but also to ensure that teachers feel empowered to use the technologies that resonate with their students' needs and experiences. In order to train teachers to be orchestrators of collaboration, professional development opportunities should be available at local, regional, and national levels. This will allow them to develop awareness of and confidence in working with digital technologies, explore the tools' potential for creative and collaborative practices, as well as develop the organizational and interpersonal skills-sets required to successfully guide groups of students in their collaborative journeys.

This can be particularly challenging on the one hand due to the ever-changing and evolving nature of digital technologies and on the other due to the varying degrees of teachers' experience of digital technologies and their associated social and collaborative practice. In this respect, professional development courses need to take place on a recurrent basis and be shorter and more practical as well as tailor-made to the teachers' level of competence. However, once armed with a more holistic, pedagogical understanding of collaborative practices as well as "trouble-shooting" experience and confidence to explore new tools through trial and error, it should be easier for teachers to develop digital and collaborative competencies and engage in more meaningful practices.

A further point for action concerns the need to reexamine the role of teachers and create time and space in their hectic school day not only for engaging with collaborative projects but also for participating in such professional development courses. In contrast to the "anti-schooler" discourses that embrace the abolishment of traditional forms of schooling and envisage the establishment of new, "virtual" types of school, the role of the teacher in orchestrating online collaborative projects and facilitating engagement with digital technologies could not be more central. Web-based school collaboration is at large dependent on the sustained enthusiasm and goodwill of the participating teachers and if schools are to harness the potential of web-based collaboration, they must view development of teachers' digital and collaborative literacies as a mainstream priority.

Toward a Framework for Future Research and Discussion of Digital Technology and School Collaboration

Despite the ever-increasing use of digital technologies in educational settings and the large amounts of research funding the field has attracted, education and technology have not yet become an area of rigorous and sustained academic study. As Selwyn (2012, p. 218) argues, "it makes little sense to pretend that the academic research that has been conducted to date in the area of education and technology has been particularly strong." Undoubtedly, this also applies to the more specialized field of school collaboration where research approaches appear to be at large rather fragmented and uncoordinated. As such the first step toward materializing the potential for digital technologies to become little more than a short-lived "fad" is to develop rich understandings of the everyday realities of web-based collaborative projects by conducting more sustained and longer-term studies. Furthermore, researchers need to move beyond asking whether or not collaborative tools work in a technical sense and open up more contextual conversations. As this book has frequently noted, there is a pressing need to consider and empirically investigate how the individuals' experiences and expectations as well as the wider school context can shape the way that web-based collaborative projects are materialized.

Within a broader educational context, I would suggest the following research agenda for action (Gouseti, 2010): (i) make better use of the existing evidence in research findings and literature and looking at the patterns emerging from the hitherto isolated studies of digital technology use so that one can critically evaluate and assess them to form realistic expectations of classroom use and inform future practices; (ii) facilitate a more sustained, rigorous, larger-scale, cross-sectional type of research in order to form a more holistic picture of the realities of web-based school collaboration practices in "real life" as opposed to "model" educational settings, leading perhaps to a clearer picture of the present and more reasonable expectations for the future; (iii) promote an interdisciplinary type of research across multiple settings and contexts in order to gain deeper and better understanding of the different elements of digital technology use in education. This will involve pulling together not only the educators and the technologists but also academic researchers from the fields of sociology, psychology, media studies, and so on to look at the many different aspects of digital technology use in educational and collaborative settings; and (iv) finally, there is a need to open up a dialogue about digital technologies and school collaboration beyond the educational and academic communities and start a bigger, critically informed conversation that will also engage parents, policy makers, employers, the IT industry, and other stakeholders. From this perspective, there is a growing need for collaborative action. Just as collaborative practices are in essence social, so too will the solutions require collaboration between educators and social policy makers, teachers and pupils, schools and the community.

Last, before the educational technology community perhaps gets too enthusiastic with the potential of the next big, collaborative tool or turns its attention, for example, toward the educational opportunities of "cloud computing" or "seamless learning," it might be worth investing more time, effort, and thought on reflecting on the present and working out ways of appropriating and supporting web-based school collaboration more successfully in the future. The messy and compromised realities of educational use of digital technologies for school collaboration should not overshadow the undoubted opportunities that collaborative initiatives entail for teaching and learning. At the moment it could be argued that too much emphasis has been placed on the "individual" (be it the teacher, student, or technology) at the expense of full consideration of the significance of the social contexts of digital technology use and nonuse in education. If we can move beyond the current hype of educational technology use, open up these contextual conversations, and work toward a more realistic and robust set of expectations, perhaps, digital technologies may be better appropriated for collaborative projects in the near future.

Conclusion

All the points raised in this chapter lead us to conclude that there is no "one-size fits all" solution that will guarantee successful web-based collaborative projects but we need to understand school collaboration "within the dialectic of the global and the local" (Selwyn 2013, p. 150). Although there may be common inhibitors as well as common expectations and aspirations shared between the range of participants, a host of factors such as the school structure and culture, classroom regimes, the particular nature, and circumstances of the project participants can determine the outcome of a web-based collaborative project. It appears that digital technologies *can* facilitate collaboration but we should be careful not to make simplistic connections between the properties of the tools and the collaborative practices that emerge when used for school linking.

As this book has suggested, participation in web-based school collaboration is not simply a matter of "harnessing" the potential of collaborative technologies. Instead, teachers' and students' experiences have shown that there is a lot more to school collaboration than simplistic descriptions of "communities of schools" and "digital learners" suggest. It is clear from this study that shifting the focus from the technical to the social appears necessary if school collaboration is to remain an exciting and worthwhile element of school practice. All of the suggestions presented in this chapter will require significant further thinking and careful development if they are to represent a realistic agenda for improvement in the field of web-based school collaboration. All in all, I hope that the discussions in this book have provided a useful starting point for reshaping our understanding of web-based school collaboration and will hopefully lead to possible changes in the future.

Appendix: List of URLs of Collaborative Programs

Collaborative Program	URL
African Revival	http://www.africanrevival.org/
AfriTwin	http://www.afritwin.net/
Arctic Voice	http://www.arcticvoice.org/
Atlantic Rising	http://atlanticrising.org/
BBC World Class	http://www.bbc.co.uk/worldclass/
Comenius Programme	http://ec.europa.eu/education/lifelong-learning-programme/comenius_en.htm
Commonwealth Class	http://schoolsonline.britishcouncil.org/projects-and-resources/commonwealth-class
Connect All Schools	http://www.connectallschools.org/
Connecting Classrooms	http://schoolsonline.britishcouncil.org/programmes-and-funding/linking-programmes-worldwide/connecting-classrooms
ePals Global Network	http://www.epals.com/
eTwinning	http://www.etwinning.net/en/pub/index.htm
Face to Faith initiative	http://www.tonyblairfaithfoundation.org/page/face-faith-students
Flat Classroom Project	http://www.flatclassroomproject.org/
Global SchoolNet	http://www.globalschoolnet.org/
Global School Partners	http://www.globalschoolpartners.org.au/
Global Virtual Classroom	http://www.virtualclassroom.org/
GLOBE	http://globe.gov/
Global School Partnerships	http://www.britishcouncil.org/nepal-programmes-dfid-global-school-partnerships-2.htm

Japan-UK live	http://www.japanuklive.org/
Link Community Development	http://lcdinternational.org/
Link Ethiopia	http://www.linkethiopia.org/
Palestinian-German School Twinning Programme	http://www.school-tp-ps.de/
School's Online	http://schoolsonline.britishcouncil.org/
School-to-School International	http://sts-international.org/
SuperClubsPLUS	http://www.superclubsplus.com/
UClass	https://uclass.org/

Bibliography

Anderson, P. (2007). "What is Web 2.0? Ideas, technologies, and implications for education," *JISC Tech Watch*. Available at: http://www.jisc.ac.uk/media/documents/techwatch/tsw0701b.pdf [last accessed August 8, 2013].

Atkinson, M., Springate, I., Johnson, F. and Halsey, K. (2007). *Inter-school collaboration: a literature review*. Slough: NFER.

Austin, R. (2006). "The role of ICT in bridge-building and social inclusion: Theory, policy and practice issues." *European Journal of Teacher Education*, 29 (2), 145–161.

Austin, R., Mallon, M., Metcalfe, N., Quirke-Bolt, N., and Rickard, A. (2006). *Dissolving Boundaries Building Communities of Practice*. Available at: http://www.dissolvingboundaries.org/research.html [last accessed August 8, 2013].

Austin, R., Smyth, J., Rickard, A., and Grace, A. (2011) *Crossing Frontiers in Education*. Available at: http://www.dissolvingboundaries.org/4/research.html [last accessed October 7, 2013].

Banaji, S., Cranmer, S., and Perrotta, C. (2010). *Creative and Innovative Good practices in Compulsory Education in Europe: Collection and Descriptive Analysis of Ten Good Practices of Creativity and Innovation in Compulsory Education in the EU27* (JRC Scientific and Technical Reports No. EUR XXXX EN). Seville: European Commission—Joint Research Centre—Institute for Prospective Technological Studies.

Barbosa, R., Jofili, Z., and Watts, M. (2004). "Co-operating in constructing knowledge: Case studies from chemistry and citizenship." *International Journal of Science Education*, 26 (8), 935–949.

Barr, H. (1991). "Social studies by electronic mail." *Social Studies Observer*, 24 (1), 10–11.

Bauerlein, M. (2008). *The Dumbest Generation: How the Digital Age Stupefies Young Americans and Jeopardizes Our Future (or, Don't Trust Anyone under 30)*. New York, NY: Jeremy P. Tarcher/Penguin.

Beer, D. and Burrows, R. (2007). "Sociology and, of and in Web 2.0: Some initial considerations." *Sociological Research Online*, 12. Available at: http://www.socresonline.org.uk/12/5/17.html [last accessed August 8, 2013].

Beldarrain, Y. (2006). "Distance education trends: Integrating new technologies to foster student interaction and collaboration." *Distance Education*, 27 (2), 139–153.

Belz, J. A. (2007). "The Development of Intercultural Communicative Competence in Tellecollaborative Partnerships." In R. O'Dowd (Ed.), *Online Intercultural Exchange: An Introduction for Foreign Language Teachers*, Clevedon [u.a.]: Multilingual Matters.

Bennett, S., Maton, K., and Kervin, L. (2008). "The 'digital natives' debate: A critical review of the evidence." *British Journal of Educational Technology*, 39 (5), 775–786.

BESA [British Education Studies Association] (2009). *ICT Provision and Use in 2009/10—Summary Report*. Education Market Outlook Series. Available at: http://resources.eun.org/insight/BESA_ICT2009_Summary.pdf [last accessed August 8, 2013].

Bigum, C. and Kenway, J. (1998). "New information technologies and the ambiguous future of schooling: Some possible scenarios." *International Handbook of Educational Change*. Kluwer: Springer.

Bigum, C. and Rowan, L. (2008). "Landscaping on shifting ground: Teacher education in a digitally transforming world." *Asia-pacific Journal of Teacher Education*, 36 (3), 245–255.

Brabazon, T. (2007). *Mobile Learning: The iPodification of Universities*, Nebula. Available at: http://www.nobleworld.biz/images/Brabazon.pdf [last accessed September 7, 2013].

Breuer, R., Klamma, R., Cao, Y., and Vuorikari, R. (2009). "Social network analysis of 45,000 schools: A case study of technology enhanced learning in Europe." 4th European Conference on Technology Enhanced Learning, EC-TEL 2009 (November 30, 2009). Lecture Notes in Computer Science, 166–180.

British Council (n.d.) *Bring the World into Your Classroom: Your Guide to International Opportunities for Secondary Schools*. Available at: http://schoolsonline.britishcouncil .org/sites/default/files/files/101347_British%20Council%20Secondary%20 E-Brochure.pdf [last accessed September 7, 2013].

Brown, J. S., and Adler, R. P. (2008). "Minds on fire: Open education, the long tail, and learning 2.0." *EDUCAUSE Review*. 43 (1), 16–20, 22, 24, 26, 28, 30, 32.

Buckingham, D. (2007). *Beyond Technology: Children's Learning in the Age of Digital Culture*. Cambridge: Polity.

Burns, M. and Bodrogini, P. W. (2011). "Web 2.0 as a Community-Building Tool." In M. Thomas (Ed.), *Digital Education: Opportunities for Social Collaboration*. New York: Palgrave Macmillan.

Cachia, R., Ferrari, A., Ala-Mutka, K., and Punie, Y. (2010). *Creative Learning and Innovative Teaching: Final Report on the Study on Creativity and Innovation in Education in EU Member States*. Luxemburg: European Commission. Institute for Prospective Technological Studies.

Campbell, N. (2004). "The Vintage Years of eLearning in New Zealand Schools." *Journal of Distance Learning*, 8 (1), 17–24.

Carr, N. (2010). *The Shallows: What the Internet is Doing to Our Brains*. New York: W. W. Norton & Company.

Caspi, A. and Blau I. (2011). "Collaboration and psychological ownership: How does the tension between the two influence perceived learning?" *Social Psychology of Education: An International Journal*, 14 (2), 283–298.

Cavanagh, A. (2007). *Sociology in the Age of the Internet*. Buckingham: Open University Press.

Chapman, C., Muijs, D., Lindsay, G., Arweck, E., Goodall, J., and Harris, A. (2010). "Governance, leadership, and management in federations of schools." *School Effectiveness and School Improvement*, 21 (1), 53–74.

Cloke, S. (2010). "The Italia-Australia Intercultural Project." In S. Guth and F. Helm (Eds.), *Telecollaboration 2.0: Language, Literacies and Intercultural Learning in the 21st Century*. Bern: Peter Lang.

Cole, M. (2009). "Using wiki technology to support student engagement: Lessons from the trenches." *Computers and Education*, 52 (1), 141–146.

Collins, A. (1996). "Whither technology and schools? Collected thoughts on the last and next quarter centuries." In C. Fisher, D. C. Dwyer, and K. Yocam (Eds.), *Education and Technology: Reflections on Computing in Classrooms*. San Francisco: Jossey-Bass.

Collins, A. and Halverson, R. (2009). Rethinking education in the age of technology: The digital revolution and schooling in America. New York: Teachers College Press.

Collis, B. and Heeren, E. (1993). "Tele-collaboration and groupware." *The Computing Teacher*, 21 (1), 36–38.

Cooley, N. and Johnston, M. A. (2000) "Beyond teacher bashing: Practical, philosophical, and pedagogical influences on educators' use of educational technologies." *The Technology Source*, July/August 2000. Available at: http://technologysource.org/article/beyond_teacher_bashing/ [last accessed September 7, 2013].

Coutinho, C. P. and Rocha, C. (2007). "The etwinning project: A study with Portuguese 9th grade students." Available at: http://repositorium.sdum.uminho.pt/bitstream/1822/6722/1/catarina.pdf [last accessed September 7, 2013].

Cranmer, S., Selwyn, N., and Potter, J. (2009). " 'Exploring primary pupils' experiences and understandings of 'e-safety.' " *Education and Information Technologies*, 14, (2), 127–142.

Crook, C. (2008). "What are web 2.0 technologies, and why do they matter?" [Online]. In N. Selwyn (Ed). *Education 2.0? Designing the Web for Teaching and Learning*. ESRC Teaching and Learning Research Programme commentary. Available at: http://www.tlrp.org/pub/documents/TELcomm.pdf [last accessed August 8, 2013].

Crook, C. (2012). "The 'digital native' in context: Tensions associated with importing Web 2.0 practices into the school setting." *Oxford Review of Education*, 38 (1), 63–80.

Crook, C. *et al.* (2008a). *Web 2.0 Technologies for Learning: The Current Landscape—Opportunities, Challenges and Tensions*. Coventry: Becta. Available at: http://dera.ioe.ac.uk/1475/2/becta_2008_web2_currentlandscapeadditional_litrev.pdf [last accessed August 8, 2013].

Crook, C., Fisher, T., Graber, R., Harrison, C., and Lewin, C. (2008b). *Implementing Web 2.0 in Secondary Schools: Impacts, Barriers and Issues*. Coventry: Becta. Available at: http://dera.ioe.ac.uk/1478/1/becta_2008_web2_useinschools_report.pdf [last accessed August 8, 2013].

Crook, C. and Harrison, C. (2008). *Web 2.0 Technologies for Learning at Key Stages 3 and 4: Summary Report*. Coventry: Becta. Available at: http://dera.ioe.ac .uk/1480/1/becta_2008_web2_summary.pdf [last accessed August 8, 2013].

Cuban, L. (1986). *Teachers and Machines: The Classroom Use of Technology since 1920*. New York: Teachers College Press.

Cuban, L. (1993). *Computers Meet Classroom: Classroom Wins. TEACHERS COLLEGE RECORD*, 95 (2), 185. Available at: http://sdexter.net/xyz/CompMeets%20 Classroom.pdf [last accessed August 8, 2013].

Cuban, L. (2001). *Oversold and Underused: Computers in the Classroom*. Cambridge MA: Harvard University Press.

Cuban, L. (2009). *Buying iPads, Common Core Standards, and Computer-Based Testing*. Available at: http://larrycuban.wordpress.com/2013/07/29/buying-ipads -common-core-standards-and-computer-based-testing/. [last accessed October 8, 2013].

Davies, J. and Merchant, G. (2009). *Web 2.0 for Schools Learning and Social Participation. New Literacies and Digital Epistemologies*, Vol. 33. New York, NY: Lang.

DCSF [Department for Children, Schools and Families]. (2007). *Guidance on the Duty to Promote Community Cohesion*. Nottingham: DCSF. Available at: https:// www.education.gov.uk/publications/standard/publicationDetail/Page1/DCSF -00598–2007. [last accessed August 8, 2013].

De Kerckhove, D. (2010). "Preface." In C. Crawley, P. Gerhard, A. Gilleran, and A. Joyce (Eds.), *eTwinning 2.0: Building the Community for Schools in Europe*. Brussels: Central Support Service for eTwinning (CSS).

DfES [Department for Education and Skills]. (2004). *Putting the World into World-Class Education: An International Strategy for Education, Skills and Children's Strategies*. Nottingham; DfES. Available at: https://www.education.gov.uk /publications/eOrderingDownload/1077–2004GIF-EN-01.pdf. [last accessed August 8, 2013].

DFID [Department for International Development] (2007). *The World Classroom: Developing Global Partnerships in Education*. London; DFID. Available at: http:// webarchive.nationalarchives.gov.uk/+/http:/www.dfid.gov.uk/Documents /publications/world-classroom.pdf. [last accessed August 8, 2013].

Dillenbourg, P. (1999). "What Do You Mean by 'Collaborative Learning'?" In P. Dillenbourg (Ed.), *Collaborative Learning: Cognitive and Computational Approaches*. Amsterdam, NL: Pergamon, Elsevier Science.

Doe, B. (2007). *Promoting School Partnerships. A Report to the Education Committee of the UK National Commission for UNESCO on the Commonwealth Consortium for Education conference on school linking* (Cape Town, December 2006). Available at: http://www.unesco.org.uk/UserFiles/File/Sch%20Linking/Report_022007(1) .pdf. [last accessed August 8, 2013].

Dooly, M., Pavlikov, J., Eastment, D., Müller-Hartmann, A., and Visser, M. (2008). "Finding the right tools." In M. Dooly (Ed.), *Telecollaborative Language Learning: A Guidebook to Moderating Intercultural Collaboration Online*. Bern: Peter Lang.

Downes S. (2005). "E-learning 2.0." *Elearn*, 2005, 10. Available at: http://elearnmag.acm.org/featured.cfm?aid=1104968 [last accessed August 8, 2013].

Du, H. S. and Wagner, C. (2005). "Learning with weblogs: An empirical investigation." Proceedings of the 38th Hawaii International Conference on System Sciences. Available at: http://www.computer.org/comp/proceedings/hicss/2005/2268/01/22680007b.pdf [last accessed August 8, 2013].

Ducate, L. C., Anderson, L. L., and Moreno, N. (2011) "Wading through the world of wikis: An analysis of three wiki projects." *Foreign Language Annals*, 44 (3), 495–524,

Duffy, T. M. and Jonassen, D. H. (1993). *Constructivism and the Technology of Instruction: A Conversation*. Hillsdale, NJ: Lawrence Erlbaum Associates.

Dutton, W., Helsper, E., and Gerber, M. (2009). *The 2009 OxIS survey. The Internet in Britain*. Oxford: University of Oxford.

Elgort, I., Smith, A. G., and Toland, J. (2008). "Is wiki an effective platform for group course work?" *Australasian Journal of Educational Technology*, 24 (2), 195–210.

Engstrom, M. E. and Jewett, D. (2005). "Collaborative learning the wiki way." *Techtrends: Linking Research & Practice to Improve Learning*, 49 (6), 12–16.

ePals. (nd) *Reaching the National Educational Technology Standards (NETS) with ePals*. Hendon, VA: ePals. Available at: http://images.epals.com/nets_whitepaper.pdf [last accessed August 8, 2013].

Europa (2013). *Launch of "eTwinning Plus" Virtual Classroom Network for Schools*. Available at: http://europa.eu/rapid/press-release_IP-13–183_en.htm. [last accessed August 8, 2013].

European Commission. (2007). *Key Competences for Lifelong Learning: European Reference Framework*. Luxembourg: Office for Official Publications of the European Communities. Available at: http://ec.europa.eu/dgs/education_culture/publ/pdf/ll-learning/keycomp_en.pdf [last accessed August 8, 2013].

European Commission. (2013a). *Survey of Schools: ICT in education*. Luxembourg: Publications Office of the European Union. Available at: http://ec.europa.eu/digital-agenda/en/news/survey-schools-ict-education [last accessed August 8, 2013].

European Commission. (2013b). *Study of the Impact of eTwinning on Participating Pupils, Teachers and Schools*. Luxembourg: Publications Office of the European Union. Available at: http://ec.europa.eu/education/more-information/docs/impact_study_etwinning_2013_en.pdf.

Eynon R. and Malmberg, L. (2011). "A typology of young people's Internet use: Implications for education." *Computers and Education*, 56 (3), 585–595.

Eyre, S. (2009). "The whole world in their hands." *Teaching, Thinking and Creativity*, 9 (4), 6–8.

Facer, K. and Selwyn, N. (2010). "Social Networking: Key Messages from the Research." In R. Sharpe, H. Beetham, and S. De Freitas (Eds.), *Rethinking Learning for a Digital Age: How Learners Are Shaping Their Own Experiences*. London: Routledge.

Forte, A. and Bruckman, A. (2007). "Constructing text: Wiki as a toolkit for (collaborative?) learning". In *WikiSym '07: Proceedings of the 2007 international symposium on Wikis*, pages 31–42, New York, NY, USA, ACM. Available at: http://www.wikisym.org/ws2007/_publish/Forte_WikiSym2007_ConstructingText.pdf [last accessed August 8, 2013].

Forte, A. and Bruckman, A. (2009). "Writing, citing, and participatory media: Wikis as learning environments in the high school classroom." *International Journal of Learning and Media*, 1 (4), 23–44.

Franklin, T. and van Harmelen, M. (2007). *Web 2.0 for Content for Learning and Teaching in Higher Education*. JISC. Available at: http://www.jisc.ac.uk/media/documents/programmes/digitalrepositories/web2-content-learning-and-teaching.pdf [last accessed August 8, 2013].

Fratter, I. and Helm, F. (2010), "The intercultural Project." In S. Guth and F. Helm (Eds.), *Telecollaboration 2.0: Language, Literacies and Intercultural Learning in the 21st Century*. Bern: Peter Lang.

Freedman, T. (Ed.) (2010). *The Amazing Web 2.0 Projects Book*. Eugene, OR: ICTE in Education, The Educational Technology Site. Available at: http://www.terry-freedman.org.uk/web2_2010/Amazing%20Web%202%20Projects%202%20online%20version.pdf [last accessed September 7, 2013].

Gee, J. P. (2012). *Social Linguistics and Literacies: Ideology in Discourses*. London: Routledge.

Godwin-Jones, R. (2003). "Blogs and wikis: Environments for on-line collaboration." *Language Learning and Technology*, 7 (2), 12–16.

Gouseti, A. (2010). "Web 2.0 and education: Not just another case of hype, hope and disappointment?" *Learning, Media and Technology*, 35 (3), 351–356.

Grant, L. (2009) "I DON'T CARE DO UR OWN PAGE! A case study of using wikis for collaborative work in a UK secondary school." *Learning, Media and Technology*, 34 (2), 105–117.

Grant, L. (with Billalobos, G.) (2008). *Designing Educational Technologies for Social Justice*. Bristol: Futurelab. Available at: http://archive.futurelab.org.uk/resources/documents/handbooks/designing_for_social_justice2.pdf [last accessed October 7, 2013].

Gray, L., Thomas, N., and Lewis, L. (2010). *Educational Technology in U.S. Public Schools: Fall 2008*. U.S. Department of Education, National Center for Education Statistics. Washington, DC: U.S. Government Printing Office. Available at: http://nces.ed.gov/pubsearch/pubsinfo.asp?pubid=2010034 [last accessed October 7, 2013].

Green, H., Facer, K., Rudd, T., Dillon, P., and Humphreys, P. (2005) *Personalisation and Digital Technologies*. Bristol: Futurelab. Available at: http://archive.futurelab.org.uk/resources/documents/opening_education/Personalisation_report.pdf [last accessed October 7, 2013].

Green, T. D., Brown, A., and Robinson, L. (2008). *Making the Most of the Web in your Classroom: A Teacher's Guide to Blogs, Podcasts, Wikis, Pages, and Sites*. Thousand Oaks, CA: Corwin Press.

Greenfield, P. M. (2009). "Technology and informal education: What is taught, what is learned." *Science*, 323, 69–71.

Greenhow, C., Robelia, B., and Hughes, J. (2009). "Web 2.0 and classroom research: What path should we take now?" *Educational Researcher*, 38 (4), 246–259.

Guth, S. and Helm, F. (2010). "Introduction." In S. Guth and F. Helm (Eds.), *Telecollaboration 2.0: Language, Literacies and Intercultural Learning in the 21st Century*. Bern: Peter Lang.

Guth, S. and Marini-Maio, N. (2010). "Close Encounters of a New Kind: Skype and Wiki in Telecollaboration." In S. Guth and F. Helm (Eds.), *Telecollaboration 2.0: Language, Literacies and Intercultural Learning in the 21st Century*. Bern: Peter Lang.

Halbert, J. and Kaser, L. (2002). "Inquiry eh? School Improvement through a Network of Inquiry." *Education Canada*, 19 (2), 1–7.

Hanford, S., Houck, J., Iler, E., and Morgan, P. (1997). "Public and private school collaborations—educational bridges into the 21st century." Forum for Public /Private Collaboration. Available at: http://www.eric.ed.gov/PDFS/ED411387 .pdf [last accessed August 8, 2013].

Hargadon, S. (2008). "Web 2.0 is the future of education." Weblogs post on March 4, 2008. Available at: http://www.stevehargadon.com/2008/03/web-20-is-future -of-education.html [last accessed August 8, 2013].

Hasebrink, U., Livingstone, S., and Haddon, L. (2008). *Comparing Children's Online Opportunities and Risks across Europe: Cross-national Comparisons for EU Kids Online*. London: EU Kids Online. Available at: http://eprints.lse.ac.uk/21656/1 /D3.2_Report%2DCross_national_comparisons.pdf [last accessed August 8, 2013].

Hauck, M. and Lewis, T. (2007). "The Tridem Project." In R. O'Dowd (Ed.), *Online Intercultural Exchange: An Introduction for Foreign Language Teachers*. Clevedon [u.a.]: Multilingual Matters.

Haythornthwaite, C. A., and Andrews, R. (2011). *E-learning Theory and Practice*. Los Angeles: Sage.

Helsper, E. and Eynon, R. (2010) "Digital natives: Where is the evidence? *British Educational Research Journal*, 36 (3), 503–520.

Hepburn, H. (2010). "One teacher, 30 nations and a day to remember" [Online]. *Times Educational Supplement*, February 19, 2010. Available at: http://www.tes .co.uk/article.aspx?storycode=6036443. [last accessed October 22, 2013].

Howe, N. and Strauss, W. (2000). *Millennials Rising: The Next Great Generation*. New York: Vintage Books.

Illich, I. (1971). *Deschooling Society*. Harmondsworth: Penguin Education.

Ito, M. (2012) *Connected Learning*. Available at: http://www.itofisher.com/mito /weblog/2012/03/connected_learning.html. [last accessed August 8, 2013].

Ito, M. and Antin, J. (2010). *Hanging Out, Messing Around, and Geeking Out: Kids Living and Learning with New Media*. Cambridge, MA: MIT Press.

Ito, M., Gutiérrez, K., Livingstone, S., Penuel, B., Rhodes, J., Salen, K., Schor, J., Sefton-Green, J., and Watkins, S. C. (2013). *Connected Learning: An Agenda for Research and Design*. Digital Media and Learning Research Hub. Available at: http://dmlhub.net/publications/connected-learning-agenda-research-and-design [last accessed August 8, 2013].

Jauregi, K. and Banados, E. (2010). "An Intercontinental Video-Web Communication Project between Chile and the Netherlands." In S. Guth and F. Helm (Eds.), *Telecollaboration 2.0: Language, Literacies and Intercultural Learning in the 21st Century.* Bern: Peter Lang.

Jenkins, H. (with Purushota, R., Clinton, K., Weigel, M., and Robinson, A.) (2006). *Confronting the Challenges of Participatory Culture: Media Education for the 21st Century.* Chicago, IL: MacArthur Foundation. Available at: http://digitallearning.macfound.org/atf/cf/%7B7E45C7E0-A3E0-4B89-AC9C-E807E1B0AE4E%7D/JENKINS_WHITE_PAPER.PDF [last accessed August 8, 2013].

Jewitt, C., Clark, W., and Hadjithoma-Garstka, C. (2011) "The use of learning platforms to organise learning in English primary and secondary schools." *Learning, Media and Technology,* 36 (4), 335–348.

Jonassen, D., Davidson, M., Collins, M., Campbell, J., and Haag, B. B. (1995). "Constructivism and computer-mediated communication in distance education." *The American Journal of Distance Education,* 9 (2), 7. Available at: http://www.c3l.uni-oldenburg.de/cde/media/readings/jonassen95.pdf [last accessed September 7, 2013].

Jones, J. (2006). "Leadership in small schools: Supporting the power of collaboration." *Management in Education,* 20 (2), 24–28.

Judd, T., Kennedy, G., and Cropper, S. (2010). "Using wikis for collaborative learning: Assessing collaboration through contribution." *Australasian Journal of Educational Technology,* 26 (3), 341–354.

Kamel Boulos, M. N. and Wheeler, S. (2007). "The emerging Web 2.0 social software: An enabling suite of sociable technologies in health and health care education." *Health Information and Libraries Journal,* 24 (1), 2–23.

Katz, S., Earl, L., Jaafar, S. B., Elgie, S., Foster, L., Halbert, J., et al. (2008). "Learning Networks of Schools: The Key Enablers of Successful Knowledge Communities." *McGill Journal of Education,* 43 (2), 111–137.

Keen, A. (2008). *The Cult of the Amateur: How Today's Internet is Killing Our Culture and Assaulting the Economy.* London: Nicholas Brealey Publishing.

Kennedy, G., Judd, T., Dalgarno B., and Waycott J. (2010). "Beyond natives and immigrants: Exploring types of net generation students." *Journal of Computer Assisted Learning,* 26(5), 332–343.

Kerr, D., Aiston, S., White, K., Holland, M., and Grayson, H. (2003). "Networked learning communities." Paper presented at the NFER Council of Members Meeting, London, October 3, 2003. Available at: www.nfer.ac.uk/publications/other-publications/conference-papers/networked-learning-communities.cfm [last accessed September 7, 2013].

Kozma, R. B. (2003). "ICT and Educational Change: A Global Phenomenon." In R. B. Kozma (Ed.), *Technology, Innovation, and Educational Change.* Eugene OR: International Society for Technology in Education.

Lankshear, C. and Knobel, M. (2006). *New Literacies: Everyday Practices and Classroom Learning.* Maidenhead: Open University Press.

Larusson, J. A. and Alterman, R. (2009). "Wikis to support the 'collaborative' part of collaborative learning." *International Journal of Computer-Supported Collaborative Learning*, 4 (4), 371–402.

Laurillard, D. (2009). "The pedagogical challenges to collaborative technologies." *International Journal of Computer-Supported Collaborative Learning*, 4 (1), 5–20.

Lave, J. and Wenger, E. (1991). *Situated Learning: Legitimate Peripheral Participation. Learning in Doing.* Cambridge [England]: Cambridge University Press.

Leadbeater, C. (2008). *We-Think: [Mass Innovation, Not Mass Production].* London: Profile Books.

Leonard, P. E. and Leonard, L. J. (2001). "The collaborative prescription: Remedy or reverie?" *International Journal of Leadership in Education*, 4 (4), 383–400.

Levy, S. (1984). *Hackers: Heroes of the Computer Revolution.* Garden City, NY: Anchor Press/Doubleday.

Lievrouw, L. A. and Livingstone, S. (2006). "Introduction to the Updated Student Edition." In L. A. Lievrouw and S. Livingstone (Eds.), *Handbook of New Media: Social Shaping and Social Consequences.* London: Sage.

Light, A. and Luckin, R. (2008). *Opening Education—Designing for Social Justice: People, Technology.* Bristol: Futurelab. Available at: http://www2.futurelab.org .uk/resources/documents/opening_education/Designing_for_Social_Justice.pdf [last accessed September 7, 2013].

Lin, H. and Kelsey, K. (2009). "Building a networked environment in wikis: The evolving phases of collaborative learning in a wikibook project." *Journal of Educational Computing Research*, 40 (2), 145–169.

Lindsay, J. and Davis, V. (2010). "Navigate the digital rapids." *Learning and Leading with Technology*, 37 (6), 12–15. Available at: http://www.flatclassroomproject. org/file/view/DigitalCitizenship_Mar2010.pdf. [last accessed August 8, 2013].

Livingstone, S. M. and Haddon, L. (2009). *Kids Online: Opportunities and Risks for Children.* Bristol: Policy Press.

Lortie, D. C. (2002). *Schoolteacher: A Sociological Study.* Chicago, IL: University of Chicago Press.

Loveless, A. (2007). *Creativity, Technology and Learning—A Review of Recent Literature.* Bristol: Futurelab. Available at: http://www2.futurelab.org.uk/resources /documents/lit_reviews/Creativity_Review_update.pdf [last accessed October 22, 2013].

Loveless, A., DeVoogd, G. L., and Bohlin, R. M. (2001). "Something Old, Something New…Is Pedagogy Affected by ICT?" In A. Loveless and V. Ellis (Eds.), *ICT, Pedagogy, and the Curriculum: Subject to Change.* London: Routledge/Falmer.

Luckin, R., Clark, W., Graber, R., Logan, K., Mee, A., and Oliver, M. (2009). "Do Web 2.0 tools really open the door to learning: Practices, perceptions and profiles of 11–16 year old learners." *Learning Media and Technology*, 34, (2), 87–104.

Luckin, R., Logan, K., Clark, W., Graber, R., Oliver, M., and Mee, A. (2008). *Learners' Use of Web 2.0 Technologies in and out of School in Key Stages 3 and 4.* Coventry: Becta. Available at: http://dera.ioe.ac.uk/1476/1/becta_2008_web2 _learnersuse_report.pdf [last accessed August 8, 2013].

Lund, A. (2008) "Wikis: A collective approach to language production." *Recall*, 20 (1), 35–54.

Lund, A. and Smørdal, O. (2006). "Is there a space for the teacher in a WIKI?" In *Proceedings of the 2006 International Symposium on Wikis* (Odense, Denmark, August 21–23, 2006). WikiSym'06. ACM, New York, NY, 37–46. Available at: http://www.wikisym.org/ws2006/proceedings/p37.pdf [last accessed October 22, 2013].

Maitles, H. and Gilchrist, I. (2006). "Never too young to learn democracy!: A case study of a democratic approach to learning in a Religious and Moral Education (RME) secondary class in the West of Scotland." *Educational Review*, 58 (1), 67–85.

Marsh, J. (2010). "Young children's play in online virtual worlds." *Journal of Early Childhood Research*, 8 (1), 23–39.

McKenna, U., Ipgrave, J., and Jackson, R. (2008). *"Inter Faith Dialogue by Email in Primary Schools: An Evaluation of the Building e-bridges Project."Religious Diversity and Education in Europe*, Vol. 6. Münster: Waxmann.

McLoughlin, C. and Lee, M. J. W. (2007). "Social software and participatory learning: Pedagogical choices with technology affordances in the Web 2.0 era." *Proceedings of ASCILITE Conference 2007 (pp. 664–673)*, Singapore.

McLoughlin, C. and Lee, M .J. W. (2008). "Mapping the digital terrain: New media and social software as catalysts for pedagogical change." In *Hello! Where Are You in the Landscape of Educational Technology? Proceedings Ascilite Melbourne 2008*. Available at: http://www.ascilite.org.au/conferences/melbourne08/procs /mcloughlin.pdf [last accessed October 22, 2013].

Meadows, J. (1992). "International collaborations in teacher education: A constructivist approach to using electronic mail for communication in partnership with schools." *Technology, Pedagogy and Education*, 1 (1), 113–125.

Mediappro (2006). "Mediappro: The appropriation of new media by youth-end of project report." Brussels, European Commission. Available at: f http://www .mediappro.org/publications/finalreport.pdf [last accessed October 22, 2013].

Meguro, A. and Bryant, T. (2010). "Finding Language Partners in Unexpected Places: Skype and Social Networking for USA-Japan Telecollaboration." In S. Guth and F. Helm (Eds.), *Telecollaboration 2.0: Language, Literacies and Intercultural Learning in the 21st Century*. Bern: Peter Lang.

Merchant, G. (2005). "Digikids: Cool dudes and the new writing." *E-learning*, 2 (1), 50–60.

Merchant, G. (2009). "Web 2.0, new literacies, and the idea of learning through participation." *English Teaching*, 8 (3), 107–122.

Merchant, G. (2012). "Unravelling the social network: Theory and research." *Learning, Media and Technology*, 37 (1), 4–19.

Miguela, A. D. (2007). "Models of Telecollaboration (3): eTwinning." In R. O'Dowd (Ed.), *Online Intercultural Exchange: An Introduction for Foreign Language Teachers*. Clevedon [u.a.]; Multilingual Matters.

Miller, V. (2011). *Understanding Digital Culture*. London: SAGE Publications.

Mor, Y. and Sendova, E. (2003) *"Toon*Talking About Mathematics." In I. Derzhanski, N. Dimitrova, S. Grozdev, and E. Sendova (Eds.), *History and Education in*

Mathematics and Informatics, Attracting Talent to Science. Proceedings of the International Congress MASSEE 2003, September 15–21, Borovets, Bulgaria. Available at: http://www.lkl.ac.uk/kscope/weblabs/papers/ToonTalking_Mor_Sendova.pdf [last accessed October 22, 2013].

Morrison, N. (2012)."The role of technology in global learning." *The Guardian,* November 6, 2012. Available at: http://www.theguardian.com/teacher-network/teacher-blog/2012/nov/06/technology-global-learning-teaching [last accessed October 22, 2013].

Muir, J. (2010). "Phone technology opens direct line to Afghanistan" [Online]. *Times Educational Supplement,* April 9, 2010. Available at: http://www.tes.co.uk/article.aspx?storycode=6040781 [last accessed October 22, 2013].

Muijs, D., Ainsow, M., and Chapman, C. (2011). *Collaboration and Networking in Education.* Rotterdam: Springer.

Naismith, L., Lee, B. H., and Pilkington, R. M. (2011). "Collaborative learning with a wiki: Differences in perceived usefulness in two contexts of use." *Journal of Computer Assisted Learning,* 27 (3), 228–242.

Notari, M. (2006). "How to use a wiki in education: Wiki based effective constructive learning." *Proceedings of the 2006 International Symposium on Wikis,* Odense, Denmark: August 21–23, 131–132. Available at: http://portal.acm.org/citation.cfm?id=1149479 [last accessed August 8, 2013].

Notten, N., Peter, J., Kraaykamp, G., and Valkenburg, P. M. (2009). "Research note: Digital divide across borders a cross-national study of adolescents' use of digital technologies." *European Sociological Review,* 25 (5), 551–560.

Obama, B. (2009). *Remarks by the President on a New Beginning.* Available at: http://www.whitehouse.gov/the-press-office/remarks-president-cairo-university-6-04-09 [last accessed August 8, 2013].

O'Dowd, R. (2007a). "Introduction." In R. O'Dowd (Ed.), *Online Intercultural Exchange: An Introduction for Foreign Language Teachers.* Clevedon [u.a.]: Multilingual Matters.

O'Dowd, R. (2007b). "Foreign Language Education and the Rise of Online Communication: A Review of Promises and Realities." In R. O'Dowd (Ed.), *Online Intercultural Exchange: An Introduction for Foreign Language Teachers.* Clevedon [u.a.]: Multilingual Matters.

O'Dowd, R. (2007c). *Online Intercultural Exchange: An Introduction for Foreign Language Teachers.* Clevedon [u.a.]: Multilingual Matters.

O'Dowd, R. and Ritter, M. (2006). "Understanding and Working with 'Failed Communication' in Telecollaborative Exchanges." *Calico Journal,* 23 (3), 623–642.

Ofcom. (2011). *UK Children's Media Literacy.* London: Office of Communications. Available at: http://stakeholders.ofcom.org.uk/binaries/research/media-literacy/media-lit11/childrens.pdf [last accessed September 7, 2013].

Ofsted. (2005). *Independent/State School Partnerships.* London: OFSTED. Available at: http://www.ofsted.gov.uk/Ofsted-home/Publications-and-research/Browse-all-by/Education/Leadership/Management/Independent-state-school-partnerships [last accessed August 8, 2013].

O'Hair, M. J. and Veugelers, W. (2005). "The Case for Network Learning." In W. Veugelers and M. J. O'Hair (Eds.). *Network Learning for Educational Change.* Maidenhead: Open University Press.

Oliver, M. (2011). "Technological determinism in educational technology research: Some alternative ways of thinking about the relationship between learning and technology." *Journal of Computer Assisted Learning,* 27 (5), 373–384.

O'Reilly, T. (2005). *What is Web 2.0?* Available at: http://oreilly.com/web2/archive /what-is-web-20.html [last accessed August 8, 2013].

Owen, M., Grant, L., Sayers, S., and Facer, K. (2006). *Social Software and Learning.* Bristol: FutureLab. Available at: http://www2.futurelab.org.uk/resources/documents /opening_education/Social_Software_report.pdf [last accessed September 7, 2013].

Öztok, M. and Özdener, N. (2007). *Information and Communication Technologies in Collaboration Projects via the Internet.* Proceedings of World Academy of Science, Engineering and Technology, Volume 24, October 2007. Available at: www .waset.org/pwaset/v24/v24–23.pdf [last accessed March 28, 2009].

Palfrey, J. G. and Gasser, U. (2008). *Born Digital: Understanding the First Generation of Digital Natives.* New York: Basic Books.

Papert, S. (1986). *Constructionism: A New Opportunity for Elementary Science Education.* Massachusetts: Massachusetts Institute of Technology, Media Laboratory, Epistemology and Learning Group.

Papert, S. (1993). *The Children's Machine: Rethinking School in the Age of the Computer.* New York: Basic Books.

Papert, S. (1996). *The Connected Family: Bridging the Digital Generation Gap.* Atlanta, GA: Longstreet Press.

Parker, K. R. and Chao, J. T. (2007). "Wiki as a teaching tool." *Interdisciplinary Journal of Knowledge and Learning Objects,* 3, 57–72. Available at: http://ijklo.org /Volume3/IJKLOv3p057–072Parker284.pdf [last accessed September 7, 2013].

Pea, R., Nass, C., Meheula, L., Rance, M., Kumar, A., Bamford, H., Nass, M.,..., Zhou, M. (2012). "Media use, face-to-face communication, media multitasking, and social well-being among 8- to 12-year-old girls." *Developmental Psychology,* 48 (2), 327–336.

Perelman, L. J. (1993). *School's Out: A Radical New Formula for the Revitalization of America's Educational System.* New York: Avon.

Perrotta, C. (2011). "Review of key studies which have informed WP2 approach to scenario development" London, iTec. Available at: http://itec.eun.org/c/document _library/get_file?p_l_id=10307&folderId=36858&name=DLFE-1607.pdf [last accessed September 7, 2013].

Pine, K. (2006). *An Evaluation of the Educational and Social Benefits of SuperClubsPLUS for Children.* Available at: http://www.take2theweb.com/pub /litton/im/images/SCP_Research_Sept_06.pdf [last accessed September 7, 2013].

Poore, M. (2013). *Using Social Media in the Classroom: A Best Practice Guide.* London: Sage.

Potter, J. (2010). "Children as creators, consumers and curators: Media education, principles and entitlement for younger learners." CEMP at the University

of Bournemouth 2010. Available at: http://www .manifestoformediaeducation
.co.uk/2011/03/john-potter/ [last accessed October 22, 2013].

Potter, J. (2012). *Digital Media and Learner Identity: The New Curatorship*. New York: Palgrave Macmillan.

Prenksy, M. (2001). "Digital natives, digital immigrants." *On the Horizon*, 9(5). Available at: http://www.marcprensky.com/writing/prensky%20-%20digital%20natives,%20digital%20immigrants%20-%20part1.pdf [last accessed October 22, 2013].

Prensky, M. (2007). "How to teach with technology—keeping both teachers and students comfortable in an era of exponential change" [Online]. In BECTA's *Emerging Technologies for Learning*, 2, 29–47. Available at: http://www.mendeley.com/research/how-to-teach-with-technology-keeping-both-teachers-and-students-comfortable-in-an-era-of-exponential-change [last accessed October 22, 2013].

Prensky, M. (2008). "Young minds, fast times: The twenty-first-century digital learner: How tech-obsessed iKids would improve our schools." *Edutopia*. June 2008. Available at: http://www.edutopia.org/ikid-digital-learner-technology-2008 [last accessed October 22, 2013].

Redecker, C. (2009). "Learning 2.0: A study on the impact of web 2.0 innovations on education and training in Europe." European Communities. Available at: http://ftp.jrc.es/EURdoc/JRC49108.pdf [last accessed October 22, 2013].

Rees, R. and Woodward, S. (1998). "Twinned schools in Ontario: A description and a comparison." *Journal of Research in Rural Education*, 14 (1), 26–33.

Reimer, E. W. (1971). *School is Dead: An Essay on Alternatives in Education*. Harmondsworth: Penguin.

Rheingold, H. (1993). *The Virtual Community: Homesteading on the Electronic Frontier*. Reading, MA: Addison-Wesley.

Rheingold, H. (2008). "Using Participatory Media and Public Voice to Encourage Civic Engagement." In L. Bennet (Ed.), *Civic Life Online: Learning How Digital Media Can Engage Youth*. Cambridge, MA: MIT Press.

Richardson, W. (2009). *Blogs, Wikis, Podcasts, and Other Powerful Web Tools for Classrooms*. Thousand Oaks, CA: Corwin Press. 2nd Edition.

Robertson, S. and Dale, R. (2009). "Aliens in the Classroom 2: When Technology Meets Classroom Life." In R. Sutherland, S. Robertson, and P. John (Eds.), *Improving Classroom Learning with ICT*. Milton Park, Abingdon, Oxon: Routledge.

Robins, K. and Webster, F. (1989). *The Technical Fix: Education, Computers, and Industry*. New York: St. Martin's Press.

Roschelle, J. and Teasley S. D. (1995). "The Construction of Shared Knowledge in Collaborative Problem Solving." In C. E. O'Malley (Ed.), *Computer-Supported Collaborative Learning*. Berlin: Springer-Verlag.

Rosen, D. and Nelson, C. (2008). "Web 2.0: A new generation of learners and education." *Computers in the Schools*, 25 (3–4), 211–225.

Rosenfeld, E. (2007). "Beginning the conversation about education 2.0." *Teacher Librarian*, 34 (4), 6–6.

Rudd, T., Colligan, F., and Naik, R. (2006a). *Learner Voice*. Bristol: Futurelab. Available at: http://www2.futurelab.org.uk/resources/documents/handbooks/learner_voice.pdf [last accessed October 22, 2013].

Rudd, T., Gifford, C., Morrison, J., and Facer, K. (2006b). *What if... Re-Imagining Learning Spaces*. Bristol: Futurelab. Available at: http://www2.futurelab.org.uk/resources/documents/opening_education/Learning_Spaces_report.pdf. [last accessed October 22, 2013].

Rutherford, D. and Jackson, L. (2006). "Setting Up School Partnerships: Some Insights from Birmingham's Collegiate Academies." *School Leadership and Management*, 26 (5), 437–451.

Scardamalia, M. and Bereiter, C. (1994). "Computer support for knowledge-building communities". *The Journal of the Learning Sciences*, 3 (3), 265–283.

Schaffert, S., Bischof, D., Buerger, T., Gruber, A., Hilzensauer, W., and Schaffert, S. (2006). "Learning with semantic wikis." *Proceedings of the First Workshop on Semantic Wikis—From Wiki to Semantics (SemWiki2006)*, Budva, Montenegro: June 11–14, 109–123. Available at: http://www.schaffert.eu/wp-content/uploads/Schaffert06_SemWikiLearning.pdf [last accessed November 7, 2013].

Scimeca, S. (2010). "Introduction: eTwinning 2.0—setting the scene." In C. Crawley, P. Gerhard, A. Gilleran, and A. Joyce (Eds.), *eTwinning 2.0 Building the Community for Schools in Europe*. Brussels: European Schoolnet.

Schwartz, L., Clark, S., Cossarin, M., and Rudolph, J. (2004). "Educational wikis: Features and selection criteria." *International Review of Research in Open and Distance Learning*, 5 (1). Available at: http://cde.athabascau.ca/softeval/reports/R270311.pdf [last accessed October 22, 2013].

Schweisfurth, M. (2005). "Learning to Live Together: A Review of UNESCO's Associated Schools Project Network." *International Review of Education*, 51 (2–3), 219–234.

Scottish Executive. (2006). *Building Friendships and Strengthening Communities: A Guide to Twinning between Denominational and Non-denominational Schools*. Edinburgh: Scottish Executive. Available at: http://www.scotland.gov.uk/Publications/2006/12/07092739/0 [last accessed October 22, 2013].

Selwyn, N. (2002). *Telling Tales on Technology: Qualitative Studies of Technology and Education*. Aldershot, Hampshire, England: Ashgate.

Selwyn, N. (2008). "Educational Hopes and Fears for Web 2.0." In Selwyn, N. (Ed.), *Education 2.0? Designing the Web for Teaching and Learning*." ESRC Teaching and Learning Research Programme commentary. Available at: http://www.tlrp.org/pub/documents/TELcomm.pdf [last accessed August 8, 2013].

Selwyn, N. (2009) "Challenging educational expectations of the social web: A web 2.0 far?" *Nordic Journal of Digital Literacy*, 4 (2), 72–85.

Selwyn, N. (2011a). *Schools and Schooling in the Digital Age: A Critical Perspective*. London: Routledge.

Selwyn, N. (2011b). *Education and Technology: Key Issues and Debates*. London: Continuum.

Selwyn, N. (2012). "Ten Suggestions for Improving Academic Research in Education and Technology." *Learning, Media and Technology*, 37 (3), 213–219.

Selwyn, N. (2013). *Education in a Digital World: Global Perspectives on Technology and Education.* New York: Routledge.

Selwyn, N., Crook, C., Noss, R., and Laurillard, D. (2008). "Education 2.0? Towards an educational web 2.0". In Selwyn, N. (Ed.), *Education 2.0? Designing the Web for Teaching and Learning.*" ESRC Teaching and Learning Research Programme commentary. Available at: http://www.tlrp.org/pub/documents/TELcomm.pdf [last accessed August 8, 2013].

Selwyn, N., Potter, J., and Cranmer, S. (2010). *Primary Schools and ICT: Learning from Pupil Perspectives.* London: Continuum International Pub. Group.

Sendova, E., Nikolava, I., Gachev, G., and Moneva, L. (2004). "Weblabs: A Virtual Laboratory for Collaborative E-learning." Presented at EduTech Workshop, WCCE 2004, Toulouse, France. Available at: http://www.lkl.ac.uk/kscope /weblabs/papers/EduTech-WCCE_04_bulgaria.pdf [last accessed October 22, 2013].

Shinners, K. D. (2001). "Public/private school partnerships: What can be learned from corporate school partnerships." Paper presented at the annual meeting of the American Educational Research Association, Seattle, WA, April 10–14, 2001. Available at: http://www.eric.ed.gov/PDFS/ED455574.pdf [last accessed October 22, 2013].

Smith, J. and Wohlstetter, P. (2006). "Understanding the different faces of partnering: A typology of public-private partnerships." *School Leadership and Management,* 26 (3), 249–268.

Smith, P., Kerr, K., and Harris, S. (2003). *Collaboration between Independent and Local Authority Schools: LEA's Perspectives on Partnership and Community Activities.* LGA research, Report 44. London: NFER.

Solomon, G. and Schrum, L. (2007). *Web 2.0: New Tools, New Schools.* Eugene, OR: International Society for Technology in Education.

Stahl, G., Koschmann, T., and Suthers, D. D. (2006) "Computer-Supported Collaborative Learning." In K. R. Sawyer (Ed.), *The Cambridge Handbook of the Learning Sciences.* New York: Cambridge University Press.

Sturm, M., Kennell, T., McBride, R., and Kelly, M. (2009). "The pedagogical implications of Web 2.0." In M. Thomas (Ed.), *Handbook of research on Web 2.0 and second language learning.* Hershey, PA: Information Science Reference.

Sutherland, R. and Sutch, D. (2009). "Integrating ICT in Teaching and Learning." In R. Sutherland, S. Robertson, and P. John (Eds.), *Improving Classroom Learning with ICT.* Milton Park, Abingdon, Oxon: Routledge.

Tapscott, D. (1998). *Growing up Digital: The Rise of the Net Generation.* New York: McGraw-Hill.

Tella, S. (1991). *Introducing International Communications Networks and Electronic Mail into Foreign Language Classrooms: A Case Study in Finnish Senior Secondary Schools (Research Report 75).* Helsinki: University of Helsinki. Available at: http:// www.helsinki.fi/~tella/95.pdf [last accessed August 8, 2013].

Thomas, M. (2011) "Technology, Education, and the Discourse of the Digital Native: Between Evangelists and Dissenters." In M. Thomas (Ed.), *Deconstructing Digital Natives: Young People, Technology, and the New Literacies.* New York: Routledge.

Turner, J. (2004). *Building Bridges: A Study of Independent and State School Partnerships*. Nottingham: National College for School Leadership. Available at: http://www.nationalcollege.org.uk/index/docinfo.htm?id=17109 [last accessed August 8, 2013].

Tyack, D. and Tobin, W. (1994). "The 'Grammar' of Schooling: Why Has It Been So Hard to Change?" *American Educational Research Journal*, 31 (3), 453–479.

Valentine, G. and Holloway, S. L. (2001). "A Window on the Wider World? Rural Children's Use of Information and Communication Technologies." *Journal of Rural Studies*, 17 (4), 383–394.

Veugelers, W. and Zijlstra, H. (2002). "What Goes on in a Network? Some Dutch Experiences." *International Journal of Leadership in Education*, 5 (2), 163–174.

Veugelers, W. and Zijlstra, H. (2005). "Keeping School Networks Fluid; Networks in Dialogue with Educational Change." In W. Veugelers and M. J. O'Hair (Eds.), *Network Learning for Educational Change*. Maidenhead: Open University Press.

Vinagre, M. (2007). "Integrating Tandem Learning in Higher Education." In R. O'Dowd (Ed.), *Online Intercultural Exchange: An Introduction for Foreign Language Teachers*. Clevedon [u.a.]: Multilingual Matters.

Vion, A. (2002). "Europe from the Bottom Up: Town Twinning in France during the Cold War." *Contemporary European History*, 11 (4), 623–640.

Vuorikari, R. and Sarnow, S. (2005). *Open Content and Source: European Schoolnet Riding the Wave*. Special Insight Reports. Available at: http://www-old.eun.org /insight-pdf/Full_Paper_vuorikari_sarnow_OSS_Europe_final.pdf [last accessed August 8, 2013].

Walker, L. (with Logan, A.) (2009). *Using Digital Technologies to Promote Inclusive Practices in Education*. Bristol: Futurelab. Available at: http://www.futurelab.org .uk/resources/documents/handbooks/digital_inclusion3.pdf [last accessed August 8, 2013].

Wang, L. and Beasley, W. (2008). "The wiki as a web 2.0 tool in education." *International Journal of Technology in Teaching and Learning*, 4 (1), 78–85.

Ward. H. (2009). "Iraqi School Logs on to Like Minds in UK" [Online]. *Times Educational Supplement*, April 3, 2009. Available at: http://www.tes.co.uk/article. aspx?storycode=6011257 [last accessed October 22, 2013].

Wastiau, P., Blamire, R., Kearney, C., Quittre, V., Van, G. E., and Monseur, C. (2013). "The Use of ICT in Education: A Survey of Schools in Europe." *European Journal of Education*, 48 (1), 11–27.

Wenger, E. (1998). *Communities of Practice. Learning, Meaning, and Identity*. Cambridge: Cambridge University Press.

Wheeler, S., Yeomans, P., and Wheeler, D. (2008). "The Good, the Bad and the wiki: Evaluating Student-Generated Content for Collaborative Learning." *British Journal of Educational Technology*, 39 (6), 987–995.

Williams, R. (1994). "The Political and Feminist Dimensions of Technological Determinism." In M. R. Smith and L. Marx (Eds.). *Does Technology Drive History?* Cambridge, MA: MIT Press.

Wintour, P. (2009). *Facebook and Bebo Risk "Infantilising" the Human Mind. The Times*, February 24, 2009. Available at: http://www.guardian.co.uk/uk/2009

/feb/24/social-networking-site-changing-childrens-brains [last accessed October 22, 2013].

Yamamoto, G. T. and Karaman, F. (2011). "Education 2.0." *On the Horizon*, 19 (2), 109–117.

Zhao, Y. and Frank, K. A. (2003). "Factors affecting technology uses in schools: An ecological perspective." *American Educational Research Journal*, 40 (4), 807–840.

Index

GPSR Compliance
The European Union's (EU) General Product Safety Regulation (GPSR) is a set
of rules that requires consumer products to be safe and our obligations to
ensure this.

If you have any concerns about our products, you can contact us on

ProductSafety@springernature.com

In case Publisher is established outside the EU, the EU authorized
representative is:

Springer Nature Customer Service Center GmbH
Europaplatz 3
69115 Heidelberg, Germany